EARLY MUSIC
Approaches to Performance Practice

JOSEF MERTIN

EARLY MUSIC

Approaches to Performance Practice

Translated from the German by
SIEGMUND LEVARIE

DA CAPO PRESS • NEW YORK • 1986

Library of Congress Cataloging in Publication Data

Mertin, Josef.
    Early music: approaches to Performance Practice.

    (Da Capo Press music series)
    Translation of: Alte Musik.
    1. Music—Performance. 2. Style, Musical.
3. Musical instruments. I. Levarie, Siegmund, 1914–
II. Title.
ML457.M4613   1986   785'.07   85-23110
ISBN 0-306-76286-2

This Da Capo Press edition of *Early Music: Approaches to Performance
Practice* is a translation from the German of the book entitled *Alte
Musik: Wege zur Aufführungspraxis* published in Vienna in 1978. It is
issued in the present edition by arrangement with Verlag Elisabeth Lafite.

Published by Da Capo Press, Inc.
A Subsidiary of Plenum Publishing Corporation
233 Spring Street, New York, N.Y. 10013

Contents

Foreword by the Translator

This book is like none other in the field. While presenting a wealth of information — historical facts, theoretical considerations, and practical suggestions — it is highly subjective in treating questions of performing early music. The author's personality and career fully justify the approach.

Josef Mertin, now professor emeritus though still active at the Hochschule für Musik in Vienna, has led at least three full professional lives. He is a superior conductor who performed Dufay, Josquin, and Schütz in Vienna at a time when Bach still sounded like a novelty. Almost all alone, he was a generation or two ahead of the present revival of baroque, renaissance, and medieval music. He is a meticulous organ builder with close to seventy instruments to his credit. He has served as organ expert for the Austrian government. There is no historic organ in Italy, Germany, and Austria that he has not personally measured or otherwise studied. All along, Josef Mertin has been an inspiring teacher whose first-hand and thorough knowledge of music permitted him to treat with equal authority history and theory, performance practices and techniques. In more than half a century as a professor, he has taught thousands of students, among whom — because of the international role of the Vienna institution — Americans and other foreigners probably outnumber local students. Many performers now famous for their contribution to early music received their first and finest training from him. His students, many of them teachers and performers themselves, will be particularly grateful for the existence of this text, which until now has been available only in German; for apart from the rich contents, it projects in many ways the special manner of his seeing and sharing a problem.

The translator, who belongs to this group, was from the beginning aware of the impossiblity of rendering even a part of Josef Mertin's personal style in a foreign language; for if we have initially called Josef Mertin's scholarly approach *subjective*, his original use of language must be characterized by the same adjective. It is full of unforgettable, spontaneously generated expressions and structures, which a German book reviewer called *Austrian* but which I prefer to call *Austrian baroque*. The meaning is always clear and the effect memorable; but what is a translator to do when he reads in the original that realization of a figured bass on paper has the "Charakter des Trockenschwimmkurses"; that false voice production may extend from "Knödeln bis zur verbremsten Stimme"; that a piano indication in Bach is ineffective "wenn drei Pulte Geiger (oder gar noch mehr) zum Kitzeln der Geige verurteilt werden"; or that "in der Scheidung von sterilem Tenor und lebensvollem Discantus wird ein Melos entwickelt, das sich aus einem Konsonanzverhältnis zu bestimmten Metrumspositionen in melodischem Aufblühen, in einem Ueberschwang der Melodiebildung auslebt"? (What the translator actually did, the kind reader will have to find out by himself.)

The preponderance of examples taken from Austrian places, collections, and composers is understandable and does no harm. Anybody noticing a discrepancy between the German and English versions may be assured that all such instances have the blessing of the author who, moreover, changed several paragraphs himself, asked for the insertion of others, and was pleased to find reinstated in the Appendix his chapter on consonance which had been cut from the German edition.

The time and effort I have given to the English edition indicate the smallest part of my lifelong gratitude and affectionate friendship for Josef Mertin.

Siegmund Levarie

PITCH DESIGNATIONS

Pitch letters in Roman capitals without further identification (C, D#, etc.) connote general pitch names without regard to a specific octave range. Definite pitches are indicated as in the following diagram:

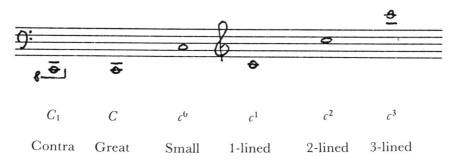

C_1	C	c^0	c^1	c^2	c^3
Contra	Great	Small	1-lined	2-lined	3-lined

Preface to the Second
German Edition

This new edition contains some revisions, mainly of Chapters 2, 6, and 7. An appendix, missing from the first edition, investigates the structural basis of musical phenomena.

Experiences with the first edition have shown that the book is capable of challenging some conventional views. It succeeds if it stimulates fresh thoughts and inquiries. Methodical and scholarly treatment of special questions, while elucidating and useful, sometimes leads students to expect "securely patented" answers. We musicians fear nothing more than a sterile fantasy. The only valuable insights are those acquired through personal doubt and work. In one's honest relation to art, one spends one's whole life "on the way."

J. M.

Introduction

On the occasion of my seventieth birthday, I was offered the chance to publish in book form my thoughts on a specific aspect of my work. Many separate publications in various journals were fused and recast to produce this textbook on performance practices.

Serious involvement with historic music obviously must utilize all musicological discoveries. Using this approach alone, however, one views the field from only a single side. Live music-making must not be subordinated to a purely scholarly treatment of the existing problems, for we arrive at decisive insights only by active musical realization of a work. A composition, regardless of period and style, is brought to real life by somebody's musical understanding and imagination. What matters is always honest effort and talent.

Occupation with early music cannot harm one's involvement with new music. It rather supplies criteria and suggestions for fresh creativity. Knowledge of early music may prove an antidote to new music which rejects any contact with tradition and which has abandoned the laws of structured sound.

My attitude to the questions treated in this book results from a lifelong commitment to the practice of music. I will deal only with problems concerning the live performance of works and therefore will not offer a scholarly bibliography. Although I personally learned a great deal from Adler, Ficker, and Fischer, I am writing as a conductor and not as a musicologist.

The chapters of the book approach the problems from various sides according to the compositional structures. The old pedagogic prescription for acquiring musical culture by writing imitations of a few dozen prototypes is not popular today, for it wastes much time and can paralyze the creation of new music. As a disciple of Hugo Kauder, however, I gained important insights precisely through this method. In a surrogate manner, this book sets about to restore that path at least in part.

Styles will not be covered systematically. I report only on matters which have touched me deeply — compositions with which I have established, with joy and devotion, an intimate relationship. The choice of works is personal and therefore partisan.

Critical comments must not be interpreted as polemics. After over fifty years of teaching, I feel in every respect committed to a conscientiously oriented position, which will remain evident.

Now to the specific chapters of the book:

Chapter I describes as concisely as possible the many historic kinds of notation and adds an explanation of the essentials of each. A performer must understand very early practices and archetypes. My demonstration restricts itself to principles, for the book is not a text on how to transcribe old manuscripts. For such work, specialized studies are available. This chapter treats what a conductor must know. It also offers comparisons with the notation of around 1910, which most musicians accept as standard.

Chapter II attempts to elucidate a fundamental problem of performance practice: the determination of the appropriate principle of movement for each masterwork by rhythm and meter. The realization of this task decides the actual worth of a performance. Factual knowledge helps to free oneself from performance conditions of 1910, which continue to dominate the concert stage, and to make music in the proper spirit of a style.

Chapter III demonstrates principles and potentials of early compositional structures. Because a moderately thorough treatment of this subject matter would fill several large tomes, we present here only explanatory extracts. The primary purpose of this chapter is to stimulate the personal acquisition of insights into musical structures.

Chapter IV treats fundamentals of ensemble formation demanded by musical structures. One encounters here the concepts of split sonority, homogeneous sonority, and their variants.

In Chapter V, questions of thoroughbass are examined from the standpoint of the instruments involved. When a basso continuo is handled by a practical musician, the whole problematic complex loses the chapter of swimming instructions on dry land and challenges the player with the particulars of the available continuo instrument.

Chapter VI turns to other historic instruments, their characteristics, possibilities, and limitations. This section, too, has to restrict itself to a survey and a few details.

Chapter VII: for the specific sound of early music, the typical manner of tuning and tempering continuo instruments, particularly the organ, is an integrating factor. Practical tuning procedures are expounded.

Chapter VIII supplies analytic support for the practical performance of a major work by Bach, of the kind a conductor must be familiar with before beginning rehearsals.

The Appendix restores a chapter omitted from the first German edition. Although music theory is not directly a question of performance practice, it should be part of every musician's thoughts and actions.

CHAPTER I

Fundamentals of Notation

This discussion of historic notations focuses on the practical work of conductors and explains only the peculiarities of the different kinds of notation. The survey is summary; the director of an ensemble for old music has to gather additional information by working his way through the basic books by Wolf or Apel.[1] Here it seems more important to show in principle what essential prescriptions for performance practice derive from notation, in what respect they deviate from the familiar image of notes, and what conventions in the historic manner of making music belonged to it. Our main effort, after all, is to realize all intentions of the composer. Only this basic attitude can carry a masterwork to meaningful fruition; this conviction has for us musicians the same principal significance as the Hippocratic oath for physicians.

In the realm of music, there exists a particular difficulty: a musical work of art gains existence only in a live performance. The older the music, the more problematic the rendition that presents the qualities of the historic work with as little distortion and falsification as possible. Our conception of music notation is dominated by the aspect of a score by Gustav Mahler, who secured the rendition of his music by differentiated instructions, by exact tempo indications and tips for the conductor. What remains open lies within the conductor's artistic judgment, depends on the qualities of the performing musicians — and all of this then defines the specific value of a particular performance. Even in the music of Brahms, security derived from notation is more precarious. The farther one moves away from the music written around the

time of the First World War, the more problematic a performance becomes, for the notation of 1910 also is that of a temporal style.

The historic practice of music has embraced many conventions
which opened up first of all to the performing musician a multitude of
possibilities for shaping music in a personal way. The older the composition, the larger the gap between notation and actual execution. The
circumstance that every temporal style and every specific sphere have
developed their own kind of notation is most strongly operative. Our
orthography and our notes are in no way appropriate to historical application. Therefore the scope of musical notation will here be considered fundamentally and according to typical methods and
manifestations.

Most generally one can state that the notation commonly used today concerns itself primarily with the definition of rhythm and melos.
A special notation for harmonic phenomena originated with the thoroughbass; it always remained a rudimentary script with all the characteristics of shorthand. The necessity (that is, incapacity) of including metric
and melodic dimensions in all their differentiations led to the disappearance of the thoroughbass as impromptu practice and to the personal as-
sumption by composers of final decisions and responsibilities concerning
all details of performance.

In many historic spheres, musical rhythm originated from symbiosis with language. Verse patterns supply the first norms for the metric dimension. This is not the occasion for debating the extent to which
the development of speech meter is not altogether a musical event. The
models thus created remain effective for a long time; today we still
respond spontaneously to such events. The emancipation of rhythm away
from speech models took many centuries of intensive procedures ever
changing with corresponding problems of style. Manifold forces and currents participate; the issue is not merely quantification or metrical accentuation. In the rhythmic shaping of a composition, many details of the
performance conventions of a period become further determining factors. A musician concerned with historic music meets in this dimension
the most severe problems. Therefore we here give precedence to the treatment of metric and rhythmic questions.

The notation of melody (that is, the writing of frequency positions), particularly in early music and considered across a wide temporal span, is burdened with characteristically specific difficulties. One
recognizes the situation best by a glance at works of genuine twelve-

tone music, where the common traditional notation is actually inappropriate. While usable for writing down Schönberg's compositions, it disavows the foundation of that music which gains its material from the mechanical division of the octave by 12 (twelfth root of two). It ignores the demand for equivalence of the tones by preserving musical currents which we follow automatically according to the orthography. D-sharp and E-flat, for instance, are in tonal music two different values, which carry tonal aspects into twelve-tone music. The lines of our scores do not convey the actual intervallic progression, for the position of halftone and wholetone steps derives only from our knowledge of the keys. A basic principle of our music-making is that in a tonal melody we do not just move from tone to tone but rather are directly propelled into the desired tonal positions by our tonal consciousness! A singer does not sight-read by dangling from one tone to the next but rather draws on his awareness of the total tonal complex in order to define single positions. Our notational technique was already based on this fact of a remembered presence of an overview when Guido of Arezzo constructed our solmization system with the mnemonic device of the familiar hymn to St. John.[2] The given hexachord is also a first sign of our orientation toward the major mode; the exact location of the semitone *mi-fa* offers the basis for the notation of intervals in Western music. The situation remains unchanged in black and white mensural notations. Historic solmization then accounts for the loose attitude toward the absolute pitch of a composition; to fix the exact pitch of a piece of music with the help of accidentals was as superfluous as it was impossible. When the church modes faded — when by way of tablatures absolute pitch could be defined and mensural notation had to make up for its deficiency in this respect — , only then absolute pitch, tied to the tuning of particular instruments, began to be notated with the help of our modern key signatures. Before then the zones of absolute pitch were approached by way of clef combinations: the *chiavi naturali* and the high and low *chiavette*.

In early stages of musical practice, composer and performer are the same person. In such a situation, methods of notation appear which are merely memory props. Pages with early troubadour lyrics, for instance, originated in this symbiosis of functions; the old manuscripts contain texts and staffless hook neumes. Such notation was not invented for this narrower purpose; one took the specific plainsong notation. There are reasons: plainsong as the characteristic sacred art of the early Middle Ages is anything but a uniform phenomenon. Wherever Christianity became the order governing all aspects of life, local musical traditions continued; and missionaries managed simply to change the function of pre-Christian vestiges which they could not cut down like a holy oak. In this manner a sacred music grew up which we call *plain-chant* and in which strongly heterogeneous elements appear. Today we distinguish between Ambrosian, Gallic, Roman, Mozarabic chants. The great monastic orders developed their own dialects. Byzantine culture influenced all the Eastern provinces. Jewish tradition supplied a whole complex, more than Psalms and Cantica, even if the transfer to Latin brought about a reconstruction and the elimination of many Hebrew particularities. Classical Greek transmission led to Christian, mainly Ambrosian hymns.

This collective whole was well served by hook neumes. They are a rudimentary notation, capable only of suggesting the general direction and course of a melody. Groups of notes can be found in an early ligature notation.[3] These staffless neumes, occurring far into the fourteenth century, have the advantage of offering any desired interpretation for every kind of tone system. The Cistercian order, reviving the ancient Benedictine rule, strives for utmost simplicity; just as its churches have no towers — except perhaps a turret above the intersection of nave and transept (towers are a later baroque addition) — so their musical practice leans toward pentatonality. Benedictines and Cluniacs move in the opposite direction.

The hook neumes change and become adjusted to new situations. Early polyphony demands exact notation of intervals. In such cases, a second kind of notation coexisted with neumes, namely, one employing letters of the alphabet, an inheritance from antiquity. Greek notation (with Phoenician letters!) flows as method directly into a letter notation with the Latin alphabet. This practice, covering the range of two and one-half octaves about great *A,* is well known but foreign to the character of chant. The famous *bilingua* manuscript of Dijon combines Carolingian hook neumes with letter notation.[4]

For the development of music, the method of making neumes to indicate exact intervals proves superior to that of retaining the musically unrevealing letter notation. The latter establishes itself only with the formation of a keyboard and the naming of the keys by letters. Now the ancient letter notation flows into organ tablatures, from which our modern nomenclature derives. In order to improve the hook neumes, the scribe eventually dug with his ivory bone a furrow into the parchment, and soon there were two furrows, thus making the approximate notation of pitches possible. Logical development leads to a staff, of which at first only the spaces were used. Writing also *on* the lines followed soon. This new notation changes the shape of the neumes. Accent neumes and hook neumes are transformed into points and "nails" (*Hufnagel*). The point neumes become the specific notation of early polyphony.

I wish to submit a few detailed comments concerning the square-shaped neumes, which since the great chant reform by the French Benedictines of more than one hundred years ago have become the universal chant notation for all Gregorian music. The rhythmic significance of the point neumes remains preserved in the square-shaped neumes. The *virga* is a long note; the *punctum,* the normal value; the rhombus, the divider. Liquescent shapes are treated as grace notes, even then written smaller. A relation to the pitch of the following main note may be signaled; the *plica* forms (*ancus, cephalicus, epiphonus*) may hide a chroma and even smaller intervals. The *pressus* is a kind of syncopation; the *quilisma,* a vocal mannerism. Groupings are written in ligatures: *pes* and *flexa* contain two tones; *climacus, scandicus, salicus, torculus, and porrectus* contain three tones. More tones can be grouped in the *neumae compositae,* such as the *torculus resupinus flexus.* Verse must be sung metrically. This is a rough survey.

The multitude of schools — for each spiritually active monastery favors sacred music — has produced a multitude of special forms, such as, for example, the sequence in St. Gallen and Reichenau. Today only five sequences remain (for Easter, Pentecost, and Corpus Domini; the Stabat Mater; and in the Office for the Dead). Antiphons were created in rich abundance; the worship of Mary has contributed much to the spread of special antiphons.

All of this is important material for a Benedictine organist. One must bear in mind that the practice of monasteries and the available ensembles influence significantly the kind of music and the individual structures. There is a great difference in the musical display of *cantores* (that is, up to three singers soloistically oriented), a *scola* (a small group with genuine musical challenges), and the psalm singers in the choir stalls. This circumstance alone leads to a variety of compositional structures.

In early polyphony, emphasis lies on simultaneous sound. Rhythm is reduced to a few metric models which effect order. The basic metric models could be written with the existing notes. In analogy to the feet of ancient verse, there are now six rhythmic modes. The first and second modes are, respectively, trochee and iamb inscribed as triplets in a tactus. The other formulas span two tactus values: the dactylus, the (practically hardly ever used) anapaest, the spondee (that is, the large value of three time units), and the tribrach (the hemiola of the former).

All early polyphony is originally traditional monophony adapted for polyphony. The tenor holds the Gregorian melody which becomes increasingly sterile and eventually may freeze into organpoints while all musical life centers on the newly composed material. The counterpart to the tenor, at first a single voice, soon grows into a group. Up to three voices unite metrically against the tenor as duplum, triplum, and quadruplum. Such compositions are culminations of the musical contribution to the liturgy. In Notre Dame organa, all voices occupy approximately the same range; one must not assume a bass for the cantus firmus.[5] The newly composed voices are raised according to the often participating boys' voices and even more so by the instruments involved. An anonymous Englishman describes the musical practice at Notre Dame. On the ambo stand three *cantores,* on the steps the boys, behind the ambo are hidden the "nonconsecrated," that is, jongleurs who play instrumental parts in ever changing distributions.[6] Above the ambo, a small platform, an "organ foot," is built onto the pillar, and the monk plays the tenor on a small *Blockwerk* organ. The simple formulas of the rhythmic modes, among which the first and third prevail, suffice to hold the performers together. (When we sang the great organum quadruplum "Sederunt principes" in 1926 under Ficker, we experienced the effect of the modes and their rhythmic impact.[7] The motion swings upward for long stretches; we were as in a trance. This music builds forms across huge spaces: in the middle section of this St. Stephen gradual, the tenor furnishes a kind of organpoint lasting over 230 tactus units.)

For ligatures, the notation of square neumes on lines requires several intricate rules. At critical moments, one could clarify metric units running across two tactus by a *punctus divisionis.*[8] What the practical performance was like—whether, for instance, one sang and played from separate parts—can hardly be established. Manuscripts like the Codex Montpellier[9] (which I have held in my hands) are far too precious and sumptuous; the notes, moreover, are too small to permit a performance directly from the Codex.

Chronologically parallel to Gregorian and early polyphonic music, a secular art has been preserved, obviously influenced by the example of sacred music. In profane compositions, the emphasis lies on language; we deal with poets who also sing, who also make music. New texts are often invented to existing melodies. Word orders create a specific morphology based on linguistic laws. Barform and types like ballade and virelais belong to a distinctly secular art.

In Notre Dame music, one already senses an emancipation from the modal orders. Modes petrify, the vital forces unfold in the increasingly differentiated lines of the upper voices. Beginning in the thirteenth century and then thoroughly in the fourteenth, the rigid modal patterns are overcome. Notes now represent precise duration values; the substance of black mensural notation is quickly gathered. The notion of tactus brings forth triple and duple divisions, and the given instructions establish the metric structure. Traditional habits become sterile, just as it had happened to Gregorian tenors in Notre Dame music. The former modes are stretched to become the superior time order *modus* of mensural notation, in which the longa or maxima is divided into breves. The brevis as metrical tempus is in turn subdivided into three or two semibreves. Finally, there follow the small orders of prolations.

The graphic image of black mensural notation still follows the norms of Notre Dame writing; single notes generally resemble in size those in our miniature scores. One performed from separate parts. In public performances, one apparently made music from memory. Perhaps an intermediary existed, like the slate of my childhood. The ensembles are small and do not employ collectives (with the exception of choir boys where each part is generally tripled as a kind of addition of three boyish minds). The professional musicians, the jongleurs, are called in whenever needed. Fixed engagements for them are rare (one thinks of the historic buildings for musicians around the coronation cathedral of Rheims with reliefs of musicians; the houses themselves were destroyed in the First World War).

Ensemble form, musical initiative, liturgical situation, quality of the performers, acoustical conditions, traditional considerations — all these have an effect and create such a multitude of possibilities that each single performance becomes unrepeatable. One can only guess to what extent diminution and improvisation participated in this practice of (mostly) singing and playing from memory. In any case, Machaut's Mass, for instance, sounds archaic compared to the experimental motets, virelais, and ballades. (In a letter to Perronelle, Machaut indirectly conceded experimentation when promising to send her a ballade only after having tried it out.)

A structural element typical of the period is isorhythm. As long as one did not rely on the newly gained consonance relationships of polyphony, one helped oneself with other structural factors. In this sense, isorhythm resembles a kind of serial music restricted to rhythm. All depends on the musical potency of the composers to transcend the intellectual schemes by intuitive unfolding of a genuinely experienced, that is, musical substance. This happens in all phases of European music whenever a masterwork outgrows merely workmanlike technique or intellectual crutches.

One of the significant revelations derived from notation is that this music dispenses with the notion of a score. Notwithstanding a long development, each individual part persists in having and preserving its own particular qualities. Just as the individual registers each have a characteristic identity, so the split sonority obeys the law of acoustic realization. Origin and compositional function distinguish the parts in essence, and notation does full justice to the given fact. The tenor is a register based on cantus-firmus tradition. One would err in always working it over the same last. One must unfold its music according to its substance, its metrical system, and its sonority. The latter reaches practically from vocal execution to the most static realizations. The motetus should usually be entrusted to a high male voice or instruments of a similar character.[10] The triplum may be sung or played by instruments identified with the upper ranges. Always plucking the contratenors is one-sided and may impair the balance of the registers.[11] For the hocket-sport, elegance of execution is indispensable.[12] Fundamental isorhythms may occasionally invite percussion instruments. In no case should the sound be homogeneous.

The music of the Squarcialupi Codex can be handled like the secular works of Machaut.[13] There are many links to the high French art. (Think of the captivity of the Popes in Avignon from 1309 until 1378, the decisive decades of the Italian ars nova.) Differences concern local details. Landini's tombstone significantly shows an organetto (the Italian term for a portative organ).[14] The secular music is strongly colored by all conventions of *hoveschheit,* the courtly posture that dominated all Europe. Many stylistic features derive from such conditions.

At the very beginning of the fifteenth century, musical practice develops in a way apparently prescribed by extramusical forces. The increasing weakness of the French kingdom shortly before the appearance of Jeanne d'Arc imparts new weight to Burgundy and her very large cities. Around 1400, Ghent has already sixty thousand adult inhabitants, Cologne only fifteen thousand. The League, strangling the French kingdom and eventually constituting itself in the Order of the Golden Fleece with head and center in Burgundy, develops its own ceremonial in order to give a religious foundation, in the image of the Holy Roman Empire, to its political power. (Seeing the Burgundian wealth in the Vienna Treasury, one understands spontaneously the significance of that new orientation.) For the manifestation of the political concentration, cults are necessary, amply supplied by religious traditions. Musical chapels are organized. A new performance practice becomes the norm. The ensemble surrounds a stand which supports a choirbook written in such large clear signs that up to a dozen performers can make music from it. The form of the notes has obviously been adjusted: all decisive notes are now large and hollow (rather than solid and black, that is, small). Maxima, longa, brevis, semibrevis, minima, and semiminima are now written as hollow notes; only fusa and semifusa, with relatively smaller heads, remain solid.

For the larger units, triple time is favored. It is classified as *perfect*. Purely musical reasons support this definition: triple time is always recognizable as such, whereas duple time in more than one rhythmic order can be misconstrued because the experience of the basic order can be dislodged by a smaller division. I wish to expound this issue in greater detail for it involves momentous decisions for a performance.

I repeat: historical practice leans on three values. Modus divides the longa into three or two breves. In this region parts move with cantus-firmus character or similar structural features. Modus by itself is nonexistent. It represents a principle of augmentation; the part always has a sterile quality, removed from musical life.

In the region of the next value, the brevis is divided into three or two semibreves. This division is called *tempus,* and all musical practice relates to this system. The semibrevis, one tactus long, is here the note one counts. Its next subdivision, the area of minims, is usually fixed at once: a dot inside the tempus sign signifies three minims for a semibrevis; no dot, two. The exact definitions are, respectively, *cum prolatione perfecta* or *imperfecta*. All further subdivisions below the minima are always duple. Thus far all tempus mensurations belong to the calm, slow semibrevis value; its duration was always slightly below one second.

Old music, however, also knows very well the concept of allegro, for which a yet smaller organization determines the meter. For this purpose, one does not choose the next smaller unit within the system of given note values but rather retains the given graphic image and devaluates the length of the notes by means of a cue given by a number or special sign. The common accelerations of the note values consist of doubling the time with a *diminutum* line or the number 2. The *diminutum* line has survived until today, but we are not always aware of the underlying principle and usually think of counting half notes in a four-quarter measure. The *diminutum* line doubles the tempo also in a triple meter, a notation still used by Bach (e.g., *St. John Passion,* middle section of the second alto aria, "Der Held aus Juda," marked *Alla breve*). One could also indicate the *imperfectum diminutum* by reversing the mensural sign. This is called *proportio dupla*.

Division of note values by three was always indicated by the number 3. In the seventeenth century, the procedure becomes ever more exact: two numbers stand one above the other, of which the lower number shows the old order and the upper number shows the newly validated order. In music of the seventeenth century, one must therefore never read a fraction but rather a relation, which has now become an exact tempo relation. The name is now *proportio tripla* when $\frac{3}{1}$ gives the cue for the duration of the notes. If one reads $\frac{3}{2}$ (it looks like our three-half measure without being it!), then it is the *proportio sesquialtera* which accelerates by "making three out of two." Rarer proportions, like *sextupla,* etc., cannot be treated here.

One other systematic order must be noted, important not only for mensural notation. The semibrevis is the divisor of the brevis; and obviously the perfect semibrevis is two-thirds as long as the same note in *tempus imperfectum.* This proportion is valid from Machaut's *Missa Nostre Dame* into the sixteenth century. After a Kyrie by Josquin in *tempus perfectum,* for instance, the following imperfect Christe is slower by that relationship (out of 3 make 2). This prototype of metric order within a total structure confronts us still in Haydn's symphonies and Mozart's music. The disappearance in the later course of the sixteenth century of the mensural prescription *tempus perfectum* has been erroneously interpreted by one's looking only at the paper: the *proportio sesquialtera* now corresponds to *tempus perfectum* as used by Josquin. To explain tempo prescriptions out of the habit of the late nineteenth century is simply wrong. Every sensitive and imaginative conductor responds to the changes of odd and even meters from one movement to the next and is glad when his spontaneously revealed insights are then confirmed by musicological proofs.

Martin Agricola, the first to describe conducting practices (he is an approximate contemporary of Gombert), says that about fifty beats per minute are the normal counting unit.[15] Transcribed into metronome indications for easier definition, in the *tempus* region the semibrevis equals 50; the *proportio dupla,* 100; the *tripla,* 150; and the *sesquialtera,* 75. The metronome indication of 50 is relative and adjustable to the actual tempo on the basis of all conceivable performance conditions. Once the special tempo has been set, however, then all other relationships occurring in the same piece are established with it! Consider a situation in the Credo of the marvelous *Missa Pange lingua* by the aged Josquin.[16] The relationships alternate repeatedly between *dupla* and *tripla.* This happens, in a certain section, not simultaneously in all the voices. *Proportio tripla* remains in some parts while other voices change to *proportio dupla.* The performance practice of that period does not know scores to facilitate coordination. The change of proportions had to be executed with utmost precision; otherwise a performance would have been impossible. Famous canonic pieces utilize change of proportion for the canonic voice and thereby achieve high polyphonic concentration. This kind of composing corresponds a bit to the high art of the Spanish Riding School. Only a very few masters like Okeghem or Josquin could afford to indulge in such sophistry without damage to the quality of the music.

In the course of the sixteenth century, the harmonic dimension increases and demands deliberate attention to special sonorities. Rhythm, in turn, becomes impoverished and foolproof in order not to distract from the new sounds. The alternation of large triple and duple divisions, a source of the full rhythmic life in Dufay's music, gives way to a one-sided primacy of the *imperfectum cum prolatione imperfecta,* that is, duple time. Only *proportio tripla* and *dupla* remain. Such is the scope of meter in the works of Palestrina. In isolated cases, finally, the metric orders fade entirely into the background. Gesualdo's madrigals leave to the notes merely a basic value and push aside any notion of tempus. In line with this composer's harmonic experiments and daring voice-leading for the intensive representation of affects, drawn-out tones stand next to a rapidly chattering parlando. Apparent tempus and even modus values and proportions follow each other without transition. Yet the seventeenth century does not pursue the path laid out by Gesualdo for

NOTE SHAPES OF WHITE MENSURAL NOTATION

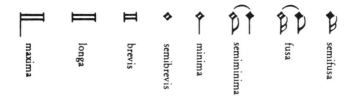

COMMON TEMPUS ORDERS

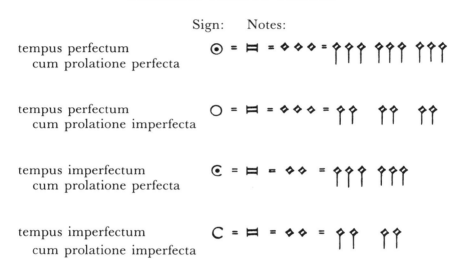

Sign: Notes:

tempus perfectum
  cum prolatione perfecta

tempus perfectum
  cum prolatione imperfecta

tempus imperfectum
  cum prolatione perfecta

tempus imperfectum
  cum prolatione imperfecta

Black mensural notation persists for a long time and hence varies according to country and period. This book cannot deal with all differentiations and details brought about by primitive, square, Franconian, French, Italian, and mixed notations or by the use of red notes (*color* for quasi modus orders of cantus firmi, etc.).

CLEFS

Chiavi naturali   High chiavette   Low chiavette
loco   a third lower   a third higher

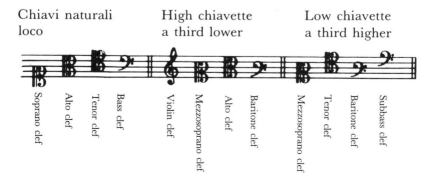

himself but utilizes all the more the orders and relations of mensural notation.

A particular problem for our singers and musicians trained on barlines is the absence of barlines from historic mensural notation. Neither black nor white notation knows our metric markers. The rhythms of the music are *quantitative* and not accentuating! By importing into high polyphony the pronounced metric accents developed in dance music, one completely destroys the charm of those melodies! A great defect in the editions of old music is the addition of barlines for the sake of the habit of performers. Even the placement of such lines *between* the staves of a score does not prevent the playing and singing of false, squeezed syncopations. An expedient solution may be van Crevel's procedure in the complete edition of Obrecht's works.[17] A little comma after each tactus value keeps the tempus orders almost invisible; what matters here is the projection of perfect and imperfect.

Mensural notation also raises the problem of absolute pitch as displayed by the *chiavi naturali* and chiavette. The former indicate the vocally appropriate clefs, namely, soprano, alto, tenor, and bass. As clefs for c^1 and f^0, they are still in use. Their location on a five-line staff permits the placement of each characteristic voice range without ledger lines. The two clefs can appear on any line to accommodate the range of a particular part. Thus one finds, as needed, mezzosoprano, baritone, and subbass clefs next to the usual and the French violin clefs, although soprano, alto, tenor, and bass clefs set the norm.

At the turn toward the sixteenth century, when fixed, almost stereotyped ensembles, particularly for instruments, begin to dominate, notation adapts itself to show absolute pitch. Apparently instruments followed two main interpretations of absolute pitch. The organ demonstrates them clearly as *cornett tone* and *choir tone*. The now mute historic prospect of the organs in the Milan cathedral, old organ remnants in Flanders and France, the original orientation of the organ on the right choir loft in San Petronio in Bologna (1470!), a report by Praetorius on the organ in the cathedral of Halberstadt, and others—in all these cases, the absolute pitch is that of the cornett tone (compared to the Paris standard a^1 of 435 Hz, a^1 sounds like b^1). Simultaneously a low tuning was also in use; Andreas Silbermann still builds on the low choir tone (a^1 sounds like f^1-sharp!). Ultimately all tuning procedures seem to relate to the old *ut* and *fa* clefs of the choral tradition. There, too, the distance of a fourth serves the rendition of church modes on absolute pitches while avoiding ledger lines in certain keys.

The question of absolute pitch becomes particularly acute with highly developed instruments, mainly organs. The cornett tone is named after the white zink (cornetto), the specific soprano instument of the cappella in large churches. Made together with the mouthpiece of one piece of wood turned on a lathe, the zink has no pitch tolerance. Musicians established in the towns submitted to trade rules, and journeymen spent years of traveling like tailors, bakers, and others. Therefore the sixteenth century needed a standardized tuning for all instuments of the same category. The particular tuning (a^1 equals b^1) is called *cornett tone* for two centuries, but it applies to the entire wind ensemble.

Questions concerning absolute pitch find answers if one proceeds from the participating instruments. Foremost the early sixteenth century declares itself in precise formulations. Clues are provided by instrument families, in which instruments of one type, as is the case with voices, fill the usual tonal space of a composition. Here the krummhorns decisively clarify questions about absolute pitch. They provide a favored instrumental ensemble for sacral halls of dukes and kings. In his preface to the Thirty-Seventh Psalm following the dedication proper, Thomas Stoltzer emphasizes the krummhorn ensemble involved in the piece (1526).[18] Krummhorns are double-reed instruments of which the mouthpiece, however, is not pressed by the lips. The reeds are enclosed by a cap so that they vibrate without restraint. The characteristic krummhorn sound derives from the player's pressing his breath through a split in the cap. Such instruments cannot be overblown! The same holds true for the family of pommers (shawms), et cetera. Here the players stick the reeds so deeply into the mouth that the space below the palate acts like a cap. Only the soprano pommer in the seventeenth century receives a shorter reed which, directly affected by the lips, permits overblowing. This soprano pommer is called *haute bois,* transmogrified by German musicians into *oboe.*

Krummhorns have at best the range of a tenth. Looking at the system of church modes of about 1500, one finds a distinction between high-pitched and obviously low-pitched modes. The hypodorian ambitus is from A to a^0 with the finalis on d^0. Mixolydian lies a seventh higher! The krummhorns, which in the early sixteenth century belong to the most popular group of sound producers because of their optimal capacity for projecting an intricate polyphonic design, now bring about an adjustment of absolute pitch: the choice of clefs for a composition indicates the pitch at which it is to be performed. Music in low modes was transposed upward; the opposite happened to pieces in modes that lie high. For a clear understanding of the situation one can profitably study the earliest collection of ricercars, the *Octo tonorum melodiae* by Stoltzer (excellent music, by the way, which perfectly presents the concept of the church modes!).[19] Pieces in the *chiavi naturali* remain in place. Hypodorian and hypophrygian are transposed upward; lydian and mixolydian, downward. The transposition is usually by a third. Organs and positives destined to accompany the cappella prove the point. They all are capable of presenting beat-free major thirds: split keys G#-A^b and D#-E^b become necessary only when one plans to resolve the chiavette by thirds. Organ builders did not favor this "extra" arrangement, for it involves construction problems. For the final choice of pitch, a key with a minimum of accidentals is the preferred one (one had necessarily to consider the meantone tuning of keyboard instruments). This means: one notates in white notation without any accidental or at best writes down a flat. One made music on any desirable pitch, indicating the absolute pitch by the clefs in the *chiavi naturali* or the two chiavette. Here one must distinguish exactly among the clearly formulated kinds of notation: in one superius part or in merely numbered parts, an extraordinary clef is not yet an instruction to transpose. One always has to consider soprano, tenor, and bass. The alto clef permits no conclusion; for the *contratenor altus,* functioning as a stopgap, fluctuates too much.

By not observing the absolute pitch range designated by the clefs, one distorts the music and sacrifices balance. Look at Palestrina's motets on the *Song of Songs*: regardless of the pitch chosen because of a certain tuning or a given ensemble, these extremely valuable motets forming a closed cycle must be sung strictly according to the clefs.[20] Or consider Monteverdi's Vesper Service[21] or the madrigals by Marenzio,[22] Schütz,[23] or Gesualdo.[24] If the chiavette are ignored, the pieces lie on a wrong pitch and strain the voices so as to produce a strange penetrance of the higher ranges, destroy the equilibrium of the parts, and ruin their expressive pronouncements.

The great cappella tradition has always and without exception understood how to adjust to the conditions of an optimal voice balance. Really high voice ranges were avoided because one considered their penetrance unsuited for polyphony. The low regions were similarly excluded because of their incapacity for design. Yet one rather conceded extreme depths to the basses than extreme heights to the sopranos. Often falsetti sang even the cantus! For madrigals, on the other hand, that

is, secular chamber music with singers, only women's voices were utilized! On the whole, however, the same basic conditions prevail. Most
of Gesulado's madrigals and a major part of Schütz's *Opus primum* are
notated in high chiavette and must be transposed.

The *Magnificat* in Monteverdi's Vesper Service must hence be performed in G major; the Psalm "Laudate," in A major. (The uppermost
two parts of the Psalm are composed for boy sopranos, the other five
parts for male voices.)

In connection with chiavette one must remember to tune sacred
music to the cornett pitch. Compared to our modern pitch, the difference is still a large halftone, by which music once sounded higher. Yet
to drive instruments deep into the regions of sharps and flats is hardly
compatible with historic tunings. (Cf. below the chapter "Historic Tunings." For the periods of mensural notation, one used Pythagorean and
meantone tunings, temperaments by Werckmeister and Kepler, and finally the three Kirnberger tunings. An exact division of the octave by
the twelfth root of 2 exists only in our century!)

The notation systems discussed so far contrast fully with another
method, the tablatures. These are instrumental notations indicating the
fingering. They differ according to instrument families; lute tablatures
are further split into several branches. Tablatures for keyboard instruments have the oldest tradition. Here one resorts to an ancient transmission of writing intervals with letters. The keys are named with the
letters gained by Boethius from Greek instrumental notation,[25] which
occurred, for example, in the *Bilingua* of Dijon in order to fixate the
Carolingian hook neumes.[26] This tradition has lasted until today; we
still name the keys according to that keyboard tablature.

Tablatures for stopped stringed instruments notate the music by
marking the finger positions of the left hand. There were tablatures for
wind players which identified the sideholes by numbers. Organ and lute
tablatures are particularly important.

Key names and fingerings on the neck of the lute, as already mentioned, define pitch exactly. For marking the rhythm, one borrows stems
and flags from mensural notation. Lacking the heads of the notes as means
to indicate duration, one must operate with note values that (compared to mensural notation) are very small and short. Therefore one
replaces in tablatures the many flags with beams. One speaks mockingly of "lute grates" because of the many crossed bars. In the tempus region,

white mensural notation stands in a 1:4 proportion to tablatures; in the prolations, even in a 1:8 proportion! A composition in tablature must be notated in values that much smaller! In the course of the seventeenth and eighteenth centuries, both methods of notation are again and again used next to each other with all their characteristics; composers employ both. Organists accustomed to keyboard tablatures write even large scores in organ tablature, as, for instance, Buxtehude has done.[27] In rare cases, white mensural notation can be used, as it were, in the opposite direction and then it looks strange, as in Handel's *Cantata spagnuola* in which he employs for soprano, guitar, and figured bass the ecclesiastic notation of 1500, moreover with the historic *color,* that is, black notation for hemiolas (recitative in white *proportio* notation become almost unrecognizable).[28] From these two extreme examples—Buxtehude's cantatas and Handel's piece written for Spanish usage—one recognizes the difference between the two systems of notation. (In Handel's time, Spain was certainly drastically backward compared to the musical situation in Central Europe. For this reason, Handel writes in an antiquated notation, but he is fully familiar with it. Consider the clear indication of hemiolas! In making music, one must not ignore such elements of meter! Modern performance practice, based on technical perfection of instrumental playing, leans toward racing the tempi without mercy and impressing the public with brilliant technique. If one wishes to do justice to all metric and rhythmic conditions and details of a master work, technical allegro orgies are naturally taboo. Handel's way of writing hemiolas could supply the necessary barrier!)

The development of lute tablatures advanced from diverse, locally conditioned musical cultures and is therefore anything but unified. In Italy one used a five-line staff which, however, represents the lute strings. The lines are interpreted in the sense in which one holds the instrument on one's lap: the lowest line corresponds to the highest discant string; the uppermost line, to the lowest string (the lute still had only five strings; for the later added sixth string, one notates in letters). Numbers on the lines indicate the fret to be fingered. Open strings are marked by capital letters. Spanish tablatures reverse the lines and orient them according to our notation: the highest line corresponds to the highest string. France replaces the numbers by letters. In Germany, lines are abandoned altogether; one numbers the intersections of string and fret. The twenty-three letters of the German alphabet plus two common abbreviations for *et* and *con* yield twenty-five signs, which suffice for the lute of the period with five frets. For the sixth fret one writes double letters or borrows the little dashes from organ tablature.

Organ tablatures are written in score. Stems and beams suffice for rhythm. Lute tablatures always remain more or less a puzzle: while notating the metric position of a tone within the measure, one thereby does not define the duration! Lute tablatures can therefore not express polyphony. All stringed instruments of the lute and viol families are in principle monophonic instruments, only subsequently trained for polyphony and then posing both technical and notational difficulties. Consider with open eyes the Pisendel Sonatas by Bach: in the fugues, voice-leading disappears when the violin technique does not permit its continuation.[29] The situation in the case of the lute is not much different.

Today only a few guitarists and lutenists are really familiar with tablature notation. One accepts transcriptions into modern notation. The notation of polyphonic music, however, must do justice to voice-leading. What is tolerated in tablatures becomes unbearable in our common notation, because we expect entirely different norms of precision. To transcribe a lute tablature, one must be a good player of the instrument, for one point remains entirely open: tablatures notate the actions of the left hand — the possibilities of the right hand are wide open. Here good players can find many solutions, particularly in the application of differentiated arpeggios.

Common to all tablatures is a typical treatment of metric units. Whenever, for instance, the requirement is *imperfectum cum prolatione imperfecta*, we now meet group formations identified by spacing or barline. Thus with retention of the mensural sign of white notation, the modern four-four time becomes visible. It has sprung from tablature! We see the connection clearly in the autograph of Bach's chorale prelude "Wir Christenleut" in the *Orgelbüchlein*.[30] Bach had to write the piece on one page, for one could not very well turn the page while playing. He notates the last line of the piece in organ tablature because it takes up half the space. The tablature permits conclusions concerning the preceding notation: the writing-down of the piece follows the tradition of organ tablatures; the quarter note thus receives the value of a semibrevis in the tempus region of white mensural notation.

If, on the other hand, one applies to white mensural notation the usual modern manner of counting the sign C in four quarters, catastrophic mistakes result which erase the real meter and spoil the music.

The tradition of white notation continues in church music and exists partly in the grand Masses by Schubert.

The eminent significance of historic notations for musical performance practice will be recognized in its full impact if one thoroughly studies the connection between the metric norms of movement and the historic manner of notation, and if one then realizes it in performance. The next chapter is therefore closely related to the consideration of historic notation.

As an appendix to the study of notation, I should like to submit one more word of advice to conductors. Whoever cares about early music must be able to read all historic clefs fluently and without transposition. Musicians educated from childhood for this profession usually have a more or less precise ear. Mastery of clefs becomes a necessity. The pedagogic methods for learning the *chiavi naturali* are not always the most practical. I therefore want to describe the method by which, fifty years ago, my teacher Eugen Zador instructed me in this skill and which seems to me very effective. The method consists in concentrating at any time on a single new clef. Zador's recipe was: soprano clef (play for miles, always just read, play nothing twice, otherwise memory participates!), then the pair of outer voices soprano-bass; after full mastery, the same procedure with the alto clef, and finally the trio soprano-alto-bass; the tenor clef follows in the same way. At the same time there is great advantage to playing Bach's *Inventions* and *Sinfonias* from a facsimile edition, where the same clefs appear. Sight-reading and transposing chiavette is more advanced, but many of our colleagues do it perfectly. The important condition is always not to learn a particular piece, otherwise one trains one's memory and does not attain fluent clef-reading. Zador used the editions of church music of the Palestrina era (*Musica Divina* publications).[31] We always had to read the rhythmic and melodic substance simultaneously. Such procedure is pedagogically correct, for otherwise a second obstacle arises in the face of highly developed rhythms.

The elimination of original clefs in editions of old music harms the issue. Such facilitation is prompted by commercial considerations in order to attract inadequately educated buyers. There is no excuse for avoiding the reading of clefs; otherwise the rich treasure of early music in the various *Denkmäler* will become ever more barren. These volumes have already been called "paper cemeteries." From clefs, moreover, one learns many important details for a performance.

CHAPTER II

Meter and Rhythm

In principle one has to remember that our Western music long ago abandoned the conditions of open, unlimited time values and has confined itself to rhythmically precise distances, similar to the fixed locations of tonal intervals. Gliding within the tonal space without firmly established intervals is analogous to music-making free of temporal markings. (In the hourly chants from minarets, for instance, Islam has retained such an attitude, because it needs for its religious effects the experience of unlimited dynamism. Emotionally charged reactions in all aspects of life belong to the totality of certain Islamic cultures.)

Before considering rhythmic phenomena in detail, we must clearly set forth two fundamentally different principles of metric formation and rhythmic qualities.

In early music before about 1700, one must carefully examine the kind of given rhythmic structure (also true for some phases of baroque music): one encounters either a quantitative meter or accentual structures. High polyphony, particularly *contrapunctus floridus*, demands practically only unaccented meters.[32] Homophonic music, dance music, etc., on the other hand, unfolds with stresses on the shared metric positions, which must be heard in performance.

The tradition of quasi free-floating lines of most chant melodies taught the Gothic musician to project rhythmic shapes without accentuation. The freer and the fuller of fantasy the development of melody, the more it rejects schematic accents. The symptom of such conduct is its openness toward rhythmically alternating time elements. Groups form

21

themselves according to diverse units of motion. "Gearshifts" are accomplished by hemiolas both *per augmentationem* and *per diminutionem*. Every performing musician must develop his ability to experience rhythmic groupings, not by mechanical tricks, but by constant efforts to carry the manifold rhythms into consciousness. Patience and sincere concern are necessary. Dufay's music offers a good field for practicing, for it demands unconditionally this kind of rhythmic structuring, far away from mechanically counting beats. Training is possible only by one's consciously dealing with both performance manners in specific compositions — with quantitative or accentual meters.

The distinction between these two metrical principles derives from elevated language. In Latin, ordinary word accents need not coincide with the verse order of poetry. Long and short syllables are placed according to the verse, thus:

$$\smile\!- \quad \smile\!-\!\smile \quad -\!\smile\!-$$
$$\text{Veni creator spiritus.}$$

The accentual attitude of most modern languages would render it falsely, thus:

$$\text{Véni creátor spíritus.}$$

German [and English] use ancient verse patterns in conjunction with modern word accents. It is this relentless scanning of accents which, among other factors, displaces the old meters. In *Wallensteins Lager*, Schiller places in the doggerel verse stresses between which the "light syllables" are interpolated. We read:

$$\text{Und wäre sie mit Ketten an den Himmel geschlossen.}$$

[Cf. Wordsworth's

$$\text{"The appearance, instantaneously disclosed,"}$$

from his *The Excursion*.] After the upbeat and the first accent, there are three light syllables. This constellation is immediately repeated. Three unaccented syllables between the ictuses — no ancient verse would permit it! There is a similar example in the *Hildebrandslied*:

"Wélaga nu, Wáltand got, Wéwort skihit."

[Cf. the Anglo-Saxon *The Dream of the Rood*:

"Swaétan on pa swífan heálfe eáll ic waes mid sórgum gedréfed."]

The old German alliterative poetry [as well as the Old English poetry] seems to be of similar nature to Schiller's doggerel [and Wordsworth's line]!

Accustomed to the accentual principle of modern German [and English], one has great difficulties in grasping quantitative meters. Again and again, the right procedure in its musical application must be trained and confirmed. A systematic clarification of metric and rhythmic questions in a particular composition must be preceded by a clear recognition of the problematic structuring of time according to the two fundamental principles.

One must further distinguish between metrical norms as orderly patterns and metrical additive procedures that spring from linear spinning-out. To the latter belongs a historically developed and still active formation of meter in which relatively small temporal elements — quasi amorphous compared to the opposite metrical procedure — produce groupings. In the Yugoslav-Macedonian region, for example, this metrical principle is well known; one finds groups of seven time units, et cetera. Miniature particles are gathered into optional large additive complexes. We Western Europeans really experience these open-ended meters only when the counted elements differ in length; for we project our customary principles of order into music using familiar groupings. The language of those regions is probably the formative element analogously to which instrumental music is then built up. At the border between the two principles lies quintuple time, as in the dance movement of Tchaikovsky's Sixth Symphony; here the five-four time is an alternation of 3 plus 2 or the other way around, depending on the musical contents of the single measures.

Additive meter is an exception to the tradition of our music. The different quality of such meter renders all the more intelligible the structural principle characteristic of Western music.

Our musical tradition has developed meters in such a manner that all our structures can be erected within the norms of duple and triple time. Whether we think of the historic schemes of mensural notation or the modern composite measures — the underlying basic phenomenon is the same. Hemiolas merely shift the count of beats from duple to triple, either *per augmentationem* or *per diminutionem*.

Our understanding of Western metric orders depends on one other basic rhythmic-metric phenomenon founded on human experience. Underlying all metrical experience is our heartbeat. A measure is set by the pulse. We sense all time units most personally in relation to that norm. The modern concept of *moderato* is identical with it. We evaluate faster or slower tempi by the distance from that basic measure (just as we interpret the plus and minus degrees of a thermometer!). When the subdivision of a beat approaches the norm of the pulse, our musical consciousness will tend to shift to the subdivision and to accept it as the basic beat. Adagio movements in duple time are thus really precarious. The easy transformation of two long values into four moderato beats creates a singular problem for conductors. Such misinterpretation is much rarer in slow triple time: such *perfect* groups in which two unaccented beats follow the main beat are almost always recognizable. Actually the reverse occurs here when the three values appear as a unit. Fast groups of threes merge and may be drawn into still larger units. Think of the scherzo in Beethoven's Ninth Symphony: "Ritmo di tre battute...di quattro battute!" The real difficulty lies in the actual performance practice, in the task of musically fully realizing an adagio in duple time. The musician has only one solution: he must carefully guard against counting smaller units than the actual adagio motion. Pulse counts are *exact* values, invariably tied to accents! For rendering persuasively a slow sovereign meter, the only method consists in subsuming all metrical positions that are not principal under that sovereignty. What we know as a baroque method for realizing the concepts *Grave, Lentement*, etc. — that *stile francese* which requires optimal dotting — may similarly be applied by conductors performing an adagio (only more carefully and in cautious doses). The subdivisors must be casually and gingerly placed in their *approximate* positions. Their subordination to the actual adagio values offers the method for a proper projection of the adagio! The importance of such aspects can hardly be overrated. If one denies a composition its proper norm of motion, then the first and decisive musical dimension is falsified; and consequently all characteristics are distorted.

From the organized echelons of note values in mensural notation, all further norms of motion derive. By taking the divisor in a *proportio* as the typical indicator for a motion, one reaches the historically fast tempi. There is no purpose to stamping them all *allegri*, for such terms have different meanings in the seventeenth century. Large metric units as well, particularly in triple time, can be musically directly experienced, regardless of heart beats (and even slower tempi). The order *modus* in cantus firmi, etc., can thus actually be realized.

Musicians around 1500 chose a standard slightly slower than the human pulse in order to manifest by this differentiation experiences beyond human measure, particularly as all significant compositions were in the service of sacred music. The technical term *tactus integer valor* defines that time value—that balanced calm attitude of a basic standard motion. It is the ordinary value in the metric region of *tempus*. According to descriptions like those by Martin Agricola, this tempo equals approximately a metronome indication of 52.[33] This norm remains valid for a long time. In special cases, its conventions last beyond the music of the Vienna Classics.

The separate regions *modus, tempus, prolatio* still occur in the seventeenth century, in the works of Schütz, for instance, in the sense that meter and rhythm structure and delimit zones and values of a composition. Consider the piece "Sei gegrüsset, Maria" from the *Kleine geistliche Konzerte*.[34] Here the metric devices of *proportio tripla*—with its hemiola and *modus*—define most effectively and genuinely musically the hierarchy of Gabriel, Maria, Jesus, and God. Gabriel's words lie in an *imperfectum cum proportione tripla*, that is, in a fluent sextuple meter in which only the naming of Maria produces the meter assigned to her, the imperfect hemiola. Maria's part signals with the brevis a new special meter, proceeding at first quasi in duple-time hemiolas entirely outside the sextuple fundamental rhythm. The "bewildered" Maria is represented in the basso continuo without relation to the meter of the Angel.

Even more illuminating is the repetition of Maria's part when Schütz places below the breves sung by Maria a pronounced trochaic *proportio tripla* bass. When Maria enters with her meter at the words, "wie soll das zugehen," the thoroughbass adjusts itself to her. At the words, "sintemal ich von keinem Manne weiss," the perplexed Maria gets muddled in the smallest note values—a typical madrigal device. The Angel's declaration of God's incarnation employs the large order of the three-beat brevis and its twofold augmentation. This feature is emphasized by the retention of the tripled basic meter in the thoroughbass, above which the large values are spanned all the more impressively. Any doubt whether composers took all these metric-rhythmic orders only as notational conventions or intellectual systems is dispelled by this concerto by Schütz, which demonstrates the possible significations of the notated mensural orders. (In connection with this concerto, one must mention that the Angel must be sung by a high voice, that is, a falsetto or the like. The new Bärenreiter edition wrongly raises the pitch by a wholetone, thereby altering the vocal character. A female alto does not fit the Angel, although the transposition was made for just this reason. The metric orders, too, appear poorly.)

Musicians will never expel long-held tones from a dynamic tonal experience by pronounced mechanical counting. Even when a very long tone is apparently held, the endpoint of the long tone is precisely composed and thus becomes a musical event by means of the diversity of consonances and positions (e.g., the beginning of the concerto on Psalm 126 by Jacob Weckmann[35]).

The tactus as the calm basic measure, as a norm of motion of the first order, has remained valid throughout the entire history of Western music. Agricola (of the generation after Josquin) describes a method of conducting with very economical, barely noticeable signs. The cappella stands next to the altar; the deportment required for this religious, liturgical position does not admit flaying arms and conspicuous gestures (nothing beyond finger motions of the conductor's hand, which rests on the choirbook). Agricola first describes the "downbeat," that is, the marking of the large note value. In the case of many persistently small note values, he recommends dividing the beat by marking the main pulse as well as its divisors. The hand is brought back to its main position (when the tactus is not subdivided) by a sweeping motion immediately preceding the next downbeat. In the manner of a *stile francese*, only the main stresses are marked and can thus be musically experienced. Conductors know that the beat inflicts itself relentlessly on the music! If one chooses a subdivisor — by markedly beating an *alla breve*, for instance, in four — one thereby has broken to pieces the large measure without mercy and destroyed an adagio. Heinrich Schütz, explaining in German many performance practices, speaks explicitly in the preface to the *Auferstehungshistorie* of "a slow appropriate measure in which consist, as it were, the soul and essence of music."[36] The era of Schütz, entirely within the framework of the great cappella tradition, still knows fast tempi only as subdivisors and apprehends them only in relation to the large overall order. *Proportio tripla* rules almost exclusively.

The various metric proportions of notation systems have been treated by theorists. Gafori's writings are well known,[37] but still Morley presents the material in a similar manner.[38] The metric structures project the same orders that are familiar from the monochord for tonal relationships. The theory scrupulously treated in regard to frequencies casts its reflection also on metric phenomena. Here a fundamental principle must be stated. In the primary musical dimension, in rhythm, the possibilities of systematic differentiations of experiences are relatively limited. In accentuated rhythm, as in dance music, the free play for the development of a proper system is rather restricted. In quantitative rhythm, on the other hand, each situation permits expansion of its details. Think of the rhythmic affluence in Dufay's music. In other words: the possibilities for the development of proper metric systems, types, and laws are limited; the rhythmic formulations *within* the erected metric orders are inexhaustible.

A methodic exposition of the principles presented yields the following guidelines for the performance of early music:

I. In multi-movement works of the Vienna classical composers and in many later works, no time measure ever exists in isolation, appropriating for itself in a quasi unoccupied space, as it were, the concept of a tempo. The masters of the romantic era, too, greatly respect the relationship of strongly contrasting elements. In the finale of Schumann's Piano Concerto, the switch in and out of hemiolas is perfectly controlled and serves as a means of formal structuring.

In early music, a "tempo" is a characteristic for a whole work. The conditions under which music is made are manifold and exert influences that can hardly be surveyed. Performances are affected by acoustics, casts, the musical qualifications of the participants, their imagination and creative force. In addition, there are the liberties of diminutions, et cetera. It is not in the spirit of the performance practice of old music to play a work twice in exactly the same manner. Each presentation of a work is different, obviously also in regard to tempo. The particular elements of a composition always remain related to each other. The internal metric-rhythmic forces are regulated by the systems of mensural notation — they are graphically fixed.

II. The conventions of metric orders and tempos were never intolerantly and mechanically followed. The baroque attitude toward affect supplies many indications in this direction — the madrigal around 1600, for example, with its emphasis on expression, be it the result of extravagant harmonies or of extreme rhythmic contrasts. For music of still earlier periods, one encounters again and again references to free play of subjective interpretations.[39] One must be able to distinguish between strict note values tied to laws of mensural notation and the op-tions of a subjective performance. Schütz again offers many excellent points of orientation. In conformity with the musical character of his works and his intent to transplant expressive values and devices from madrigal and concerto to Protestant church music, he concretely registers deviations from the strictly factual type of motion, as indicated by the *mensura*, by additional explicit prescriptions. He writes out the Latin terms *tarde* and *praesto*. The performer's task is to determine the extent to which these instructions are capable of influencing the situation set by mensural notation. Various passages in compositions by Schütz make it clear that these two terms function as an attribute to the given tempo relations, which stem from the conventions of sixteenth-century mensural music. They are instructions to intensify the particular character of a piece or section. They are not real tempo markings! Schütz moves out of these special sections without any caesura or explicit retraction; a new mensural sign cancels the addition of the attribute. The instruction is similarly erased by the entrance of instruments or by changes in the situation of the section superscribed by special instructions. Schütz employs also the words *adagio* or *presto*. The terminology adjusts itself to the place of publication (Italy in the case of the *Symphoniae sacrae prima pars*) or the Latin text. At the end of the second section of the concerto "O quam tu pulchra es," the precept *adagio* does not occur in the various voices at the same moment but rather at the respective entries of the pertinent theme.[40] The different parts insert themselves into the *adagio* one after the other. This concerto shows that the staggered instructions do not reflect mistakes or imprecise orthography but rather the deliberate disposition toward expressiveness. The Latin or Italian tempo indications are certainly not modern measures of time but cautiously used attributes of the actual temporal orders given by notation. It is important to comprehend that mensural notation relates the sections of a composition in secure proportions to each other and thus lets the work arise as a whole.

The meaning of the term *tactus* as a measure of time depends on many circumstances. Church music with its aesthetic precepts and resonant acoustics requires a characteristic tempo. Secular music admits of considerably faster tempi, which may exceed 60 beats per minute and approach the human pulse. For the performance of early music, exact metronome markings are out of place. Each musician has his own individual nature and temperament; and many factors make themselves felt to create a persuasive performance that springs from the best vitality of singers and players. A musician's personality must have free play in such matters. Technical know-how obviously enters.

The Italian or Latin attributes differentiate the strict conditions of mensural notation, in line with the general excitation of all musical means for expression, for affect. This tendency softens the relations of mensural notation, of which the gradual dissolution advances in very small steps. Unconditional subordination to norms is superseded by deference to the peculiarity of a composition and the accompanying facts. Personally I am convinced that at all occasions musicians of our Western civilization have known such tolerances. In the music of the seventeenth century, the composers prescribe the desired interpretation and thus begin to write it down. The concerto "De profundis" by Nicolas Bruhns presents an extreme case.[41] The organ music and cantatas of this composer, who died young, show so many typical characteristics that one need not wonder at the extravagant occurrence of additional tempo indications. It would be wrong to interpret such indications as "modern." Bruhns must be understood in the context of organ practice where both notation in tablature and the tradition of mensural notation prevail. (At the beginning of the concerto, the minima, current in the seventeenth century, defines the beat. A metronome marking of 54 should suffice, variable down to 48, even 46, and up to 60. The relationship of the separate sections to each other is regulated by the laws of late mensural notation.)

III. To define the tactus of a particular piece, one must first know without doubt whether the manuscript followed the practice of mensural notation or of tablature. The relationship between these two methods of notation is not always 4:1. In Malipiero's edition of Monteverdi's *Orfeo*, the dance pair "Lasciate i monti" is transcribed in such a way that after the vocal tripla the following instrumental postlude appears in only halved note values of that *proportio tripla*; the tripla is notated in minims instead of semibreves, hence just a 1:2 relationship.[42] Instrumentalists expected to find a notation as it was common in tablatures, but they also had to be able to read mensural notation (cf. the calm ritornelli in the third act of *Orfeo*). Bach's works show clearly his use of both methods of notation. Consider the Credo in the B-minor Mass.[43] The seven-part fugue at the beginning has the *diminutum* line, which halves the value of the brevis. In the autograph of the thoroughbass part, lines above the second to fourth quarters and the sixth to eighth quarters mark the retention of the harmony for the duration of a semibrevis. We deal here

with archaic white notation and count the semibrevis, that is, two very
calm beats per measure and hence the historic *tactus integer valor*. Beating four halfnotes would go against the notation and be wrong. The pulse
of the large values is confirmed by the structure of the fugue. The appearance of the theme toward the end *per augmentationem* would otherwise not remain practically comprehensible for a hearer but dissolve into
a series of organ points. Bach never wrote paper music; if the structure
of a movement does not render a direct experience, the error lies in our
wrong interpretation. The fugue has as subject the Gregorian intonation formula and takes the place of the intonation according to pre-
Reformation practice. The attitude of the fugue is determined by this
function. The word "Patrem" initiates in a "modern" alla breve the text
assigned of old to the cappella. Here one moves in a calm *tempo ordinario*.
In the next section, "Et in unum," the diminutum line is eliminated;
the quarters in this movement, notated in the manner of tablature, count
like the halves before.

In his *Versuch,* Philipp Emanuel Bach no longer cares to explain
historically the possibilities of writing the same music in normal, doubled, or halved note values.[44] He merely records how a musician reacts
to these differentiated notations. He finds that large note values carry
the piece into the sphere of sacred art, where the style of church music
is considered deliberately archaic, ponderous because of its situation and
tradition, and where it is employed only when an approach to up-to-
dateness seems undesirable. Philipp Emanuel interprets notation in small
note values, on the other hand, as an instruction to play the music fluently
and even hastily. For Bach's son, the conventions of mensural notation
and tablature are no longer recognized as the causes of principles of notation. Of all cappella principles, today only the alla breve has remained
valid.

IV. In Bach's works, the pieces in the specific cappella tradition
can also be delimited by their engagement in expression, in affect, in
the attitude of the performers. Pieces in the tradition of sacred music
leave the singers and players much less room for personal interpretation. Wherever one finds the old notation, the old tactus prevails with
a beat slightly slower than that of our heart, that is, about the historic
standard of 52. In all notations outside these ties, the norm of the heartbeat establishes itself as *tempo ordinario*. This is true for all music not written down in that special cappella notation. When Bach notates in
tablature tradition, one should be guided by *tempo ordinario*. When, on

the other hand, he evidently resorts to white notation, we should approach the music through the old *tactus integer valor*. Quite apart from this differentiation, the fundamental validity of relations is maintained.

V. The relationships among the separate movements of a composition are then fractured by dance music. The traditional pair Reigen-Hupfauf (or Allemande-Courante, or Pavane-Gagliarde) obeys the relation of *imperfectum* to *proportio tripla* (or to *proportio sesquialtera* if one considers the later appearances of the duple-time first movement with its minute metrics). As long as the variation suite dominates, the various movements of the suite remain related to each other. In the French suite, however, the freely added movements of sarabande and gigue never found themselves tied by any relationship. The sarabande always stood in isolation with its typical alternation of iambs and trochees (the Roman proscription of its being danced!) and its very different origin.[45] The quick English or the siciliano-like Italian gigue is in turn separated by the sarabande from the primary pair. In the eighteenth century, any ties are further dissolved by the participation of then modern dances, often exotic. In Dresden, for instance, Polish aristocracy swarms around the Saxon Elector, who is also King of Poland, and thereby carries specifically Polish society music to central Germany. Similar situations bring about an exchange of dance types from England down to Italy. Paris of the last French kings admitted an abundance of dance variants. The dancing masters created in continuity ever new variants of the social dances which thereby gradually lost their sharp definition and particular character. Bach's B-minor Suite for flute contains neither movement of the original dance pair; the only remnant from the French suite is the sarabande but stylized as a piece of absolute music through canonic voice-leading.[46]

VI. The thoroughbass offers significant suggestions for the clarification of the main tempo, of the tactus. The bass line by itself as well as the essential harmonic events prescribed by the figures offer a much clearer reading of the basic motion than the upper voices. In concertizing parts, moreover, the diminution may be written out. It would be a great mistake to apply a millimeter standard, as it were, to a free melody flowing in smallest note values in an attempt to box it up in a diminutive meter. Such procedure would turn an adagio movement into a tedious moderato. Pieces marked adagio show the norm of the motion best in the bass line and in the harmonic rhythm often revealed by cadential tendencies.

In a *proportio tripla* by Schütz, fast harmonic progressions may occur in the separate tripla values (cf. *Opus Decimum,* concerto "Ich werde
nicht sterben").[47] Here we deal with a prototype. A fast harmonic rhythm
belongs to the nature of genuinely fast movements. The clearest possible graphic representation of the metric situation is essential. The Schütz
piece has an *imperfectum*, that is, duple meter subdivided in the next lower
order by triplets. Our modern six-eight measure would do justice to the
concept and situation. In it, even the duple order of the dotted quarters
is always present (a six-eight measure notated in tablature is nothing
else but an *imperfectum cum prolatione perfecta!*).

Looking at the whole problematic complex of tactus, one realizes
that contrary to our modern attitude toward tempo questions, the rules
and conventions of the old notation practice do not indicate tempi but
metrical structures. In early music, multi-movement compositions want
to be taken as a whole. Metrical relationships of the parts to each other
are significant. The question of a correct tempo cannot be answered by
a metronome number, because many separate factors differing with each
performance make themselves felt. Notwithstanding these resistances
against rigidly precise performance conditions, the specific metric and
rhythmic demands must be met. In view of the dissimilarity of historic
notation, a multitude of prescriptions must be optimally understood and
musically realized. Chronological limits for the validity of such prescriptions can be set only with difficulty. For a variety of reasons, composers
resorted to archaic notation manners. Today we still accept Philipp
Emanuel Bach's patently effective method of differentiating through note
values slow, normal, and fast tempi. Summarily one must emphasize
again that a composer's metric orders and systems must be unexcep-
tionally respected. Notation in long note values must not be ignored
in order to "count out" rhythmic details in a foolproof reduced but inappropriate meter. In Church music, historical notation can be found beyond the Classic period.

VII. For the realization of metric and rhythmic structures, the
placement of stresses is a practical method, of which the fundamental
significance has not yet been clarified and evaluated. In accentual music, the distribution of stresses defines the character. Because note values
often pile up, mastery of often complicated rhythmic details becomes
dependent upon a subdivision of the main pulse, particularly in the case
of a conductor's inadequate talent or deficient training. Unfortunately

a true rhythmic, dynamic task is all too often bypassed by a performer's executing metric details. (Inadequate rehearsal schedules in opera houses are to blame for the negligence attached to purportedly artistic events. The poor conductor then saves himself by putting on blinders and riding to the end of the opera through thick and thin at high speed and with painfully metric beats.)

Everything depends on placing the form of conducting and each detail connected with it in the service of the structure of a composition. The practical question is: where are accents required or admissible for a definite musical situation, and how many? Here one must decide: is the piece built in a large meter, in a fundamental measure, or does a composite meter allow the allotment of subaccents? Such problems affect primarily the slow movements. In a quiet siciliano (as in Bach's Double Concerto for Two Violins),[48] the task consists in presenting the four dotted quarters and through them the fundamental meter of the twelve-eight measure. Failure to realize the hierarchy of the four differentiated single accents robs the piece of its large order and thereby ruins it. In very fast movements, larger groupings can also be found. I refer again to the scherzo of Beethoven's Ninth Symphony with the markings *di tre battute* or *di quattro battute* — instructions which must become audible in performance.

One need not interpret metrical instructions in old pedagogic writings too pedantically. They often address beginners and employ elementary methods which must be evaluated as such. More is revealed by the character of a composition, as defined by the Italian quasi-tempo indications. One plays andante with a minimum of stresses and accents. The "walking" character is musically best realized by the elimination of subaccents — if at all possible, only by the main accent at the beginning of the measure. An adagio is destroyed by one's cutting up four sixteenths into two groups of two-times-two with a little squeeze on the third sixteenth. Again: the main accent comes into its own only when the smallest note values nestle into it. Tasteful operation of this *inégal* principle is the central issue of a practical knowledge of style. In this life, one never learns to find the absolutely correct measure. One is always on the way to a better solution of one's tasks. Musicians continually gain new insights and are grateful for the beautiful sensation of improving themselves.

In the context of tactus, the execution of syncopations can be objectively considered. The various possibilities are:

1. Syncopations displace the accent. Hence they do not increase the number of stresses but shift them.
2. Syncopation brings additional accents. A properly inherent accent is surpassed by a following syncopated accent.
3. The dominating orientation remains that of the metrically spaced order. The main accent, enclosed, as it were, by the syncopation, appears in a forced "squeeze." Through the diversity of beating time and its influence on performers, this last method has gained excessive currency even when stylistically and technically inappropriate.

The situation may be elucidated by an example from Bach's *Magnificat,* the alto aria "Esurientes."[49] Bach notates the flutes not by means of ties: [musical notation] , but he rather lengthens the dot: [musical notation] . In short, he does not wish to carry the prolongation into the musical consciousness of the flutists. For this metrically involved piece, one must decide among the three procedures mentioned above. (1) The first measure has only one accent, namely, on the entrance of the syncopation, free of coarseness — a delicate shifted accent. The basic beats appear only in the accompaniment. (2) The first sixteenth note in the flutes retains its metric accent, the accent on the syncopation follows. A doubling of accents has occurred; an element of dance becomes clearly noticeable. (3) The main beats prevail. Within each syncopation, the positions of the second and fourth quarters are marked by a little squeeze. The syncopation loses its force, and a mechanically metrical principle violates the rhythms. Hence procedure (3) may be ignored. The decision lies between (1) or (2). Execution (2) has much to commend itself, for the singer's text later confirms it. But execution (1) is also possible if one considers how much the regular pulse accents appear, anyway, in the accompaniment. This whole example shows how many decisions a conductor has to make and how many details he has to weigh carefully before beginning the first rehearsal!

VIII. The practical task before us is to find the best modern way of conducting sacred music (that is, the larger ensembles) of the fifteenth to seventeenth centuries. Division of the large value of the semibrevis (the tactus value) into four conventional beats is unacceptable, because it would protract and ruin the tempo and moreover impose an organization of metric accents on a work of a different nature. Small ensembles respond well to the "homoeopathic" manner of conducting described

by Agricola; and if a situation requires more gestures, the outline of
the old beats can be enlarged and differentiated. This kind of direction,
in any case, requires of the performing singer and musician full and
responsible participation and it safeguards the personal involvement identified with chamber music.

For a better understanding of the situation, we shall survey the
forms of conducting practices in Western music (and no more than name
the foot-stamping practiced by the choir leader in the orchestra of the
Greek theater; in this book, such primitive methods need no more than
a fleeting reference):

1. *Cheironomy.* — The hands, by position and fingers, give rhythmic as well as melodic instructions in aid of memory. This technique
was used for Gregorian chant, for instance, for groups singing from the
choir stalls and for similar occasions.

2. *Conducting with appropriate percussion.* — Sacred polyphonic music from about the twelfth to fourteenth centuries requires that the unit
of the tactus be marked. We read nowhere of visible signals given by
a responsible musician. Order of the metric flow could be maintained
by instruments with a pronounced attack and definite percussiveness
(triangle, bells). We have reports of the Notre Dame practice that the
singers of the discant voices executed a common swaying motion of the
upper parts of their bodies, thus uniting themselves into a group. In
secular music the ensembles were so small that conducting was and is
against the spirit.

3. *The scepter staff of Ockeghem.* — In the fifteenth century, a staff more
than a meter long and richly decorated, was the external symbol of the
importance and role of a responsible director. In a picture (the Paris
miniature is reproduced in *MGG* 9, 1840) Ockeghem holds the staff in
such a way as to preclude the possibility of tactus beats.

4. *Visible aids with fingers and hand.* — Counting rests on one's fingers
enables the pausing performer to remain metrically involved. With such
economical signs he remained tied to the ensemble as if he were singing
along (cf. the Ghent Altar). The same principle subsequently governs
actual conducting motions of hand and fingers. In sacred music, only
a very small ensemble had to be coordinated and not led in the sense
of modern conducting. Motions of hand or fingers concerned only the
downbeat, which could be subdivided for shorter metric units by a return
motion equally exact and marked. In the absence of barlines in classic

mensural notation, nobody considered beating "figures" of any kind. Perfect and imperfect tempus arrangements are written down only at the beginning of a piece; during the piece they become more or less intelligible only through the course of the composition, varying with style and character. Thus the downbeat of the hand indicates only the beginning of the tactus. Any subdivision of the tactus in three or two parts (*proportio tripla* or *dupla*) could be signaled by exact return motions: as trochaic triple measure (2 plus 1) or even division (1 plus 1). Beating figures originated much later from the organization of tactus groups created by accents. The change was brought about by homophony, dance music, and similar types. We first hear at the beginning of the eighteenth century of conducting by grouping beats into figures. The practice initiated in France. Gradually the beats in various directions familiar to us were established. Parallel to this development is the appearance of barlines taken from tablature notation; they are not placed after each tactus but after a tactus group oriented by accents!

Polychoral music was kept orderly by hand signals (vertical tactus marking as usual). A first director gave clearly visible tactus signs, and assistant conductors relayed his indications.

5. *Conducting with a big baton in the French theater.* — Ockeghem's scepter staff appears transformed into the long baton with a polished ornamented metal knob at the upper end. Whipping motions could mark only the main beats; the knob was clearly visible in the darkened theater. In critical situations, the lower end of the baton was hit against the floor and thus dictated the meter in a penetrant manner. This technique is reported to have been used so frequently that it became almost the rule. One poked fun at it. Until today, many military band conductors mark the accent by an upward beat and do not differentiate groups within the measure. In a way, the drum major marching ahead of the band has inherited Lully's staff and uses it for his own mischief.

6. *The "battuta."*— The name reveals the derivation from Italian performance practice. The fist holds a rolled-up music sheet and gives jerking signs with it, similar to the whipping of Lully's baton. In the early eighteenth century, the conductor began to beat figures. He also clapped the music roll against the music stand and thus marked only the tactus sequence. All these methods of conducting concern only the keeping-together of the ensemble. There is in principle no intent to influence "interpretation," for which reason strong musicians like Handel disdained

the battuta. (Cf. Goethe's *Italian Journey*: "Venice, 3 October [1786]...Church of the Mendicanti...here is the conservatory...the females perform an oratorio behind the trellised gate...marvelous voices...such an Italianate Latin that one has to laugh at moments...it would have been a great pleasure if the cursed conductor had not so impudently clapped the meter with a roll of music paper against the gate as if he were dealing with school children during a lesson...he rather wants to have his presence noticed by this clumsiness...I know that this is the French manner, but I should not have thought it of the Italians, and the audience seems used to it.")

7. *Directing from the harpsichord.* — It originates with playing along on the spinet *colla parte*; we have a picture of Lassus using this method of directing. In the thoroughbass period, the harpsichord part is ideally suited for this kind of conducting, the common practice in the theater and in instrumental chamber music.

8. *The "standing fiddler" as director.* — The bow arm of the concertmaster can be very well observed by the ensemble; and when he pauses, he can employ the bow as metric indicator. From this direction by the concertmaster as "standing fiddler" stems the baroque concert practice of having the soloist play along in the tutti sections. Bach conducted in this manner. Mozart reports in a letter from Paris (3 July 1778) that the rehearsal of his symphony went so badly that he should have liked to direct with his violin.

The practice of direction by the concertmaster has survived; in dance music, the leading violinist, on his feet, has become the actual conductor.

9. *Batons and beating of specific figures.* — One may doubt that Carl Maria von Weber introduced this method as something entirely new (he did so for the theater; conducting with a baton was already common in church music — in this manner the young Mozart conducted his "Orphanage" Mass). Nicolai's baton (and also Hans Richter's) was barely two handbreadths long and relatively weighty; one felt it in one's hand, and it gave the conductor the sense of beating. Mahler, Nikisch, and the following generation (Richard Strauss was a master of this kind of conducting) used a thin baton of twice this length, made of bright wood clearly visible in the orchestra pit. Because of its length, it projects small movements of arm and hand proportionately enlarged. Its minimal weight, moreover, helps the conductor physically to last for the dura-

tion of a long opera. Beyond the metric positions, he can also incorporate minute details. From Weber over Nicolai, Mendelssohn, Richter, and Brahms to Mahler and Strauss, these forms of conducting span an arch within which the executants met increasingly intensive demands for specific expression and involvement by gaining greater control over the particulars and qualities of a performance.

In our contemporary conducting practice, two variants of the technique of "beating" have evolved: directing a choir and directing an orchestra. The former is concerned with vocal attack, with breath support, sonority, and specific methods of singing aimed at developing tone; round, swinging motions are the basic principle. Instrumental music, on the other hand, needs to be guided by the ductus of the beat; all time values lie at the decisive moment of their beat "at the bottom." The old traditional beat is always the basic form of every distinct act of conducting.

Modern conducting technique can be adjusted to meet the demands of early music: in triple meter, avoid the pronounced horizontal beat on "2" and instead repeat gently and sparingly the vertical beat on "1." Thus "3" becomes an accentuated return. What one conducts are trochaic triplets! In quadruple meter, too, it is best to weaken the beat on "2" in a similar manner. When strongly marked, it indicates the nineteenth-century norm of counting small units. There is no early music which tolerates six marked beats; the same is true when conducting nine and twelve. One must carefully guard against setting a series of separate accents which knock apart the overall large meter. The beat on "2" is dangerous!

I have no doubt that a change in the notational norm (white mensural notation versus tablature) clearly prescribes the extent to which the musical performer may become personally engaged. White mensural notation calls for concentration on optimal realization of the compositional design; attention rests on the elevated texture. If a section then follows in the note values of a tablature, the music is set free for personalized interpretation — hence exploration of affect, liberty with diminution, less rigid obligation toward the prescribed rhythms, and under circumstances the charge to vary a *da capo*. Bach's entire output contains this kind of instruction for an appropriate performance. It is common in his chamber music to delimit exalted polyphonic sections with their particular texture from music admitting lusty and carefree playing. In Bach's period, this alternation of notations is common practice. Look, for an example, at Pergolesi's *Stabat mater*. Whoever lacks courage to assert his personal interpretation in a masterwork should recall C. P. E. Bach's disdainful judgment: "Nothing seen but notes, nothing seen but numbers..."

CHAPTER III

Principles of Musical Structures

An exposition of the multitude of forms in Western music would fill books. Here we shall only try to present prototypes, archetypes, which may guide a sensitive musician toward an independent recognition of structures. The serviceable terms in this search are *form* or *design* or *texture*. (The French term *dessin* is used in German, which has no real equivalent.)

What is generally known as form originates in our capacity to store musical substance in our memory. Consciousness transcends the momentary and gains the possibility of an overview. Musical talent and training develop an increasing ability to apperceive a composition more or less as a whole — a specific quality of a true musician.

Musical substance can be remembered and consciously stored only when it is structured. Music is in every respect a temporal phenomenon, whether one deals with metric-rhythmic formations or with laws of tone and melody or with a cadence shaped by melody and harmony: in each dimension, the potential of a structure exists. One encounters here both the particular aptness of a principle as well as its limits, the transgression of which turns the plan of a composition into an arrangement on paper. There are many developments of which the formative powers were falsely evaluated and finally abused. Think, among other examples, of isorhythm which in all its most differentiated appearances actually ran a fruitless course, relinquished and eventually abandoned by genuine musicians. In the disciplines of high polyphony, too, deviations beyond the proper limits occur when sheer hybris permits merely intellectualized procedures. Compare, for instance, canonic artfulness in the work of Josquin and Philipp de Monte.

Enlargement of norms given by tactus and meter leads to the creation of phenomena like phrase, period, etc.; but this formation is equally carried by melos and harmony. A point of origin for these orders is the community of poetry and music, where strophic structure and musical shaping are deeply identical. A quantitative procedure corresponding to additive metrics may participate, but also an order from the musical-metrical sphere (like measures put together *per augmentationem*). For an additive series, the single element must not be too large or it cannot serve as a numerator. Homophony appropriates such orders, or there is at least one dominating part which carries the order. This principle creates the prototype of form by repetition. In practice, repetition is always paired with a dynamic element. The Gregorian Psalm tones offer a good example. In each Psalm, the length of the verses varies considerably. The articulation by initium, tenor, mediatio, tenor, and finalis (melodic introductory curve, recitation tone, middle cadence, again recitation on a tone, and final cadence) is so subliminal that the closed form of the verse is not challenged. The adjustment of the textually different verse lengths in the tenor sections contributes its share.

If the single building stone becomes too large, it must be structured by itself. This basic organization soon reveals its own form principle. Division in two halves is the first stage. Duality is established and with it a form of counterbalance. In the differentiations and further developments of this form principle, the two "scales of the balance" do not always have to contain identical matter. Two different pieces may be related to each other. (This type is often called Prelude and Fugue. We rightly think of *The Well-tempered Keyboard.* Playing these paired movements as if they were unrelated belongs to a very poor tradition. Unspoiled, unprejudiced players have long known these connections and can realize them musically.) The very condition of equilibrium is not always valid. The placement of the musical center of gravity, for instance, can make of one movement an introduction and of the other the main event. In specifically counterbalanced forms, however, equilibrium remains a structural element. Barform supplies a good example of counterbalance. Apode and epode (*Aufgesang* and *Abgesang*) relate to each other and are yet different. The apode is formed by the repetition of a strophe (*Stollen*). This enduring form is heard in the   *minnesongs* of Neidhart (to name an Austrian); it dominates the major part of Protestant chorales.[50] Singing the familiar beautiful chorale "Aus meines Herzens Grunde" from Bach's *St. John Passion*, one experiences in an exemplary way the forces of this form.[51] The opening strophe is sometimes repeated at the end, in which case the form becomes closed and creates a recapitulation barform. In the background of the formal logic of sonata form, the recapitulation barform is recognizable. It contains in a nutshell the whole sonata form. Repetition after a contrast produces a frame—the principle of a closed form. Closed form itself permits a multitude of variants, from a simple da capo to all rondo types and the Vivaldi concerto form.

Let us look at the artistic aspects and solutions by way of at least a few models. Much can be learned from singing and playing Monteverdi's ciaconna "Zefiro torna."[52] The ostinato bass is only one *tempus* long (equivalent to approximately one measure). Above this foundation, Monteverdi leads the two tenor lines so freely and spontaneously that their metric behavior becomes independent. At the beginning, even the ciaconna bass is fooled and shifts into trochees. Then the note values of the voices stretch as in a modus. Every further section brings above the ostinato new variations of the most diverse extensions. The ostinato bass appears seventy-six times yet never becomes a Procrustean bed! Toward the end, Monteverdi interrupts the flow of the ciaconna by two recitative episodes. (Here one can profitably study the nature of the Neapolitan sixth. The way in which it arises from the tonal minor sixth and in increasing intensification reveals its true character is more instructive than the dry treatment of the case in many harmony textbooks.) The ciaconna interrupted by the insertions now admits the addition of a coda with virtuoso vocal runs, which become understood as a necessary closing formation.

Binary form offers an abundance of examples and of diversity of procedure. Because the binary principle underlies all old dance music, a survey of this type seems to the point.

Artful composition of dance music occurs relatively late. The Black Dance Book of Margarethe of Austria (writing in gold and silver on black parchment; the book actually belonged to Maria of Burgundy and originated at the time of her grandfather, Philippe le Bon, in the middle of the fifteenth century) contains in plainchant notation only melodies meant to be unfolded into fashionable dances by improvisation.[53] This collection of *basses danses* typically indicates in a special writing below the notes the steps and modalities of the dances to be executed, but it does not concretize the music! The jongleurs and minstrels involved with dance practice were so familiar with each detail that writing-out the dance music was superfluous. Only after the turn to the seventeenth century does a plenitude of artfully composed dance music become available. At the beginning, the traditional variation pair Reigen and Dantz seems to have supplied a model. (First the Reigen in duple meter. The tempo is determined by the dance modality of a divided step — heel to front of foot — and the formation of the row of dancers. It was a kind of stepping dance. Then the row split up into couples, one gentleman and one lady, and now this and now the other partner turns under the raised arm of the other. The music moves in *proportio tripla*, hence the Dantz is often called *Proporz*. Watching folk dances, one encounters many social dances trickled down and adjusted to another milieu. In this sense, all folk art is not a primary creation but the cultural goods of upper circles filtered and adapted for other conditions.) In a logical and simple development, the original pair was enlarged to more than two movements while preserving variation technique. Great variety of texture attaches itself to dance music. Peuerl and Posch offer tidy dances for four and five parts.[54] Somewhat later dance music restricts itself to an upper voice and thoroughbass while still revealing good technical qualities, as, for instance, the dance music composed by Emperor Leopold I (whose imperial daughters learned to dance to his fatherly music!).[55] Whereas Posch and Peuerl (to give Austrian examples from the beginning of the seventeenth century) still dispose three sections for each dance, stretched by repetition to double length, binary dance movements subsequently become the norm. At the same time, however, the variation suite has yielded to the French suite in which the original allemande-courante pair is followed by further new independent dances. Significantly, purely musical considerations establish groupings by contrast. The sarabande stood under Papal ban and later was therefore never danced. The finale placement of the gigue is also best explained by musical necessity. Fashionable and quasi exotic dances are met with increasing interest and invade dance suites. Soon the minuet occupies its sovereign position. One would like to know more about how this old music was danced. The absence of concrete and unambiguously recorded annotations makes clarification difficult. While expecting contributions from historically expert dancers, we musicians remain dependent upon interpreting details of our own subject matter. We know that in baroque dance music, accents and their occurrences coincided with steps and dance figures. At the court of the

last French kings, the Parisian dancing masters created ever new fashionable variants of dances; their differentiations increasingly dissolved the
original types. In music that was actually danced, the metric relations
among the suite movements become of secondary importance because
the executed dances each demand a precisely defined tempo. Here historic
dance experts could confirm or correct on the basis of their own laws
what we musicians only suspect and sense. Society structure, rank, conventions, and costume also contribute! Such differentiation and developmental effusion appear, for instance, in the "Hofballmusiken" of the
Concentus dedicated by Johann Joseph Fux to the composer Emperor
Joseph I.[56] Finally one must bear in mind that the harpsichord had
long appropriated the suite and initiated a development of pure instrumental music only loosely connected with music actually danced.

Within the flood of dances, often short-lived fads, the typical binary structure continues to assert itself. Valid in the dance music of Lan-
ner and the Strauss family, this order in all its musical dimensions, from
phrase and period to their various modifications, experiences development and fulfillment. With this music, we reach the threshold of our
century.

Sacred and other secular music produce even more complex and
differentiated forms and types. Their variety prohibits a systematic treatment of each proper structure in this book. I want to limit myself to
one movement from the Cantata 78 by Bach, which I have performed
repeatedly ever since the early twenties and which offers highly interesting
structural features.[57] A prerequisite for the analysis of the first movement is acquaintance with the formal model provided by the closing
chorale "Herr, ich glaube." The chorale is in barform with a minimal
variant in the second strophe which intensifies the bass line by a low
G. The epode typically modulates into the relative key and then utilizes
the cadences of the return for the dynamic shaping of the barform as
a whole. Now the first movement of the Cantata, as text and organization show, is a chorale prelude which follows the structural model of
the chorale. The barform of the chorale here determines the large architecture. The movement is moreover a strict chaconne with the typical four-measure ostinato which runs through the entire movement. The
chaconne type forces also the cantus firmus into a triple meter, from
which it frees itself only occasionally by hemiolas. In line with Bach's
technique of composing, the ostinato moves from the bass into other
ranges and even suffers contrapuntal mirroring so that it appears in ever

new differentiation. The movement is further organized by instrumental sections with their own thematic material and by separate vocal developments of each line of the chorale. This aspect produces a Vivaldi concerto form; only the last ritornello is pyramided above the ending of the last chorale verse and reduced to its first half. The instrumental ritornello itself is a barform in miniature. The music above the first statement of the chaconne bass is repeated as in an antistrophe. There follows, exactly twice as long, an epode with the chaconne theme in the upper voices accompanied by scale lines. These observations yield for the main piece of the Cantata fivefold formal concepts, all of them realized by the compositional process. One might claim that the barforms large and small, belonging to a most familiar form type, had been introduced unconsciously; but the Vivaldi concerto form, the chorale prelude, and the chaconne realize a compositional plan in a highly deliberate structure. In this summary survey, single details have not been mentioned. Yet many more insights can be gained from the voice-leading technique, the large harmonic architecture, the special madrigalisms of each verse line, the polyphonic devices, et cetera. True, this piece offers a particular concentration of formal ties, but every work by Bach requires utmost attention for a performer to do musical justice to it.

Apart from the three formal archetypes — repetition, counterbalance, and closure — it is equally important to recognize the principle of a genuine musical phenomenon. In music, the length, the extent of single units, need not be kept. Just as the slide rule diminishes or enlarges a mathematical measure by logarithms, so a comparable change of musical magnitudes is always possible! Already the Nibelung Strophe [or Spenser's *Fairie Queene*] develops the dynamic principle of enlarging the last half-line of each strophe to shape the ending by way of an additional verse foot. This kind of enlargement or contraction of detailed elements has been practiced in all style periods in order to develop within a formal principle a special dynamism. The stronger the metric building stone of a composition, the more noticeably effective the breaking-out of the norms. The formal opening-up of a particular unit for the purpose of transplanting it to a sphere of new norms dilutes the contours of the building stone and deprives it of its limiting marks. Themes become motives, complex organisms fall apart. Out of these opened-up single elements arises a new, specifically dynamic, musical architecture which, depending on modulatory means or intensification of the thematic substance, may grow into large structures, into crystal druses. These constitute the actual developments of compositional practices. Here one must not think exclusively of sonata form. In the case of the motto aria, for instance (and equally valid in pure instrumental music), Bach's compositional practice admits after the initial statement of the motto any conceivable dynamic formal development. The role of *dessin* becomes very influential. Within the context of changing magnitudes, the reprise deserves attention. The best examples are supplied by Schütz, whose masterly musical forms always possess the character of something organically grown and fully developed out of an inner necessity. Music by Schütz demonstrates the subtlest reprise formations.[58]

Another structural principle of a completely different nature arises from the procedures and techniques of polyphony. For this complex, the concept *dessin* or *texture* has long been in use. From the polarity of a sterile tenor and a vital discantus, a melos springs up which, out of consonance relationships at definite metric positions, fulfills itself in flourishing abundance of melodic formations. The scanty positions of dependence on the tenor cannot hinder an unfolding toward *contrapunctus floridus*. Thus particular responsibilities develop in the play of polyphonic lineament. The early formations out of the principle of discantus gradually achieve ever greater significance and lead to a rich treasure of possibilities, rules, and laws which developed independently of the principle of formal equilibrium. The term *dessin* or *texture* thus comprehends all schemes of polyphonic voice leading, from discantus to the modalities of strict interdependence, that is, to canon and the dux-comes relationship in imitative counterpoint.

The two orders of structuring—formation by metric norms or by conditions of contrapuntal procedure—need not be mutually exclusive, although special intensity of one musical responsibility will usually be at the expense of the other. A through-imitated motet by Josquin or a fugue from *The Well-tempered Keyboard* fulfills laws of both voice-leading and form. In a Bach fugue, the voice-leading mostly takes place within the plan of a Vivaldi concerto form, because two principles here support and build each other mutually. But one also finds obligations arising from voice-leading which cause the magnitudes of the formal elements in the concerto form.

An excellent example of melody developing according to its own laws is the beginning of Okeghem's setting of the Marian Antiphon "Alma redemptoris mater."[59] The rhythmic dimension is decisive for this music! The tenor develops its melos, derived from the Gregorian antiphon, by

rhythmic energy. The first dotted note causes by a kind of initial igni-
tion the explosion of a melodic development, whereby this dotted note
defines the metric measure for this beginning. After the exposition of
the space of a fifth, and a brief pause, the climactic octave, as in the
Gregorian model, is reached. With it, a transition is prepared to a meter
of double length. Simultaneously, the discantus melody has entered at
the cesura before the second ascent. It retains the momentum and the
smaller metric standard while the tenor transfers to a large meter. One
must sing again and again the rhythmic and melodic arch of this in-
genious beginning of a motet until it spends itself in the unison of both
parts. One comprehends and absorbs the beauty and proper logic only
by feeling and touching the inherent forces of each note. (Just "tap" the
course of the tenor in order to taste the pure rhythms!) One cannot say
more about the beginning of this motet without experiencing it and its
structure in a live music situation. I hope, however, that the understanding of only one part of a truly artistic phenomenon may lead to further
private study and affectionate empathy with a master work. Details can
be read about in specialized texts on the musical logic of polyphonic
textures. This book does not wish to ruminate.

Textural structure derived from canon (earlier called *fuga*) keeps
at first to the simplest discipline, even when the canon becomes the actually effective ligament. The connective power of canon is employed
by Dufay in his Christmas Gloria — a canon in unison above two lower
trumpet parts which represent tenor and contratenor.[60] Soon this technique of composing suffers exaggeration. According to the attitude that
"art must also be artificial," the elevated canon technique becomes an
end in itself. *Canon in diapente* or *epidiapente* is passable; one must only
avoid pushing the canon into a modulatory circle (although such course
is sometimes calculated). Imitation at other intervals can only be approximate if the tonality is to be preserved. The mirroring of intervals
is mostly tonal; only in exceptional cases can a master operate with real
mirrors. More frequent are modifications of the measure of the canonic
theme. In this regard, Okeghem and Josquin demonstrated their superior skill as composers. The line extends up to the *Musical Offering.*[61]
By leading the royal theme also through artful canonic techniques, Bach
indicated to the Prussian king the traditions and cultural roots of his work.

I have often performed the *Musical Offering* and was always confronted by the problem: should one really present such compositions
to a general public, and when is this public simply out of place because

of insufficient insight into such work? In Potsdam, Bach assumed that one canon today, another canon another time, would be tackled for deciphering and performance. After all, he had not offered the king resolved pieces in score but rather in reduced notation in which a title like *Quaerendo invenietis* approaches mockery (apparently taken amiss by the king who did not reward Bach by a present), all the more so as this canon admits of several solutions. Until today we cannot really consider the *Canon per augmentationem in contrario motu* as resolved. The abbreviated solution by the pupil Kirnberger does not prove its final authenticity. The most persuasive solution of the canon has been offered by Friedrich Smendt who limits the *per augmentationem* to the length of the theme.[62] One could believe that the old gentleman is still mocking us today!

The dedication copy does not clarify the sequence of pieces. The engraver placed canons on the copper plates by utilizing every free space. A real cycle set by Bach exists only in the trio sonata. I can imagine the following order of the pieces in the *Musical Offering*. First the improvised fugue *a tre* followed by the six-voice ricercare (Bach uses the antiquated name because of an acrostic). Then the canons, which can be separated into canons *to* the theme and canons *on* the theme; the canonic fugue might well close this group. Now the procedure reverses: the polyphonic treatments of the royal theme are followed by fresh music-making in the trio sonata, which cites the theme in both allegro movements. (N. B. Bach's biggest trio sonata!) The finale, in divertimento tradition, combines both form principles in a playful gavotte for trio-sonata players, which at the same time realizes one of the most difficult canonic tasks: *Canon in diapente per contrario motu* with exact intervallic mirroring, that is, major becomes minor and vice versa. One must try to write such a canon over a thoroughbass to get an idea of Bach's accomplishment!

This work by Bach transcends all textural confinements. One must play the six-part fugue (note the alla breve and the particular placement of barlines which marks even semibreves as main beats) in order to experience spontaneously the formal orders which organize and build this giant fugue. Genuine formal aspects and high polyphony here coexist. The *Musical Offering* shows how long this kind of legitimacy of *dessin* remained effective. Classical and also twentieth-century composers have dealt with questions of polyphonic texture under the aspects of their contemporary music, although here the invention of thematic material and voice-leading remains bound by formal norms. Schubert's fugues in the great Masses in E-flat and A-flat have been criticized for lacking energy and invention compared to the other movements. The fault really lies with the conductors who do not recognize the cappella notation of the fugues and offend against the fugue finales by counting small note values. Bach's *Art of Fugue* offers the best systematic survey of the concept of fugue.[63] The possible technical procedures are shown in the separate fugues in sharp characterization and concentration (emphatically stated: the *Art of Fugue* wants to be played!). Having analyzed this work, one can then properly evaluate any situation within a fugue on the basis of compositional principles. I recommend for study Wolfgang Graeser's score with his annotations. Such study will lead to proper insights and personal interpretations of the whole complex issue of fugue.

CHAPTER IV

Ensemble Types: Split and Homogeneous Sonorities

The terms *split* and *homogeneous* sonorities concern basic structural qualities of compositions and their realization in sound. Both terms make sense only for music in several parts. Split sonority is adequate for textures combining voices of different origin and attitude. A distinction between sacred and secular music is here at first not to the point, because the structures of both kinds are governed in early polyphony by common compositional techniques. Secular music lived off the crumbs dropped from the table of sacred music.

In early polyphony, such as the motet, the tenor always offers Gregorian material which, however, usually consists only of somehow sterilized fragments. One took sections out of *Graduale* melodies deprived of all structural features except the melodic interval. All life was concentrated in the newly added voice (or two and even three new voices). The very compositional plan calls for a contrasting execution of tenor and discant, that is, for split sonority. The tenors without text should be played on a suitable instrument. The discantus is vocal, perhaps doubled in ottava by an instrument. The absence of a text in certain sections of the discantus practically proves instrumental execution. The tenor line may be given to a big fiddle or the front register of an organ of the period. Significantly this register, playable by itself, is called *tenor* (the 24′ *principale*, for instance, of the organ, of 1470, in San Petronio in Bologna). Assigning the often very long note values of the tenor to other instruments is not logical. A viol might cope with the tenor parts of secular music. For the Notre Dame organa, the tenor needs the early organ. In secular music, polyphony up to three voices is achieved by actual independence of the newly composed parts. The well-known motet "Pucelette" places above the vestige of a *Graduale* melody the chanson of a troubadour and at the top a street song.[64] It is as if polyphony wished to prove what heterogeneous musical worlds it was capable of binding. The question of sonority is easily answered: the tenor is played on a big viol, the two upper voices with text are sung. The plan of the little piece demands the simplest performance. "Elevation" of the voices by instruments would do too much honor to the piece. The upper voices are vitalized by the text which must remain in the foreground. Conductus compositions (with an original tenor melody) are related to motet behavior and can therefore be treated analogously.

The parallel organa develop an entirely different principle. Metric equalization is here the decisive factor. Primitive conditions are of little interest to us musicians. A practical conductor's attention can be riveted only from the point on where a compositional principle serves an artistic statement. Faux bourdon (as a somewhat later special case) is an early field for experimentation, and it lasts a long while! Dufay closes his three-part sacred chanson "Flos florum," for instance, with purest homophony and complete renunciation of metric formation.[65] Tenor and discant follow the organum principle of contrary motion. The contratenor tosses around as a stopgap; a tritone progression makes vocal execution of this part unlikely. In short, for a piece in pure homophony in which no part violates singable norms, vocal performance (with homogeneous sonority) is probable. Errors are often committed. Bukofzer, for instance, transcribes Dunstable's motet "Quam pulchra es" in homogeneous sonority because all parts have a text.[66] One has to remember, however, that the addition of words in such almost homophonic pieces provided highly welcome assistance to the performers restricted to separately notated parts. I consider a performance by three vocalists musically wrong, for the tenor and contratenor parts are here treated as in the chanson "Flos florum" mentioned earlier. The tenor could be sung, but the contratenor in Dunstable's setting is a paragon of unsingability! I would assign a lute to contratenors of this type and let a viol play the tenor. Then the specifically singable part remains for the voice. In pieces like this one by Dunstable, one could double the discantus at the octave by a portative or recorder. The voice part of this motet is a falsetto alto. This anticipatory consideration of a chanson from the middle fifteenth century acquaints us with a standard type which easily serves as a model for similar cases.

Many difficulties confront us in the work of Machaut. His reputedly archaic *Missa Nostre Dame*, tied to the tradition of sacred music and destined for a solemn liturgy, probably grew out of an experimental situation.[67] Nothing else like it exists (the Mass of Tournay does not bear comparison).[68] Machaut employs several particular compositional techniques of which the methods and disciplines submit to a more highly oriented creative force. Isorhythm taken as technique has here a rather subordinate significance. There are connections with the Gregorian Advent Mass "Cunctipotens genitor Deus"[69] and, in the triplum of the Credo, to the Gregorian Credo IV.[70] Considering what Machaut expects of the singers in the Gloria and Credo, one might assume that almost all parts could be managed by voices; but this would go against their character derived from an older convention. The tenor needs its own sonorous profile. So do motetus and triplum. The contratenor has no text in the Sanctus and Agnus movements; its musical behavior, too, seems to point to a suitable instrumental execution. Tenor and contratenor in the Gloria and Credo movements contain brief instrumental bridges (always the same music in the Gloria; different music in the Credo except for the identity of the first and last interludes). Corresponding to the team of triplum and motetus, contratenor and tenor are harnessed together. A stereotyped cast of performers is hardly credible. Among the three dimensions of rhythm, melos, and harmony, the diversity of rhythm is evident. Many compositional relationships enliven this dimension. The melos functions independently within the laws of tetrachord and Church modes. Linear forces ruthlessly run over harmonic concerns! Leading tones, now possible in the procedure of the *subsemitonium modi*, appear exclusively for linear reasons. All these techniques of composition demand split sonority.

There is the question of the instrumental means serviceable in that era for sacred music. The absence of any harmonic foundation helps us decide on the choice of an appropriate sonority. The great octave is hardly touched; it would not be justified by the kind of quasi harmonic relationships. From the long list in *Remède de Fortune*, instruments can be selected which will produce a balanced energy for a specific movement or section.[71] If the Mass was actually performed (although we have

no documentary proof) at the coronation of Charles VI in Notre Dame
in Reims, one must nevertheless remember that the liturgy was assigned
exclusively to the cathedral choir and that the cappella stood right at
the altar. The five big musical scenes salvaged from the Maison des Mu-
siciens wrecked in the First World War are very instructive.[72] Wind
instruments and perhaps one or another supporting stringed instrument
participate. The use of the organ is uncertain. To assign one register
to one part of the Machaut Mass is highly improbable; and for doubling the cappella in order to support it, the instrument and the playing
technique of the time are not yet mature enough. One might think of
a portative, but neither it nor the earliest *positif de table* is at home in
a church. May one ponder the employment of carefully involved, very
small timpani, triangle, and a kind of cymbals? They are secular instruments, and the accentuation of metric structures seems equally
problematic. I can rather think of an occasional marking of tactus values,
if only in order to keep the cappella together; for there was no conducting in the modern sense. Many instruments were readily available for
the existing tasks. There were straight and transverse flutes, pommer
types, zinks, large trumpets perhaps with a slide (the trombone does
not appear until one generation later), large and small fiddle forms. The
psaltery is negligible amidst the energy display of the Mass. The early
lute, too, would not lend the contratenor a balanced sound. One aspect
must be stressed: just as the structure of the Mass is highly differentiated, so the best suited instrumentation must be found for each movement or important section. The relationship of the first Kyrie to the
Christe, for instance, clearly suggests one of tutti to solo.

Historical instruments of that era have not lasted into our time.
We have to use a later set of instruments. Also in regard to the singers,
one must not think of our choirs and their modern training and voice
production. A few male voices, a male falsetto, and a few boys should
here suffice (the royal cappella maintained a boys' school from the beginning of the thirteenth century). The more sparing the ensemble, the
more effective a change of sonority.

Motets, ballades, rondeaus — apart from virelais — originated in
quite different compositional plans. Machaut's ballades are specifically
pieces favoring split sonority. A flute for the triplum, a good tenor capable
of falsetto in the upper range for the motetus, for the tenor a viol, and
in the contratenor a lute — in this distribution, "De toutes flours," for
instance, will sound very good.[73] This arrangement will prove that there

is no problem to playing E in one voice and E-flat in another. Such apparent clashes are not offensive with parts assigned to strongly contrasting timbres. The musician learns that at that period melodic laws originating in the tetrachord carry greater significance than a sometimes scanty harmony. This recipe for ballades with minor variants serves also rondeaus, et cetera. The motet requires an instrument for the sterilized tenor. It could be a viol, for a lute is a poor match against two male voices. The same viol plays the instrumental part in virelais.

Hurdy-gurdy and different types of bagpipes were utilized for soloistic music. Original music of this kind, however, will seldom be found. Such music grows out of organpoint and organum techniques. Any halfway good player depended on his own invention and execution. A special chapter later in this book will deal with the historic instrumentarium.

With the fifteenth century the Netherlands era of Western music begins. We have already said a few things about it. From the standpoint of ensemble formation, it is initially manifold with a highly differentiated and dispersed sonority. Among the significant compositions, we shall consider Dufay's powerfully profiled Introitus written for the consecration of the Florence cathedral in 1436.[74] Triplum and motetus sing the praise of the city, her wise administration, the intelligent men and the beautiful women and girls. The actual Introitus text is pushed away and stays within the range of a sterile-sounding tenor and the contra; these two parts are vocally barren and belong to instruments. Looking around the cupola and recognizing the local performance conditions, one my conclude that the ensembles were well adapted and gradated but not burdened by large numbers. The compliments of the text were certainly intended to be heard and understood. At the time of the consecration motet, the tenor trombone perhaps already existed. Otherwise the instrumentarium of the Machaut period was still valid. Yet the instruments never cover the essential vocal tasks. They organize the work and characterize the registers, they decorate and give festive accents, they dominate the space. Such was their function then, and we today should proceed accordingly.

Another piece noteworthy because of its sonority is the "Gloria ad modum tubae," also by Dufay.[75] At the festive Christmas performance in Brügge, I have been told, the field trumpeters of Duke Philippe le Bon stood on the triforium gallery, Gilles Binchois, then still a field captain, in the foremost rank. The children who had to sing the canon at the unison stood at the ambo. The instruction in the Trent Codices is very clear: *Fuga* (i.e., canon) *duorum temporum*, the second entry after two tempus units. The actual tempo for this music cannot be chosen without regard to the resonance of the large hall. A pulse of 52 for the tempus unit, which here defines the beat, has proven serviceable. The blaring fanfares at the end need a subtle broadening. The trumpets are the large instruments in cornet tone (on D!). The Gloria demands to be lifted to D major. We have repeatedly performed the piece with the historic trumpets of the Vienna Kunsthistorisches Museum and the Vienna Choir Boys; the composition belongs to the most persuasive from the middle of the fifteenth century. This discussion of specific performance conditions clarifies a number of details (a canon in discant register moves above a trumpet part split in two, thus extreme separation of the vocal substance from the trumpet share in tenor and contratenor).

As another example of performance practice, I now submit Dufay's "testament" motet, "Ave regina caelorum."[76] This work of his old age places the voices in the center. The melos of the main lines stems from the Gregorian antiphon "Alma redemptoris." The two two-voice sections at the beginning of the motet move in characteristic Dufay rhythms which must be musically realized beyond all beating of time. The *tempus perfectum cum prolatione imperfecta* demands for each semibrevis the *tactus integer valor*. The strongly contrasting insert with the prayer "for a good death" surprises by its clear homogeneous vocal sound. The contrast of the two texts is worked out in the composition and need not be emphasized by a conductor obsessed with externalization. If one has at one's disposal very good singers, trained in the realization of such subtle rhythms, then a vocal performance is the best solution. A conductor planted in front of the ensemble (or in the apse of a church misused for a concert platform) is entirely inappropriate. We always gathered around a stand. For difficult pieces, I had written a large score. I always sang along and after sufficient rehearsals hardly ever resorted to a conducting hand. Three boys capable of coping perfectly with Dufay's intricate rhythms are hard to find. We substituted women's voices of which the sexual characteristic was unobtrusive. The separate sections of the motet present ever new performance challenges according to their compositional technique. The rhythmically complicated section for three voices before the end requires the three best and most musical soloists. Anyone beating small units ruptures the glory of Dufay's rhythms and produces inevitably wrong stresses on syncopations. Now a performance

of the motet in this manner does not yet yield a pronounced homogeneous sonority. Within the framework of vocal possibilities and moreover
sustained by the clear rhythmic structures, singers are quite capable of
giving to each of the diverse sections its appropriate character. Gregorian
relations of cantus-firmus quality, free lines of the *contrapunctus floridus*,
chordal connections, differentiated text recitation, etc., demand the personal involvement of the singers every time. One condition for the vocal ensemble is the assignment of high male voices for the alto. They
need not be stars. Popular contratenors with their excessively cultivated technique (of which they are actually the servants) often impregnate
the situation with a perfume inappropriate for the honesty of the alto tasks
in that music. To repeat: around the middle of the fifteenth century,
the voice parts gain access to sonority, to harmonic sounds. The basses
now dip down to *F*. Instruments reach even farther. The organ in San
Petronio, referred to earlier, extends the range of the keyboard to subcontra G_2! This should put one on one's guard. The structure of the vocal chorus must be consistently and unbrokenly built up from the bass
to the boys. Above the highest male voice (for which the term *altus*, high,
is very significant) lies the boy soprano. Female altos have the character of a low voice; their participation, because we hear them as a lower
voice, would break up the whole vocal structure.

If one compares this Dufay motet with one by Josquin, such as
"Benedicta es coelorum regina," one is much more tempted to involve
instruments.[77] The composition distinguishes between carriers of the
cantus firmus in the metrical system of modus and contrapuntal lines.
The cantus-firmus parts move in canonlike imitation. This situation
might occasionally admit instrumental execution of the discant parts.
The circumstances change: at the words "Te Deus Pater," Josquin's most
personal style begins to dominate. Lapidary themes generated by the
words and intertwined in plain imitation remind one of the *Missa Pange
lingua*.[78] After sections with fewer voices, the composition concludes the
first part with the intensive sonority of six voices. The following bicinium, in attitude and texture, is a clearly contrasting middle section. Based
solely on the swift meter of *Imperfectum cum prolatione imperfecta*, this section plays the role of a fast allegro distinguished by a certain brilliance
of the two-voice texture. The following finale reverses the *proportio*: imperfect division is replaced by *tripla*. A large energy curve produces concentration and intensification carried by the triplum meter. At the end
of the third section, the main duple meter returns. The final Amen ca-

dence culminates on a monumental consonance including the upper third!
If one looks for an ideal supplementation of the voices in this motet by
instruments, a set of old trombones offers a possibility, backed by bassoon and (for the upper ranges) zinks or their equivalents. In such motets,
stringed instruments used soloistically are out of place; and used in sections, they can badly disfigure the composition. Singing and blowing
are based on breath. This community of condition relates singers and
wind players. They share all questions of phrasing and breathing. One
might consider the participation of an organ positive, mainly for the bicinium of the middle section. With all profiling of the varied structures
of the movements, the sublime grandness of this motet rests on the co-
hesion of the compositional and sonorous means. One can employ a
minimal choir, a wind ensemble embracing all ranges, perhaps also a
positive (if the right one is available; a thoroughbass positive would not
fit) or a good regal. A time beater, provoking false syncopations at the
very beginning, would be out of place.

The motets by Dufay and Josquin discussed above outline a path
which leads from medieval split sonority to an increasingly more
homogeneous ensemble type. Conjoined to it and offering a second reason
for this development is the total involvement of the tonal space, primarily
through the inclusion of a genuine deep bass region upon which a closed
sonority begins to be built up. Josquin's work contains also perfectly
clear forms of sonorous homogeneity: in the motet "O Domine Jesu,"
he fully respects the Good Friday situation which excludes instruments
and musically striking means and structures.[79] Here one needs only male
voices. The rhythms run the simplest possible course. Homophony
dominates. Only at the very end of the five separate motets does Josquin
permit himself to fill the tonal space with imitative polyphony. These
motets deserve to be better known!

Secular music after Machaut is marked by the chanson. The arch
spans from cases of the best and most ambitious musical means to simple, almost primitive two-part writing. A good example is Dunstable's
chanson "O Rosa bella."[80] A subtle four-part texture manifests instrumental execution with an added voice. This chanson aroused enthusiasm;
it was followed by a flood of parodies. For this piece, one desires a string
tone. It is sufficiently intimate and leaves to each player a great selection of possible articulation and sonority for each phrase, for each rhythm,
for each tone. The melodically poorest part may be plucked (it is always the contratenor that suffers melodic abuse; when only a few voices

are involved, that period manages to allocate to this part a kind of harmonic aspect; only through Okeghem's mastery does the chanson "Ma bouche rit," for instance, gain full equivalence for the contratenor).[81] From "O Rosa bella" a thread runs up to the viol consort in the days of Dowland. The concept of chanson remains a direct model for song texture, regardless of whether the texts are Flemish or German. Italy went its own way. From the relevant pieces of the Squarcialupi Codex until the frottola, we encounter a particular, specifically Italian development.[82] (To acquaint yourself with a typical and attractive piece, perform the music of the laude "Ave Mater," wrongly attributed to Oscar von Wolkenstein.[83] It is contained in an old Venetian collection.) With a secular text, the frottola follows a similar line. More about it later, as also about the French development.

German lied texture is for us a significant domain. The rich abundance of the transmitted pieces stems from the immediacy of literary relations. The Lochamer Songbook is indispensable (this manuscript collection was a kind of album of a Nürnberg bourgeois girl, a pupil of Paumann's; her first name was Barbara, as we read in an amorous dedication).[84] Each detail is typical for the category around the middle of the fifteenth century. Handsomely composed pieces for three parts are represented by tenor songs ("Der walt") and discant songs ("Der winter"). The collection contains songs for two parts and those with notation for only the sung melody. This circumstance, too, is significant: it subsumes the whole species from the Neidhart type up to fully achieved three-part composition for tenor, cantus, and contra. The proximity to early organ music with its craftsmanlike attitude again has consequences for the lied texture, which supplies the model. In the case of the Lochamer Songbook, the connection of its best pieces with the Burgundian chanson is self-evident. In spite of the proximity to the Paumann circle, I do not recommend the execution of the nonvocal parts on a *positif de table* (see the engraving by Meckenen in the Vienna Albertina).[85] This kind of small organ is always used soloistically. The standard instrumentation for these songs consists of recorder, viol, and lute, whereby the human voice usually displaces the instrument corresponding to its range.

The category then spreads considerably. Special masters of song composition arise; the arch spans from Hofhaimer past Isaac, Stoltzer, Senfl until Lassus. It is important to remember that all these songs are intended for one and exceptionally (perhaps when the voices move in canon) for two soloists. The human voice is accompanied by instruments

which usually act more fluently in the manner of *proportio*. This repertory does not belong to a chorus. Both sides would suffer, an unnecessary situation for the present music scene. Only few, musically superior
pieces can endure being dragged from intimate music-making onto the
concert stage. This literature is best performed at home.

The category later effaces the type. In the sixteenth century, the
imitative motet has a parallel secular type, chanson and madrigal, which
in turn now require vocal execution. Josquin ever and without exception demonstrates his superior technique and quality. Even a somewhat
ribald text like "Faute d'argent" is composed in a style of unsurpassed
exquisiteness.[86] Pieces of utmost simplicity and beauty, like "Mille
regretz," establish the standard of the species. This vocal type, too, begins to spread, loses much of its depth, and becomes real social music.
Jannequin, whose chattering jests taken in moderation are quite nice,
suffices as one name among many.

After the middle of the sixteenth century, the secular analogue to
the motet covers a wide field: the typical madrigal intensely cultivated
for about a century. In the works of Lassus, of Marenzio, Monteverdi,
Gesualdo, and Schütz, it serves as a real playground for good invention, it demands technical quality, it is a laboratory for experimentation, and it offers the additional advantage of being in great demand
by publishers and music lovers. In the social situation, the rich trades-
folk in Venice are not considered equal to the aristocracy. The children
of Venetian shipowners find in musical activity a real chance for social
advancement. The first conservatories are established, and treatises offer
an introduction to musical practice. Anybody concerned with early music should carefully study and utilize the recorder treatise by Ganassi
(1535).[87] As with Josquin, five-part writing is the rule. Here, too, the
normal case is a *tempus perfectum cum prolatione imperfecta* with only an occasional interruption by *proportio tripla*. The madrigal being the preferred
field for experimentation at the turn toward the seventeenth century,
it permits the use of musical means for highly personal expression. Harmonic features are unsparingly used to convey affects, not always conjoined with good taste. In the fifth and sixth books of Gesualdo's
madrigals, such means become ends in themselves.[88] This attitude toward
harmony renders also rhythm desolate; long drawn-out note values alternate abruptly with hectic rapid motion.

This entire species from Josquin's "Mille regretz" until Gesualdo's
sixth book of madrigals is vocal chamber music, elevated social music,

and accessible to women's voices. Two soloistic female sopranos sing *cantus primus* and *secundus*, followed by male alto, tenor, and bass. This music appears in printed part books, a circumstance which causes the disappearance of ligature notation and withal a substantial simplification of white mensural notation (notes are printed with movable type, Petrucci).[89] This musical repertory, too, admits instrumental participation — partly to secure a difficult harmonic progression, let us say, with the help of a lute, and partly as the result of a vital musical practice which allowed participation in any suitable occasion and for any available performers. This whole setup hardly recognizes the concept of an audience in opposition to the performers. The music makers wish to have their pleasure and fun by being active! Viol sets, recorder choir, voice ensemble (supplemented by the lute when not complete), krummhorn choirs in the early sixteenth century — all these possibilities entered, although instrument families are clear indications of ensemble forms and thereby represent genuine bonds. Three Roman female singers known as virtuosos first introduced works by Gesualdo, which means that in this case tenor and bass were spontaneously given to the lute. One fact must not be overlooked: in the madrigal, the composition student learns how to handle obbligato voices, he learns how to employ all musical means and feels the challenge of original invention and varied techniques. This happened to Heinrich Schütz when studying with Giovanni Gabrieli (see his Opus primum, the *Italian Madrigals*).[90]

At the beginning of the seventeenth century, we find the first deliberately fully composed scores. The possibilities offered by the circumstances of the era are again concretely realized by the very best composers. The decisive landmarks in this development are Monteverdi's *Orfeo*, his Vesper Service for Mary, the great Psalms by Schütz, etc. The Vesper Service also shows for the first time precise instructions for the organ registration.[91] The "Sonata sopra Sancta Maria" employs the instruments exactly according to their potentials. The quick dotted violin strokes, the behavior of the boys' voices, etc. are specifically thematic. The litany call of the boys ("Sancta Maria ora pro nobis") stands in a kind of modus relation to the sonata. Similar situations occur in abundance in Monteverdi's music. Giovanni Gabrieli's instrumental canzonas, among them the "Sonata con tre Violini e basso se piace," also belong in this nexus.[92] What the given conditions determined for the most varied performances of Lassus's music has now become explicitly composed in deliberate notation with consideration of the acoustical qualities of the place.

To all detail is now added the *concertare*, the virtuoso quality prescribed by the composer or delegated to the soloist. By way of improvised diminution, this show of personal virtuosity was equally possible in sixteenth-century music and even earlier. There are areas particularly receptive to this art of improvisation while inadequate mobility denies participation to some instruments. Ganassi's *Fontegara* seems to me to remain the most important treatise on diminution.[93] This textbook on playing the recorder consistently refers to the vocal art of diminution as the model for ornamentation. If one remembers that there exist printed diminutions sanctioned by Palestrina[94] of his Song of Songs motets, which are among his most sublime and beautiful compositions, then one can appreciate how thoroughly the art of diminution permeated a musical practice which did not automatically exclude from it these works of high polyphony. One must never ignore a basic quality of early music: artistic and artificial are one! One finds no artistic achievement without a conspicuous measure of artificiality! Today nobody would think of bespattering those marvelous Palestrina motets with the quasi "historic" diminutions, particularly as they reveal a penetrant lack of talent. There are, on the other hand, many instruments of which the character and playing potential demand diminution. Here the recorder is particularly active, then the violin, and finally any instrument capable of virtuosity. The best example of vocal diminution is the third act of Monteverdi's *Orfeo* with the diminution written out by the composer.[95] It occurs in the big aria meant to gain Orfeo admission to the underworld by musical means. The virtuoso display in this piece determines also the behavior of the instruments. Monteverdi invests everything that good instrumentalists of the period could offer. The parts of the violins, zinks, and of the large harp match that of the singer in regard to virtuoso exhibition. The instrumental "artificiality" is quasi realized in the composition, whereas that of the singer is merely sketched. If the tenor singing Orfeo lacks adequate specialized training and vocal talent, the only way out of this area is suitable simplification of Monteverdi's diminutions! Braking the tempo and ruining it only in order to cope with the diminutions are beyond discussion!

A considerable distance remains between, on the one hand, the principle of changing sonorities along with thematic material specifically tied to it and, on the other hand, instrumentation proper as we use the term today. In all old music practice, the cardinal rule *variatio delectat* offers the clue to the employment of changing possible sonorities appropriate to the musical structures. In the first half of the eighteenth century, the use of timbre by differentiated mixtures is still an exception. When in the siciliano "Et misericordia" in the *Magnificat* Bach[96] employs muted violins and the low register of transverse flutes, this very difficile and "modern"-sounding timbre presents a special case compared to the orchestration in his other works. As a rule, Bach's instrumentation originates in the compositional structures. The separation into choirs is still founded in the tradition of the seventeenth century, and the selection of instruments is influenced by types. The conduct of chamber-music conventions is practically never disturbed, although certain instruments are favored for concertizing and others relegated to a ripieno atmosphere. The violoncello, for instance, in the hands of Bach always has a ripieno flavor. In pieces particularly engaged with affects, Bach sends the violoncello into *tacet* (e.g., Brandenburg Concerto No. 5, slow movement, *affettuoso*, violoncello tacet). As violoncello piccolo, on the other hand, it functions soloistically (among others, in the Cantata, "Bleib bei uns").[97] Bach is very familiar with historic ensemble types, which he uses according to tradition. The motet "O Jesu Christ, mein's Lebens Licht" renounces a thoroughbass foundation (composed for the outdoor funeral service at the grave of Governor Count Fleming).[98] Orchestration: three trombones, white zink, and two other similar instruments marked *lituus* in the score which continue to puzzle us (for the musical reason that these *litui* have to blow distinctly accompanying notes in a rather high register, I believe these instruments to be also white or mute zinks). Between the separate sections of this highly typical six-part wind texture, the verse settings of the chorale named above are introduced one by one, whereby the winds support the voice parts in a kind of *colla parte*. The first large instrumental section then concludes with a ritornello in the manner of a Vivaldi concerto form with *da capo* disposition. For the actual performance, further chorale strophes were probably sung. Bach later adapted this beautiful pious music for a performance in church by arranging it for strings and continuo. As another example of prominent contact with tradition, I refer to Bach's arrangement of Palestrina's *Missa Sine nomine* in the Aeolian mode.[99] It consists of what at the time of Bach was known and used as *Missa* in the Protestant liturgy, namely, Kyrie, Christe, Kyrie, and the Doxology. He uses the traditional instrumentation for large halls: two zinks and three trombones *colla parte* with the voices. The direction of a performance by the Thomas Cantor elevated the foreign work of another composer to the rank of his own compositions for which he was responsible. The direction of compositions not by him was usually assigned to the prefect of the Thomasians, but Palestrina's Mass was conducted by Bach himself.

In conclusion I wish to repeat: modern performance practice distinguishes radically between chamber music and music for some collective body. In the latter, a conductor interposes between work and performers. A modern conductor's claim to leading an ensemble reaches from the justified and necessary direction of a large orchestra or chorus to the placement under tutelage of small ensembles. The latter is out of place. The smaller the group, the more sparingly the conductor must interfere, always with the proviso of adequate preparatory rehearsals. Here the performers' genuine knowledge of all musical factual qualities of a composition is to be sharply distinguished from mechanical training for perfection, as for a recording session, et cetera. This polished smoothness may be stylistically entirely irrelevant for a particular piece. The good director of an ensemble for early music will try to make his co-workers musically responsible! Only then can a performance gain that intensity which stems from the quality of all performers. The real joy in chamber music is the evocation and increasing maturation of the participants' best formative powers. One ought to approach early music from this standpoint!

CHAPTER V

The Thoroughbass Instruments as a Key to Continuo Problems

I shall submit only supplementary thoughts to the existing historic and contemporary writings on this theme, wishing to share with music students the many experiences I have gained during decades spent confronting this problematic issue. This chapter proceeds not from an interpretation of figured-bass notation, its shorthand and symbols, but rather from the instruments. Figured-bass notation has been amply explained by historic as well as modern writings. The realization on a particular instrument, however, has been hardly touched because it always remained a topic of practical instruction. Yet the realization of a figured bass loses its artless woodenness only when the manner of playing and the sonority of the particular continuo instrument are comprehended and musically projected.

There is a close relationship between figured-bass realization and the art of diminution, for both are based on improvisation practices. In older standard works, the improvisation appropriate to an instrument is sometimes explicitly prescribed. In the preface to the *Historia von der Auferstehung Jesu Christi,* Schütz demands diminution by the keyboard instrument or, respectively, by a viol![100] Restraint in matters of thoroughbass must not degenerate into musical impotence. The time of dry, untalented accompaniments seems to have passed. Anyone plagued by inhibitions should remember Philipp Emanuel Bach's disparaging judgment: "Nothing seen but notes, nothing seen but numbers."

All this applies to the *improvised* continuo! If one has to *write out* a figured-bass part, then one inevitably ends up in understatement and falls prey to prudishness.

The improvised thoroughbass is a task for "today." The continuo part confronts the player with tasks to be mastered within the given situation for making music. Such ability furthers and sharpens musical presence of mind as well as creative participation. In the practice of thoroughbass, certain conditions must be respected, otherwise performance problems often create insurmountable obstacles. One of such conditions concerns the selection of the proper continuo instrument. Historic continuo practice initially was served by the already existing instrumentarium, which was subsequently adapted to the new tasks. This was the case with lutes, with certain organ types, and with plucked keyboard instruments.

Figured-bass notation is a stenography of harmonic events. As long as the triad is identical with the very concept of harmony, one works well with the figured abbreviations. The method of notating harmonies in basso-continuo manner has all the advantages of easy recognition, optimal appropriateness, and economy of demands on intellectual concentration. As the challenges and problems of realization presented by a figured bass become more complicated, the continuo loses its practical value. The possibilities of stenographic notation are overgrown by the increasing inclusion of tones formerly rated as "voice-leading dissonances" and now taken obligatorily at their full musical face value. One recognizes the situation by the spread of symbols. In 1711, Heinichen uses one dozen; in the new edition of the book, there are already thirty![101] Rameau sets threescore signs for half that many chords.[102] Mattheson wants ten more.[103] With Rameau, an extreme is reached and the principle led *ad absurdum*: he puts in one hundred and twenty![104] Telemann, a practical musician addressing also the music dilettante, tries to cut back but fails to establish a useful system.[105] Thoroughbass ran aground by wishing to participate in the rational comprehension of formerly improvised elements.

Figured bass was not an original invention but stems from older reduction procedures. Both the cappella and private house-music circles resorted to support by especially suited instruments. In the sixteenth century, two instrument types become involved: the cappella is almost obligatorily joined by a keyboard instrument which uses either wind or strings. Depending on the situation, it may be:

(1) A regal, being easily transportable, is favored by the Imperial cappella, which had to accompany the Holy Roman Majesty to all places of political activity. (See the engraving by Weiditz, "Emperor Maximilian I in Augsburg hearing Mass": in the cappella under Heinrich Isaac, Hofhaymer plays the regal *colla parte*. The picture gives a mirror image because it was worked directly on the copper plate!)

(2) An organ positive served the same purpose. One played a kind of organ reduction in tablature.

(3) Lassus is often portrayed playing along on the spinet. For madrigals and similar forms, this practice helped intonation and rhythm as well as the direction. In church, the spinet took its place primarily in a group of plucked stringed instruments. When Schütz refers to a *coro di liuti* in the multi-choir psalms, he means a group of lutes or theorbos and the spinet. The lute by itself was always problematic. It could play along only sketchily. Yet in modest circumstances it became involved in incredible services. Luther reports on his first High Mass in the diaspora. He solemnly intones the Gloria: "And there sat in the choir stalls the sacristan and plucked the Gloria on the lute, and I had a difficult time remaining serious." From the lute stems the tendency toward radical simplification of a *colla parte* task. Significantly, a special lute type evolves for the early operas, capable of essentially outlining the bass line and also realizing the harmony. The chitarrone becomes the practically decisive instrument, which first gives concrete shape to the basso-continuo situation.

This survey of the conditions shortly before the actual thoroughbass period may be taken as a first introduction. Because the lute with its inherent difficulties in thoroughbass matters has radically fashioned the treatment of a continuo, we may start our explanations with this special case.

1. Lute and Lute Continuo

In its early forms, the lute is actually a mandolin type (it stems from the Moorish region; *al ud* means "of wood"). It has paired metal strings, is plucked by a plectron, lies in the discant range, and is a melody instrument. Later one plays it with single fingers, uses gut strings, and enlarges the instrument. The shaping of the body remains always the same. Staves cut as for a cask and set in a hooplike strip of wood produce the hollow body. On it lies a very thin, flat top with a soundhole. (Soundholes of stringed instruments, also of viols and fiddles, certainly do not exist merely to let the sound escape; these breaks in the table cut the surface and vault tensions, thereby rendering the top elastic and capable of resonance.) The body continues at the upper end into the neck of the lute. The pegbox bends away from the neck at a right angle so as to give the strings at the change of direction on the saddle a maximum of friction and grip. The neck is knotted with frets. The fingers of the left hand press down behind the frets so that the vibrating string becomes exactly and pointedly defined by the fret. The lute experienced a first bloom in the fourteenth and fifteenth centuries, initially as a tenor instrument in the virelais, etc., later for the playing of contratenor parts. The earliest lute music proper is not documented. The lute has five open strings, makes good use of paired stringing, and strengthens the bass register by octave courses. Tuning in fourths (the fingers of the left hand span exactly a fourth across the frets) with a third in the middle does justice to diatonic music and could even be a Moorish heritage. In the sixteenth century, a lowest bass string is added. The most common type is a G-lute, created by the addition of the lowest pitch value (the strings are tuned to G, c^0, f^0, a^0, d^1, g^1). A somewhat smaller lute on A was also popular. The German names for the strings proceed from the highest pitch: *Quintsait* (fifth string), *Sangsait* (song string), *Mittelsait* (middle string), *Kleinbrummer* (small growler), *Mittelbrummer* (middle growler), *Grossbrummer* (big growler). The old instruments never formed strict, narrowly confined types; each instrument exhibits structural individuation. Look at the beautiful lute with an ivory body which the Innsbruck lute maker Georg Gerle built for the "Welserin": the lady must have had very tiny hands, for the neck of the instrument is extremely narrow.[106]

This kind of lute was inadequate for continuo matters. To increase the effect of the bass and to relieve the left hand, strings are added which receive their own, separate pegbox. Because wound strings were still unknown, the second pegbox for the bass tone lies at almost twice the distance from the bridge. These bass strings do not run above the fingerboard and are tuned as the case requires. Because of the extraordinary length of the strings, the instrument, now called *chitarrone,* usually dispenses with double courses. One economizes very much with the number of strings to protect the instrument against deformation by the string tension. Monteverdi's *Orfeo* prescribes two chitarroni.

Outside Italy another thoroughbass lute type develops, the theorbo. Here wound strings were available for the bass positions, and the second pegbox now moves directly behind the first. The theorbo probably grew gradually out of reconstructed large lutes: the thin lute tops suffered tonal damage after a relatively short time; and when a top was renewed, a new bridge was made with additional bass strings and a special bass pegbox affixed to the neck in the manner of the little "rider" (this is the name of the specially placed peg for the highest string; this method, too, served to add to the lute one more, the sixth, string). Such adapted types are referred to as "theorbized lutes." Finally, this development leads to the large virtuoso instrument associated with the name of the French lutenist Denis Gaultier.[107] Tuning in fourths with a third in the middle yields to a D-minor tuning: two four-six chords above each other, with single strings for the two highest pitches. Because of the high tension, these two single strings sound very well (another technique perhaps participates at the time, namely, an approach to the guitarist's hand, which would supply the reason for leaving these specific melody strings single). The other courses are doubled at the unison, below *A* at the octave. This lowest tone on the fingerboard is followed by an entire diatonic octave tuned to suit the piece to be played. This was the disposition of the large Hoffmann lute[108] which Bach owned. Twenty-four strings have to be tuned — a bothersome procedure often ridiculed.

Among all thoroughbass instruments, the lute is most tied to the given playing conditions and most remote from a simple harmony exercise. Significantly in this case, common notation rather than the pertinent tablature was used. Only exceptionally was a continuo part transcribed into tablature, probably in order to help a player not trained for continuo tasks. There exist, for instance, continuo parts in German tablature for operas by Hasse. They have led some people to the conclusion that a plain chordal realization of the lute continuo was normal. This inference is erroneous. It is up to the player to vitalize with his right hand the plain chordal notation of positions for the left hand. The French art of lute-playing knows the so-called covered or closed play. The chordal positions are notated; but on the basis of these prescribed tones, the right hand adapts the notation through neighboring notes, passing tones, etc., in the direction of linear playing. The technique of the great English lutenists, such as Dowland, made possible the performance on a lute of a typical chanson and even (with minor simplifications) the whole of a composition like "Lacrimae" (a ricercar of five obbligato voices for a viola-da-gamba consort). That period was the apex of lute playing. Dowland, too, employed "covered" playing, that is, the lutenist sets his left hand on the chord position and plays further desirable tones into this complex by the action of single fingers. Slant lines indicated that certain finger positions were to be held. This practice reveals that in the early seventeenth century the concept of harmony was utilized in its full significance. Good lutenists knew perfectly how to resolve such harmonic complexes into a specific linear lute texture, according to the most opportune possibilities of the right hand. In this connection, the French players refer explicitly to a *separationes* style. It is the opposite of the *cracle* by which the circle around Dowland designated lute-playing limited to chords. The characteristic of the lute continuo, in any case, is the adjustment of musical features to the given situation, from thumb arpeggio to rarified texture.

How a lute continuo actually sounded in detail, we can only try to reconstruct from a knowledge of lute music and from a few precedents. The lute, we must emphasize, is the instrument best suited to project a continuo with a minimum of display. Among the existing pieces of concrete continuo realization, the arioso "Betrachte, meine Seel'" from Bach's *St. John Passion* stands in first place.[109] The ensemble is carefully orchestrated: the baritone voice is accompanied by two violas d'amour, lute, and string bass (the latter marked pianissimo). Bach fully composed the continuo aspect and notated it in *chiavi naturali* (discant and bass clefs). Pizzicati mark the space of half notes, which thereby create a kind of large adagio. The two violas d'amour enter after the beat. Recurring ties consistently recreate the situation similar to the one established by the beginning and by the pizzicato basses. Melodically and rhythmically, the voice has a recitative character, quite apart from the absence of any formal relation to the commonly used aria types. This ensemble contains the most beautiful lute continuo of Western music. The right-hand thumb pursues a continuo motion; and the harmonic substance, always after the beat, is stretched across the most sensitive, composed arpeggios, with an occasional insertion of runs carrying passing tones. This E-flat-major arioso is obviously not a common continuo case; it has always seemed to me the ideal dream of a lute continuo! Bach realized this most difficult situation because such quality cannot be improvised! (The specific quality consists in the musical perfection of the lute part of which the concentration lies beyond any improvisation.) One wonders whether to provide a lute continuo also for the following, equally subtle C-minor aria. The aria, in any case, is a virtuoso piece for the tenor, requires similarly the violas d'amour, and makes considerable demands of the thoroughbass, which a lutenist could meet very well. He must, however, not be charged with a detailed execution of the bass line! Careful occasional rakes and thin texture could alternate.

Bach's funeral ode on the death of the Grand Duchess Christine calls for two lutes.[110] The score gives no apparent, conclusive information about the use of the lutes. One could conceivably adhere strictly to the score and play only the written notes. The siciliano aria in the first part, however, needs more. What is the situation in this work by Bach? The opening chorus is richly orchestrated, a broadly flowing *grave* in the manner of a French overture with optimal dots (the upbeats to the dotted sixteenth notes to be played as short as possible!). In this full orchestra, the two lutenists probably only play along with the bass. For the given texture, a continuo by the lutes would be far too thin and incapable of carrying the ensemble. Here one needs an organ continuo and, because of the presence of the lutes, also harpsichord participation. Today one often makes the mistake of not giving the continuo sufficient sonority. The continuo sound must bind together the manifold array of the most diverse ensemble formations. Only in very delicate and subtle ensembles is a lute continuo the right type for producing the proper sonority and correct tonal balance. In the "bell" recitative, the lute parts are exactly written out; this section has nothing to do with a thoroughbass part. The following siciliano is such a case of subtle ensemble formation for which one may request of the lutes a real continuo (unless one chooses the cheap solution of using the lutes for the bass line and assigning the continuo task proper to the harpsichord). Bach's employment of two lutes for the funeral ode was certainly in response to the (incidental!) availability of two lutenists. In Leipzig, lute participation depended on such facts. Players of the instrument, to be sure, existed, because around 1730 the lute was still ably practiced! But the average lutenists cling to tablatures and to specific, that is soloistic, performance. What Bach asks goes beyond the capacity of everyday dilettantes! He therefore writes out essential parts in common notation, in which the *chiavi naturali* appear to him appropriate. In the siciliano, I would let the better player cope with a fitting lute continuo while withdrawing the other player to execute the bass line. In the closing chorus of the first part, the lutes are tied *colla parte* to the vocal bass. The tenor aria at the beginning of the second part could be handled like the siciliano. In this movement, the two violas da gamba take the lute bass in diminution. Considering the array of instruments, one ought to give to each lute

its own continuo. The lutes are prescribed again in the closing chorus
where they double the continuo bass line. Any attempt to let the lutes
do more in this movement would be useless in face of the ensemble.
The funeral ode reveals, in any case, that Bach employs the lute equally for continuo tasks, for *colla parte* amplification of the bass line, and
finally for concrete participation (bell recitative) in an ensemble.

  Quite different is the role of the chitarrone thoroughbass in Monteverdi's *Orfeo*.[111] In some places, the score clearly specifies the use of
the chitarrone. One remembers the historical practice that in an opera
the harpsichordist and lutenist always sat next to each other and played
from the same part. This fact shows that the minutest coordination and
also alternation was possible and even intended. The *Orfeo* score (see
the facsimile in the Malipiero edition) lists all the participants, that is,
also the exact orchestra players, together with the information that the
orchestra was placed *behind* the stage in an exactly defined "stereo position" of left-right. We also read old reports according to which *Orfeo* in
Mantua was played without scenery. A barrier of little laurel trees yielded
to an opening in the middle and two side entrances. Above this barrier,
contact between singers and instrumentalists was easily established in
chamber-music fashion. One recognizes the characteristic of antique
theaters where the action also occurred on a long, narrow strip in right-
left motion. In contrast to other operas of the period, some music of
Orfeo was concretely written out. Exact study of the score leads to a number of important clues for the performance. From the manner in which
the chitarrone was used, we conclude that each musical situation called
for the appropriate continuo instrument. An extreme case is the accompaniment of Caronte by a regal. A vast number of scenes and pieces
specifies the *organo di legno* (cf. below, p. 89). The chitarrone is repeatedly mentioned in the context of different vocal and instrumental conditions and finally for very subtle and careful performance by itself. The
strophes of the prologue can be realized in varied ways. The character
of Musica, going quasi to and fro with strophic variations on the same
bass model, is accompanied once by the lutenist on the right, then by
the one on the left. The dance movements also call for the chitarrone,
which is highly qualified to project metric orders. The more difficult
the musical situation, the less instruments share in the continuo; ac-
curate coordination with the singer is best provided by a solo lutenist or
harpsichordist.

  I must repeat that the different lutes were often used as linear bass
instruments. Bach lets them reinforce the bass line in the funeral ode.

Monteverdi's very specific and detailed instructions in *Orfeo* far surpass the common practice of his day. The *Orfeo* ritornelli are written out, and the traditional notation fixes the metric orders and tempi. For all these reasons, I consider rigorous detailed study of this opera indispensable for a conductor.

I wish to submit some of my own experiences. The bass strophes of the prologue, for instance, can well use a bass gamba. The accompanying lutenist will have all the more freedom if he is not the only one responsible for the bass line. We once even used the harp for two prologue strophes only to avoid repetition of a musical situation. Similar is the approach to the strophes sung by Orfeo at the beginning of the second act (these strophes are today best transcribed in accordance with the meter, otherwise the three-beat hemiola might not be promptly comprehended and musically correctly realized). The rhythms of Orfeo's ritornelli and strophes (after the chorus "Dunque fa degno Orfeo") should also be shown in additive meters. This opera calls for at least two first-class chitarrone players who must work with their material for a long period. If one must minutely write out a continuo part, one will hardly find a solution which after a week still appears really convincing. Continuo is in its innermost essence an improvisation, by the standard of which it must be judged. The possibility of an *Orfeo* performance depends primarily on the singer of the title role and then on the lutenists. While dwelling on the lute continuo in Monteverdi's music, I should also like to recommend some of his monodic madrigals, for example, "Come dolce hoggi l'auretta," a lovely, serenade-like piece for three female sopranos.[112] For such cases, the chitarrone is the only proper instrument. It adjusts itself to the level of the gentle piece. The thoroughbass of this music must not become luxuriant but rather be treated simply and plainly, as is appropriate to the musical qualities of the piece; for factual essentials, the lute continuo takes first place. Monteverdi wrote a multitude of such pieces. (A guitarist planning a concert would considerably enrich his program by such pieces. Good guitarists are numerous. The guitar is so closely related to the lute that substituting for it is absolutely justified. After all, denying a modern pianist the *Well-tempered Keyboard* would be equally absurd.)

Another thoroughbass situation facing the lute involves the "string swarm"; spinet and lute (occasionally more than one) together in a group were appreciated in the seventeenth century as carriers of a specific sound. In early music practice, this is one of the few cases of genuine accumulation. What led to this heaping of plucked instruments was probably the weakness of a single lute in a large room. Yet already the sixteenth and even the fifteenth centuries knew such sound effects (see, for example, the coronation liturgy in Reims which refers to the sound of lutes and stringed instruments as typical of the royal cappella). In a multichoir psalm by Schütz, an ensemble of plucked strings must be used as a swarm to achieve the desired balance — this is Schütz's *coro di liuti*. At such occasions, effective strumming will not be avoided. Private music-making further favored the use of lutes. The wide propagation of the different lute types contributed its share. The early monodic song, too, and its analogues were mostly performed with lute accompaniment. Only in the eighteenth century do the lutes relinquish their role first to the harpsichord and finally to the early pianoforte.

There are many compositions the intricate sonorities of which require an adequate lute continuo. Let us examine Bach's *Actus tragicus* in regard to the instrumentation.[113] The autograph of this cantata from Bach's youth is lost, but two conforming copies by pupils permit us to assume an identical score. According to Pirro, this cantata most probably served as funeral music for Bach's uncle Lämmerhirt (his mother's brother), a city counselor in Erfurt and a wealthy furrier. He had left fifty ducats to Bach, who received the same amount, large for the time, again at the death of the widow Lämmerhirt. Pirro's suggestion gains much probability from the chorales taken from the Gotha Songbook and further from Bach's way of gathering Bible sentences for a cantata text. The instrumentation indicates that the music was not intended for church. The subtle sonorities make one imagine a restricted space for the performance, perhaps the living room in the house of the deceased. The traffic conditions of the period would not have permitted Bach to arrive in time for the funeral ceremony in Erfurt. The occasion for the performance of the cantata may well have been the execution of the last will and the payment by the notary in September 1708. Bach liked this intensively expressive work of his youth. He never orchestrated more cautiously: two alto recorders, two gambas, and thoroughbass to the four voices. In the closing chorale, the diminution of the cantus proves that solo singers were intended. A harpsichord continuo is possible; but far more charming, differentiated, and yielding is a lute continuo, which we have used repeatedly. The two recorders present a special problem. Tuned in F, they would move up the cantata by a wholetone and thereby badly shake the balance of the voices. The notation in French violin clef, the warrant for a baroque alto recorder, in connection with the downward transposition by a wholetone (like B-flat clarinets) hints at a lower tuning for the recorders, perhaps in analogy to the older choir pitch. For this cantata, one needs two recorders in E-flat (or in D), which have to be made to order. After many serious endeavors on behalf of this music, I have come to the firm conclusion that E-flat alto recorders are best. Transverse flutes are not admissible; they would spoil the soft weeping of the flutes in the overlays of the Sinfonia. A large lute for the continuo can adapt itself discreetly to all occurring musical conditions.

In detail: in the two gamba parts, the Sinfonia contains an almost realized thoroughbass. Thus the lute need not supply massive harmonies. The tempo of the Sinfonia is identical with that of the following chorus, "Gottes Zeit." In the Sinfonia one counts large time units, the accents limited to the minims. "In ihm leben wir und sind wir" moves in *proportio tripla*, that is, a dotted halfnote in the place of a halfnote. The shift back to the beginning is *subito*, without ritardando blurring. This movement strongly relates to a French overture; it ends on a half cadence, modulating to the relative minor. Now follows the little tenor aria above the ostinato bass à la chaconne (but in duple meter!). In this movement, the second gamba goes with the thoroughbass in sparing diminution. From this fact one may conclude that the cantata dispensed with the otherwise common violoncello for the thoroughbass. Directly after the tenor aria comes the tripla "Bestelle dein Haus." This bass aria cannot be played on F alto recorders; here E-flat recorders are obligatory. This proportio-allegro is followed directly by a kind of chorale arrangement. The combination of three texts is paralleled by three kinds of structure. The text from Jesus Sirach is arranged as a fugue of the lower voices. To this is added the aria-like madrigalism of the soprano with the text from The Revelation of Saint John. The third text is not worded: the recorders in unison play the chorale "Ich hab' mein' Sach' Gott heimgestellt." The chorale must not be overpowered by the singers! The two recorders in a low register are not capable of developing intensity and power. Acknowledging these circumstances, one arrives at a balance of sound in the cantata. The way in which this movement runs down at the end in the diminution of the soprano, and the thoroughbass dries up ahead of it in a *tasto solo* situation, and the voices dissolve in parallel lines and secondary-dominant chromaticism — all these details have a density of madrigalesque affect unequalled in Bach's works! The following alto aria (before which a small cesura is possible, even necessary) is usually spoiled by a wrong tempo. The correct tempo is the same as in the baritone aria 'Heute wirst du mit mir im Paradies sein." With a lute continuo, the scale passages of the thoroughbass and sparing harmonies favor the correct metric treatment. The section of the quasi aria for baritone is joined immediately to the chorale arrangement. Possibly the soprano could share in the projection of this cantus firmus. After a pause of a few heartbeats, the finale offers a last chorale arrangement and a fugue on the last chorale verse. The diminutions in the soprano mentioned earlier are significant. This finale, too, cannot bear more than four singers, otherwise the tonal balance is destroyed. From the old *tactus integer valor* for the chorale lines proper one shifts to *tempo ordinario* at the beginning of the closing fugue. Nowhere does this cantata show the chorale in the simple four-part setting usual in other Bach cantatas. Bach here does not renounce chorales; he uses them in various types of chorale arrangements. I see therein further proof that this work does not belong in a liturgical situation, as do other specific church cantatas, but that it was written for a particular occasion, namely, as Pirro suggested, the service for the dead in the Lämmerhirt house. Whether one cares to accept these special circumstances or not, the text with Bible quotations and chorale verses certainly produced by Bach himself (the only cantata not suffering from the poor quality of the usual cantata texts), the texture, the particular attitude and expression of this music — all this is so singular and individual that one must not let the music bypass any of these facts in a performance! (The absence of a . recitative perhaps also suggests the absence of a harpsichord in a performance.) The lute continuo will succeed only if the player possesses far-reaching knowledge and experience in the field of historic lute literature. (Guitarists fed exclusively on virtuoso pieces are inadequate to such a task. Only by practically playing early lute music can one gradually gain a vocabulary that then becomes disposable by association and permits the execution of a lute continuo.) No other continuo instrument is so intimately tied to its playing technique! It must be extensively tried out! Italian canzonas and arias (Caccini et al.) offer a rewarding testing ground. Accompanying a singer will lead particularly well to that familiarity with thoroughbass tasks which provides valuable clues for a performance.

2. Organ Types and Organ Continuo

Thoroughbass confronted the organ builder with concrete tasks which led to the creation of a specific type of instrument and of organ registers. Here, too, an existing instrumentarium and playing practice were bent to serve the continuo. The keyboard made the organ particularly predestined for the presentation of polyphony. Although the positive for playing continuo is a special case, I wish to make it part of the discussion of all organ forms, because the type of thoroughbass instrument can be better understood in an overall context.

The role of the organ in Western music begins with the adaptation of the ancient hydraulis by organ-building monks for the ambitions of sacred music. The sophisticated system of a water compressor and pistons, which gave the hydraulis its name, is replaced by wrought-iron bellows. The pipes are mostly made from a tin-and-lead alloy. The increasing difference between the largest and smallest pipes (the hydraulis pipes all have the same width) automatically leads to new methods of mensuration. The relation of plate length to plate width is of primary importance (when the pipe material lies on the work table as a tin plate, the relation of length to width is easily calculated by proportional compasses). The old organ instruments at first contained exclusively flue pipes. For an understanding of this principle of tone production, a concise exposition of the physical events is necessary.

The tone of a flue pipe originates in a coupled system. An air ribbon escaping from a narrow flue or windway is blown against a cutting edge (the upper lip) where it creates vortices and thus a tone. In steady alternation, the oscillating airstream passes the lip first on one side and then on the other. The whirls thereby produced alternatingly rarefy and condense the air. This edge tone functioning as power source is coupled to an air column incited to vibrate sympathetically by the continuous change between plus and minus of the edge tone. It is essential that the pitch of the edge tone, given by the tempo of the oscillating air leaf, matches the frequency of the air column. (The length of the oscillating air stream that initiates the motion determines the pitch of the edge tone inasmuch as the time needed for the air ribbon to flow from the flue to the obstacle has a role in determining its frequency. Low wind pressure keeps that value small, higher pressure increases it.) The air column confined by the body of the pipe acts as the resonator through which the waves pass at the speed of sound. According to the physical law correlating the slowest vibration to the pipe length, the situations at the two ends of the vibrating space are always of opposite nature, that is, air pressure increases at one end at the same moment that it decreases at the other. Air compression at one end (wave crest) corresponds to rarefaction at the other (node). If the frequency of the agitating vortex agrees with an overtone of the resonating air column, the vibrating resonance will sound the correspondingly higher pitch. Production of overtones is called *overblowing*. If the resonating air column does not find the way to the outside air at the otherwise open pipe end, that is, if the pipe there is closed, the stopper or cover reflects the wave. It runs back, finds at the lip a vortex of opposite phase, and issues with it to the free outside air. The pitch of such a stopped or covered pipe thus equals that of an open pipe twice as long. Because air-pressure variations are strongest at the point where the wave is reflected from the cover of the pipe, no node can form there and hence no first overtone (octave) of the pipe. Therefore, stopped pipes have only odd-numbered partials. When the walls of the resonating body are not parallel but either narrowing or widening, this shape, too, greatly influences the overtone constellation. As narrowing increasingly damps the pipe, the overtones disappear more and more. In a conical pipe, the node of the partial tone sounding the octave lies beyond the middle; and further divisions for the formation of partial tones become ever more complicated. Flutes narrowing toward the open end have correspondingly more decorous overtones. The reverse shape gives the overtones a penetrant sound; it also perspicuously develops ecmelic overtones (those which have no place in our tone system). These facts of physics yield the following possibilities for building an organ.

The energy of an organ stop is determined by the width of the lip and the amount of air (which depends on the height of the mouth and the wind pressure). The lip width can vary from one third to one ninth of the circumference (practically one operates within one fourth and one eighth). In the first case (with greater width), the resonating air column is violently agitated, particularly with somewhat high air pressure. In the second case, good organs vary from about 40 millimeters of water column as the mildest wind (the Antegnati organ of 1583 in San Giuseppe, Brescia) up to the strongest wind pressure measured in a historic organ of 90 millimeters (in the Hofkirche in Innsbruck, built by Jörg Ebert in 1558). These two organs have contrary musical intent.

The width of the pipe (in relation to the width of the lip) defines the tonal concept of fullness. Ample pipe width and narrow lip (for minimal, gentle agitation of the air column) yield a tone that carries best. The vortices as the immediate carriers of energy agitate a wide pipe without forcing it; and the vortices themselves pass directly into the medium of the surrounding air. The result is an optimal transmission from the initial vortex to the wave which hits our ears. In the contrary case of wide lip and relatively narrow pipe, the tone carries poorly because the overenergetic vortices, tearing off upon contact with the air of the medium, cannot flow over. Such a stop sounds penetrant and rough from nearby, and faint and poorly assimilated from the distance. More successful vibration systems easily push it aside.

According to the resonating body, we find the following types:

Open pipes with parallel walls.

Stopped pipes with parallel walls.

Half-covered (canister-stopped, chimney flutes into the lid of which a narrower open pipe has been soldered which lets part of the wave pass through. Such pipes sound similar to open pipes but are more quiet because the pierced cover makes the tone a bit sick).

Conic open.

Conic stopped.

Reverse conic open.

A last group are overblowing pipes. A narrow mouth makes the agitating whirl so fast that it provokes the first overtone of the pipe. Here one must bear in mind that such procedure creates a different overtone spectrum. The fundamental vibration (first partial tone) disappears; the harmonic series begins at the second partial tone (stronger overblowing eliminates further overtones from the bottom up). Thus observed, overblowing is really a sonorous phenomenon of its own.

The attack of a flue pipe is an event that can be analyzed. At the moment the ray of air squirts out, it shatters at the edge of the lip. This first, explosive agitation creates the first overtone of the pipe as a forerunner (transient). As soon as the air ribbon begins to oscillate regularly, the forerunner dies out and the fundamental arises, followed by all overtones made available by the pipe dimensions and the kind of voicing. Because of air inertia, the forerunner is somewhat too low: the open pipe sounds approximately the leading-tone seventh; the closed pipe, the tritone above the octave. If the straight edge of the upper lip were cut into a curve, the specific transient frequency activating the main tone would be eliminated. The forerunner disappears, and the overtones are also strongly reduced. The transverse orchestra flute, for instance, is equipped with this tonal character. The player's lower lip covers half of the round mouth hole. The remaining semicircle possesses tolerant distances to the "windway," the opening of his mouth. By rolling the flute toward or away from his mouth, the player changes the distance from flue to edge. Together with a differentiated pressure of his breath, the player can now produce forte in the low register and piano in the high register. The recorder, with a straight edge at the upper lip and a fixed distance between flue and upper lip, is incapable of such tasks, notwithstanding the hole for overblowing (the width of which one can delicately control). Precisely regulated breath pressure accomplishes only overblowing (together with appropriate covering of the hole for over-blowing). By controlling breath and intonation with various articulating syllables, however, one can develop forerunners on the recorder.

Transfer of these principles to the organ shows that different conditions of the buildup process permit the tone to be influenced by the key action. With a rigid transmission from key to valve, one can quickly tear open the valve and thereby bring forth a penetrating forerunner. Or one can press the playing valve gently, and the transient phenomenon becomes subdued. This control over the build-up process affords all kinds of possibilities for influencing the tone by means of touch and articulation. Old organ music is thus deeply tied to historic organ building. Tone differentiation through touch is best achieved on small instruments. In this regard, a small organ really has a fine, genuinely musical advantage over a large instrument!

There is no strict coupling between the frequencies of the edge tone and the resonating air column. The whirls, that is, the frequency of the edge tone, can be somewhat controlled because of the rather intolerant frequency values of the resonator. In a flue pipe, a slightly too low mouth (the distance from flue to edge) creates more overtones; a relatively high cut renders the tone poor in overtones and dull. If the height of the mouth is so narrow that its value corresponds to the octave, then the pipe over-blows. The tolerance with which the edge tone submits itself to the tone frequency of the "steering" air column is relatively great; but for voicing the organ, the measurement of the height of the mouth offers a possibility of differentiation so that one can predetermine how rich (or poor) in overtones a register or part of it should become. Notwithstanding the linkage of the height of the mouth and the pitch of the pipe, one can thus influence the overtone distribution of a pipe by making the mouth high or low. One must, however, remember that a healthily voiced pipe needs its proper *optimal* mouth. Certain props for voicing—favored around 1900 as "beards" on the pipe lips (also known as ears) to direct the airstream — have been recognized as wrong and are being cut back to the simplest forms. As in a historic instrument, a good modern organ pipe should have dimensions, materials, and wind pressure conforming properly to the desired sound.

The sounding substance disposed in an organ is almost inexhaustibly variable, and its organization is crucial for the construction of the instrument. In spite of archetypes and prototypes, typical and individual forms are susceptible to such freedom of variation that, together with the acoustical conditions of the hall, no organ design can or should repeat itself.

For the sake of completeness, we shall now discuss also the special qualities of the second kind of organ pipes, the reed pipes. In an organ, the reed stops all involve striking tongues. An elastic brass tongue is larger than the plane it hits. Air pressure thus makes the tongue strike periodically. The flowing wind finds the tongue (which is slightly bent) somewhat detached from the shallot and carries it along, as a draft closes a door. The brass tongue is thereby stretched against its bend. After hitting the edge of the shallot, the elastic tongue bounces back and thereby opens the path for the next air current. The vibrating tongue divides the air stream into a series of separate impacts (similar to the principle of a disk siren). The tone created by reeds is noisy and rich in overtones. Procedures were soon developed to alter the initial situation of a pure reed tone, to vary the sound and to ennoble it. If an instrument consists exclusively of tongues and shallots (besides the blocks which hold these elements together), the reed pipes can be arranged in conformity with the width of the keys on the keyboard. The result was a small, mobile instrument, the regal.

At an early stage, small and then ever larger and more complicated resonators were attached to the block. The first shapes were small funnels. Such regals generally sound as if they were bawling; the stop is then called *calves' regal* (Kälberregal), *old-women's regal* (Altweiberregal), or the like. Later the funnels were replaced by little tubes with parallel walls, topped by various kinds of caps. At the same time, reed-pipe registers become incorporated into organs; now there is room to make the resonators as long as the flue pipes. The result is a coupled system, similar to that of the flue pipe, except that the brass tongue is far less tolerant toward the resonator. If under certain circumstances (cylindrical caps) the frequency of the vibrating tongue stands in no exact ratio to the air column of the resonator, the pipe remains silent. Much information about the type is gained from a consideration of the register *krummhorn* (named after the wind instrument). On the wind chest, there stands the boot (corresponding to the reedcap of the wind instrument), a hollow box into which is stuck the actual sounding pipe, that is, block, shallot, and tongue with tuning wire (the name of a movable crook by which one can change the length of the vibrating tongue and thus tune it). Above the block, there is soldered a tube with parallel walls into which the tones created by the vibrating tongue are conducted, producing a coupled resonance. From experience one knows a similar case (valid, by the way, for all pipes, hence also for flue stops). If you stand in a tunnel and shout toward the opening, the outside air throws back the sound vibrations as if there were a firm closed door at the tunnel opening. The cause of the return bounce are the totally different conditions of the air outside and inside the cylinder. The sound waves thus run back from the open end. When in the case of our krummhorn tube the reed begins to vibrate, that is, at the first arrival of air, a pressure wave runs along the cylindrical tube, bounces back from the outside air, and wanders back to the reed (where the impact of the returning wave helps detach the reed from the shallot). The wave thus makes the way twice; the length of the resonator corresponds to the measure of the stopped flue pipe. Meanwhile the tongue has been pushed down on the shallot. The compressed wave is followed by one of rarefied air. Then the chink between shallot and tongue opens again for the next pressure wave. Because here reed frequency and tube length must be precisely attuned to each other, the effect of the resonator is optimal. In the krummhorn organ stop, the waves always run only a plus-and-minus course (compression and rarefaction) and are reflected at the open tube end. Hence the lengths of the tubes match the lengths of stopped flue pipes. The krummhorn produces only odd-numbered partial tones! In this very old reed stop, the tubes were placed at equal distances across the whole range of the keyboard; hence a characteristic of its sound is that the bass is not preponderant. This is a specific quality of most reed stops with funnel resonators. The reason lies in the smooth transition from the inside to the outside conditions. Even if there is some bouncing back at the open wide end of the funnel, the returning wave is consumed by the sloping wall of the cone. Consequently resonance is affected only by the path of the wave toward the outside. The funnels on reed stops are thus just about as long as open flue pipes, but there is no exact relation of resonator length to reed frequency. By thus varying the tube measurements, one could develop a whole set of organ registers. All such registers contain the *complete* overtone series!

From these norms of reed pipes, all kinds of organ registers and instruments derive.

The regal is an independent reed instrument, a parallel to the *positif de table*. It has rudimentary resonators (no resonators at all in early instruments) which influence the pure reed sound only moderately. It is restrained most readily by narrowing the tone outlet. The common regal type with civilized tone and usable balance across the whole range of the keyboard is called *rankett*. Here the reed tone travels through a short narrow krummhorn tube into a superposed cap, from which it egresses through a few narrow holes.

Experiments with regal resonators have been manifold and adventurous. The effect of tube shapes and the highly varied sounds led to the incorporation of reed pipes into organs. As organ stops, they are called *regals,* after the name of the independent instrument. That independent little reed organ emerged among renaissance organs when the newly built large instruments combined the individual historic types in one unified playing arrangement. The new big organs contain first of all the former *Blockwerk* (of which one is reminded by multi-choir mixtures, a rear set, etc.). Then they absorb the small church positive, which takes care of virtuoso passages because of its greater mechanical agility. The regal follows, initially without a separate keyboard and playable from the great organ. In the seventeenth century, the single-reed stop is joined by a few flue stops that fit into the space. Because this collection is placed in a little enclosure below the main pipework, it is named *Brustwerk* after its position. Simultaneously it receives its own keyboard. The organ pedal serves at the beginning only the lowest zones of the manual; it is merely a help for the player. Soon, however, it takes over by itself the lowest zone of the great organ. It becomes an independent bass instrument, always in closest relationship to the great organ. Within certain ranges, the pedal keyboard controls stops for the projection of different cantus firmi. Because the huge pipes require much space, the pedal work is assigned its own position in special towers on the sides of the main pipework. The positive being by nature small compared to the main organ, the latter receives in certain regions a genuine partner, the *Oberwerk* or swell. France develops separate units for the performance of a pronounced individual part. Spain has its cantus-firmus works. All these various "works" of the great organ pay increased attention to the reed stops, of which a considerable number is absorbed in the separate work units.

Italy did not have much use for the sound of reeds and tolerated the regal only as an independent instrument (if nevertheless an organ contains the regal register, a radical separation by cut-off valves prevents the simultaneous playing of organ and regal). France and Spain demonstrate the opposite extreme: strong participation by reed stops in the great organ defines the sound. North Germany, too, gives tongues a considerable share but insists on unified sonority.

A discussion of organ types usually ignores one issue: Catholic countries know only organ arrangements derived from Gregorian chant. Protestantism proceeds from the central element of the Lutheran liturgy, the German chorale. With emphasis on the German language and the liturgical factor of the "community in Jesu Christo" unified by the community chorale, an entirely different cantus-firmus substance is here employed. It has its consequences in organ music and obtains its adequate instrument. Compare organ arrangements based on Gregorian cantus firmi from Cabezon to Froberger with the chorale arrangements of the Protestant organists. One quickly recognizes the different challenges facing the organ builder. Gregorian tradition, concentrated on diatonism and limited range, develops as an extreme case the Spanish organ. The German church hymns demand a specific supply of organ registers, as finally required by the highest musical qualities of the chorale preludes by Bach.

Reed stops with long, fully formed resonators derive from two basic categories: voices with conic tubes (variants of the trumpet) and krummhorn forms. By differentiating width and length of the tubes, the former group can satisfy the standard and energy level of the organ to which the stop is assigned. German krummhorns are narrow, French krummhorns are wider and more colorful. Between the trumpet and krummhorn types, there are several transitions. The dulcian stop has tubes which begin as very narrow trumpets and then convert into a cylinder. This is not the place for a description of the many reed stops, which can be studied in specialized books.

After these introductory explanations, we now turn to the historic types of Western organs.

The early organ is bound by Pythagorean consonance laws (one suspects that the pipes on the hydraulic instrument were already ordered according to consonances; if so, the knowledge credited until now to the age of Hucbald must be pushed back to the early Christian era).[114]

Whatever the case, two paths lead from the ancient hydraulis: one to the gothic church organ, the other to the portative. The first case tends toward increasing enlargement. The second approach produces the smallest possible type.

In our previous discussion of Notre Dame music, we have said a few things about the church organ, which eventually became the musically dominating instrument in large spaces. The keyboard is still limited to about two octaves. The basic set of pipes provides a real connection to Notre Dame music. It comprises the small octave—perhaps a few tones below—and ends upward at the two-line octave. Those very early instruments permit registration for two tasks: bringing into play the basic set and involving the totality of sonorous means. On the basic set, a structure of consonances is erected like the one which until today dominates the principal or diapason system of the organ. The technical solution is provided by a so-called chiselled wind chest. Into a post of nut wood (some carpenters still call it a chest), about three to four feet long, one foot deep, and two inches thick, channels are chiselled from below (the French foot at 0.3248 meters is 2 centimeters larger than the English). These channels are closed lengthwise by leather-covered valves. A wind chest positioned below the chiselled block is connected through ducts with the bellows. From the upper side of the block, separate bores lead into the channels. Directly on the bores stand the pipes. Rigid mechanisms connect the valves with the keyboard. By opening a valve, one sounds all pipes standing on that particular channel. For the basic set of pipes, special smaller valves are provided; a kind of second keyboard permits playing only the basic set (through a kind of nonreturn valve, the basic set receives the necessary wind from the main channel). The crude forge bellows are wedge-shaped. The calcant (= stamper, bellows treader) stands with each foot in a kind of wooden shoe. With one foot he raises the top plate of one bellow while with the other foot at the same time he presses down the other, previously raised bellow. Large organs have sets of paired bellows. Early organs are encumbered by action made of wrought iron—like all work details of those earliest organs, a basically rustic contrivance—, by very simple and even primitive tools, and by insufficient experience. This organ without registers is called *Blockwerk* (*block* or *ploch* is the term for the technically decisive part, the wind chest).

Later additional valves are successfully built into the chiselled channels, permitting whole rows of pipes to be engaged and disengaged. Pulls which move the additional rows of valves must be hooked in; when disengaged, the levers spring back. Hence the term *spring chest* is used for this construction. The array of pipes — foundation and consonance sets — planned for one tone, for one key, can thus serve a flexible registration by way of such racks of valves which can block the connection from channel to single pipe. The wind valve or pallet is connected with the key and admits wind to the entire channel. Sounding a pipe row depends on interlocking the valve racks arranged by registers. These valve racks cross the course of the channels at right angles and serve to engage and disengage the pipe rows.

For the subject matter of this chapter (and for Western musical culture), the development of the small-organ type is more important. In a portative, the single, initially diatonic set of pipes stands on a small wind chest and is played by way of simple pins (similar to the buttons on the accordion keyboard). The sitting player places the instrument on his left upper thigh (the dancing jongleur carries it on a strap across his shoulder). The player's left hand operates a bellow. The hand must pull up the bellow; and briefly the instrument, like a singer catching his breath, has no wind at its disposal. The dimensions of instrument and bellow were such that a full wind supply corresponded more or less to a singer's breath. The player's right hand played a discant part on the keyboard buttons. Toward the end of the fifteenth century, a real keyboard replaces the buttons. This development takes place on a slightly larger instrument, the *positif de table*. Both hands now play on a proper keyboard; the former buttons are covered by keys. The hands are at right angles to the course of the wind chest and the pipes. On a portative, where the hand forms approximately a forty-five-degree angle with the course of the instrument, buttons serve the technique of the hand better than keys. The *positif de table* now has two bellows which alternately provide wind but have to be worked by a second person. Initially the *positif de table* also has only one set of pipes. Utilizing the experience with the great organ, one later tries to dispose a set of octaves above the basic set. As in the little positive, the pipe rows can be blocked not by valve racks but by a movable thin board inserted between pipe and channel. When all borings lie above each other, the register sounds. By sliding the board a bit, one closes all borings belonging to it. One speaks appropriately of a slider chest. Developed for the small organ, this mechanical principle serves such conditions very effectively. For more wind and large wind chests, the valve racks of the spring chest were technically and functionally the better construction.

For a better understanding of the tonal structure of an organ, one profits greatly from acquaintance with a special type of European organ, incomparable in the clarity of its structure and of the realized musical tasks: the old Italian organ. It employs only one kind of pipe, namely, the open pipe with parallel walls, and deliberately aims at homogeneous sonority. The oldest, still playable large instrument stands in San Petronio in Bologna, the church in which Charles V was crowned. It is a rood-loft organ (at the bridge to the choir, the church had a huge rood screen). The instrument has therefore two prospects, one facing the choir, and the other facing the nave. After the demolition of the rood screen, the organ was moved to the choir gallery and finally during the baroque period framed by a stucco case. Inside the latter, the large gothic case of 1470 stands intact (San Petronio is the largest gothic church in Italy; only the inside was completed, façade and outside remained a torso). Toward the nave, the organ has a 24-foot prospect: the largest pipe sounds subcontra G_2. The prospect on the other side is smaller by one octave. At the time it was built, the organ had a large manual and, to assist the player, a pedal keyboard which permitted him to play the lowest zones also with the feet. Subcontra G_2, A_2, B_2-flat, and B_2 were accessible only to the feet. From contra C upward, one could use either hands or feet (the pedal range was two octaves). The pedal is an aid for the player whose hands cannot fully cover the excessive span of the keyboard. For low pitches, the feet entered. The entire sounding material of the organ is thus playable by way of a large manual and auxiliary pedals. It contains two categories of pipes intimately related to each other. The main set of pipes belongs to the category slightly later called *principal* or *diapason*. The primary task of the organ was to play the standard texture of contemporary church music. The mensuration of the pipes is decisive. By measuring octave values in the proportion of the golden section, the Italians found a method which frees the width of the pipes from its relation to the length (pipe lengths followed monochord measurements, but already in the tenth century a correction of those proportions was applied to actual pipe lengths; Codex Bernelius[115] and Hucbald[116]). Of significance is the choice of registers disposed in the organ. The deliberate aim of the instrument is an optimal homogeneous sound. The basic stop, in San Petronio still marked *ténor* (after about 1500, the name is *principale*), is joined in order by: octave, superoctave, fifth above the superoctave, the third octave, and then ever higher sets of octaves and fifths. The Italian organ counts the intervals in relation to the basic set. The resulting structure is *principale*, VIII, XV, XIX, XXII, XXVI, XXIX, and (in very large instruments) still XXXIII and XXXVI. The pipe lips of the principal structure measure about two ninths of the circumference. Together with mild wind pressure, they produce a singing tone, somewhat restrained and extremely cultivated. In Flanders, France, and Germany, the same organ category measures the lips at one fourth of the circumference. Together with much higher wind pressure, the character of the sound is essentially harder.

Italian organ builders also discover the method (reminiscent of the egg of Columbus) of adapting the organ to the space via the compass of the bass zone. Instruments in a small space have the limited range from c^0 to a^2 (the top of a^2 is never exceeded). In somewhat larger halls, organs reach down to great F or C. Huge churches activate the octave below down to contra C_1 or F_1. San Petronio, as said earlier, has a subcontra G_2. The book by Dom Bedos on organ building gives the following instruction:[117] measure the longest unobstructed path the organ tone may take, that is, from the lip of the register *montre* (principal) to the farthest point in the church, take a twelfth to a twentieth of this distance, and use this number as a clue for the footage of the pipe on great C.[118] This method is excellent and offers still today the best solution. It was first followed by Italian organ builders; hence the very different ranges of manuals in old Italian organs. The gigantic space of San Petronio admits a 32′. The lower the pitches of an organ, the higher the overtones it must employ. The Italian organ recognizes only single sets of pipes, no rear set like the German organ and no mixture. Only in the eighteenth century do Italian organs follow the general European influence by combining the registers of the uppermost harmonics in *ripieni*.

Other kinds of pipes in old Italian organs are *flauti in ottava* and *in quintadecima*. They are wide pipes with narrow lips (the width of the lips measures almost that of an equally large diapason, but the range is almost double). Two registers usually are tuned to octave and superoctave. The tonal energy is modest, the carrying power great. The addition of flauti rounds off the organ tone and makes it brighter and subtly colored. Only octave sets, after all, are involved; a set of fifths, ignored by the old Italian organ, would strongly tinge the sound. One additional flute register makes the sonority of the basic set stand out in the discant range. It is second narrow diapason set tuned with beats. The register is known as *voce umana*. Monteverdi's scores, which often prescribe the registration, also indicate the use of this "alteration" by the *voce umana*. The large organs of Italy show one more peculiarity: the registers are divided into bass and discant halves, making the restriction to one manual more acceptable. One must not associate this division with "terraced" playing, trio situations, and the like, which are far later practices. A bicinium, on the other hand, can be very well performed.[119] The great motets of the Josquin period never sound clearer and more beautiful than on this type of organ. Evaluating the possibilities and particularities of the old Italian organ, we find that every situation in a composition of the time is extremely well served by the practical, precise structure of the tonal substance built on the disposition of separate overtone series.[120] The gentle, mild wind (water column of about 40 mm) enables the organ, moreover, to take care of thoroughbass tasks. If still gentler organs were wanted, one built the instrument with wooden pipes of very thin walls. The most beautiful piece of this type is the *organo di legno* in the Silver Chapel of the Hofkirche in Innsbruck. In the relatively small hall of the funeral chapel for Archduke Ferdinand and his wife of the rich Welser family, the organ, with utmost tonal clarity and tonal distinctness, is wonderfully civilized. It demonstrates by its nature the aesthetic law of economy of sound, which so many modern organists constantly violate by excess.

The second organ type, apparently formed in Flanders and then spreading with certain alterations through France, South and North Germany, and even the Spanish realm, proceeds from a completely different principle. The ever larger positive seems to be at the core of the development. No large structuring takes place, as in the many separate overtone series and tonally unified substance of the Italian organs. A few sets of pipes are expected to provide rich tonal differentiation, and hence the registers are basically varied. The limited space of a small instrument presupposes stopped pipes. Recognition of the demand for both stopped and open registers eliminates the chance of building a self-contained sonority. Now one makes a virtue out of a necessity and deliberately yokes together extreme differences of sound. Reed stops are developed and incorporated into the system.

As said earlier, the Italian organ never uses reeds together with flue pipes. Any regal found in an old instrument is separated from the labial organ by a cutoff valve. The intonation of regals suffers at the slightest temperature fluctuation. This fact, too, separates the pipe categories. The Flemish, French, and German organs then experiment with reed stops with long tubes. The most varied timbres can be developed and are utilized. As an explanation, we describe the choir organ in the Hofkirche in Innsbruck (the most important, fully preserved instrument, unique in quality and size!). Following an imperial order (to build first of all a church, the Neustift, for the proper placement of the elements, scattered throughout Innsbruck castle, intended for Emperor Maximilian I's elaborate tomb), a top organ builder was engaged, Jörg Ebert, of Ravensburg, who carved the date 1558 in the keyboard rail of his organ. The quality of the organ is extraordinarily high. By a whole set of coincidences, it was possible to put the instrument back into its original condition; only two reed stops had to be reconstructed. For the latter, much information was available. During the last war, the original pipes, together with the bronze statues of Maximilian's tomb, were stored in a mine. Later additions were deposited in the *dogana* of the Innsbruck castle, where they were destroyed by bombs. Thus there were external reasons for restoring the original condition of the instrument, which succeeded excellently. The Innsbruck instrument supplies the norm and key for the performance practice of organists in the second half of the sixteenth century. Many stylistic problems solve themselves when this organ is played. The instrument combines three organ types in one arrangement: the old organ for large halls, the positive, and the regal. The chest of the main work or great organ (as we would say today) is played from a manual and also from a pedal keyboard (exactly as in an old Italian organ). The latter is only an aid for the player and does not possess its own sounding voices. The regal, placed below the wind chest of the great organ and operated by a tracker action that can be disengaged, is played from the keyboard of the great organ, the manual proper. The range of these two dispositions is from great C to a^2 (without C-sharp, D-sharp, F-sharp, G-sharp, and g^2-sharp). The positive adds a further independent organ type (on a lower manual), recognizable as an octave reduction of the great organ. In this respect, the independent positive has become united with the organ. The positive has the typical range of the type: great F to a^2 (without F-sharp, G-sharp, and g^2-sharp). Because of its typical formulation, the disposition may here be quoted with the names of the original contract:

"In the great corpus. In the manual: an open *Fletn* [principal], a *zudeck Fletl* [stopped at the same 8′ pitch], octave [4′], fifth [actually twelfth, hence 2⅔′], *quintez* [corruption of quintadecima, hence superoctave 2′], a rear set [great mixture with the special name of the gothic great organ, five-to tenfold choir], *Ziml* [cymbal, twofold], *Herndl* [sesquialtera, twofold, overtones of fifth and third], *Pusaun* [trumpet 8′, reconstructed]. In the *Positiff:* an open *Fletl*, a stopped *Fletl* [principal 2′, gedackt 4′], a mixture [three- to fivefold], a *Ziml,* a *Herndl.* In the *Brust* [front set]: a regal [funnel regal 8′]."

As a specific alteration, a *zitter* was added (a valve tremulant). . Originally the organ could not couple the positive to the great organ. Domenico da Pozzo, of Milano, painted the doors of the prospect, and Hans Perkhammer, of Innsbruck, made the wood carvings. Compared to an old Italian organ, this one has more than double the wind pressure (90 mm water column) which gives the tone density and force. Consequently the instrument is not meant to serve virtuosity. Each tone carries such significance that the organ is best used *colla parte* with cappella literature. This is true not only for Innsbruck. Instruments of the early seventeenth century, of which there are several in Austria of high monumental value, have exactly the same general tonal quality. On such an organ, one should play the chorale arrangements by Hofhaymer on "Salve regina."[121] Similar original organ music will be hard to find. Schlick's *Tablaturen etlicher Lobgesang* of 1512 are suitable.[122] Several collections of the period contain, anyway, intabulations of Masses and motets. One can learn a great deal from the existence in organ tablature of all sacred compositions by the Fleming Jacobus Vaet, the *Kapellmeister* of Emperor Ferdinand (who ordered the construction of the Hofkirche)![123] One must not even think of playing a thoroughbass on the Innsbruck instrument. This type of organ renders with utmost clarity everything that happens on the keys. Already Italian toccatas sound trivial and painful, and subliminal harmonic accessories as required from a continuo part are all the more unplayable on this organ.

The large organ of the seventeenth century develops very logically. In large spaces, the task is divided between manual and pedal regions. A good example survives in the abbey Aigen-Schlägl in the Bohemian Forest. Built by Andreas Putz, of Passau, in 1634, it was a rood-loft organ with two prospects. After the demolition of the rood screen, it was moved to the West choir gallery. The organ has a large common wind chest for the main work and the pedal, thereby demonstrating the unity of the substance.

More significant is the West organ of the abbey Klosterneuburg, which I wish to describe. It, too, is the work of a Passau master, Johann Georg Freynd, and dates from 1642. It is the only organ in Europe from that period preserved in almost all its parts. It is worth discussing because of its high quality and its role as a sounding monument. Freynd dismantled two large choir organs of which he reused many parts in the new West organ. One of those older instruments had been built by Jonas Scherer in 1556. Inside Freynd's organ, there are registers which immediately reveal their origin in an older instrument. The "Festive Organ" in Klosterneuburg shows the following organization. The historic large-hall organ is divided into manual and pedal regions; but, as in Schlägl, the unity of the arrangement is evident. It contains a huge principal pyramid, standing on 16′ in the pedal, and on 8′ in the manual. The grand mixture (modeled after the rear set of the blockworks) with twelve to fourteen pipes per key is typical. The principal structure adds to the diapason the octave, fifth (twelfth), superoctave, and cymbal. These stops alone create a principal choir that dominates the space. It is joined by a structure of stopped pipes, wide flutes, and gemshorn (the name for a conical organ register after a historic wind instrument, a kind of recorder made of chamois horn). Thus a second, basically different tonal organism comes into being. The good timbre combinations of these labial pipes are countless. Then there are also reed pipes: *pusaun* (trombone) on 8′ in the manual, and on 16′ on the pedal (these reed stops were lost at the beginning of the century and had to be replaced). The tonal structure of the pedal is independent in details and adapted to the specific pedal conditions. The 16′ trumpet still existent in the manual is not historical but an addition of 1947.

The tonal structures of manual and pedal are now joined at the octave by the positive. From the very beginning, one tried to find an optimal place for the positive now made part of the large organ. One cut open the parapet of the choir loft and moved the positive into the breach. Because all old organs of that period, for technical reasons, were played from a kind of cupboard (the playing arrangement, today called *console*, stands under the organ prospect in a niche of the substructure of the main body), the positive is located at the player's back, hence the name *Rückpositiv*. Compared to the heavy great organ, the positive is better suited for the performance of diminutions because of its dimension, tonal function, stereo separation of sound, and easier playability (smaller valves, etc.). Compositions for the organ have always respected and utilized this circumstance.

Since the beginning of the seventeenth century, the initially independent musical instrument regal has turned into a separate part of an organ. The reeds are joined by a few labial stops which fit the space, and together they form the *Brustwerk*. In Klosterneuburg, it has its own keyboard (manual 3) and contains the registers 8′ rankett, 4′ gedackt, 2′ principal, and 2′ gemshorn. The seventeenth century deliberately develops the tendency toward music in large spaces, which in isolated cases had existed in earlier practices. Think of the Mass at the inauguration of the Salzburg cathedral (by Benevoli?) and its unrestrained joy in stereo effects![124] Composing, playing, and building all relate to the organ on the same level; for church music finds itself unified, and the organ assumes to a great extent the tasks of the cappella. The formation of the maximal sound of the organ is of interest. Around 1600, when the playing of coupled stops was made technically possible for the organist's fingers, the only coupling introduced was that of rückpositiv to manual. At that period, no other couples were made, for they yielded litle sound and made no sense.

The positive of the West organ in Klosterneuburg is not suited for thoroughbass tasks. The tonal relationship of the positive to the great organ is far too concrete and penetrating to permit any continuo realizations. In Klosterneuburg, the church musicians (singers, instrumentalists, and continuo) were stationed on the choir gallery. The West organ remained for occasional *alternatim* music-making and perhaps *colla parte* playing with cappella music, on the whole, however, for pure organ music at festive entrances.

At exactly the same time, the church of the Franciscans in Vienna received a new organ. It has been preserved but also variously maltreated and now lies practically fallow. A cure of all wounds is unlikely because of lack of interest and money. The great organ and pedal have a tonal substance similar to that of Klosterneuburg; but the much smaller hall of the Franciscan church influenced the disposition of registers, their mensurations, and the production of pipes. The organ stands in the apse of the church on the central axis. The high altar, a century younger, with a big theatrical prospect and a painted canvas background, spoils the optical and acoustical situation. The instrument stands on the level of the church floor. The positive occupies the elevated position normally taken by the brustwerk. Choir stools surround the organ, and the historic cappella stand is located before it. Here every kind of contemporary church music was performed. Something is new: the old Franciscan organ (built by Hans Wöckherl, civic organ builder and organist at the cathedral) contains a clearly defined thoroughbass positive! The proportions of the pipes fully meet the challenge. The stop "gedackt in die music" (the popular Austrian term is *copula*, which does not express the continuo qualification) has a strong bass register which carries well. Starting around f^0, the pipe mensuration is radically reduced; at d^1 it reaches its minimum, which is retained. Only the highest discant is again permitted to emerge a bit. The range of the player's right hand with the continuo harmonies is hereby tonally restrained — a manifestation of the special continuo positive. This particular arrangement has a musical reason: for the projection of the bass line, neither bassoon nor violoncello joined the positive, which thus had to assert itself alone. The favored literature included Viadana's *Cento concerti ecclesiastici* and similar pieces. There were no boys in the cappella, falsetto voices sang the *cantus* and *altus,* a tenor and a bass completed the ideal setup of a vocal quartet. The group stood around the lectern in the choir space. This situation explains the pipe mensuration of the positive. The mensuration of all other registers in the positive of the Franciscan organ derives from that curve. The positive shows individual characteristics in regard to its tonal material, tuning, and special keyboard. From the middle of the bass clef to the top of the treble clef Wöckherl chose double positions for $G^{\#}$-A^{b} and $D^{\#}$-E^{b} for which he built double keys, channels, tracker elements, and pipes. This arrangement proves meantone tuning and simultaneous concern for the demands of continuo playing. The organist, obliged to participate in *every* key, could do so only with such double keys. The positive of this organ is evidently a continuo instrument. Wöckherl's quality shows: to preserve the tonal unity of the organ notwithstanding the specific individuality of the positive, he adjusts the mensurations of the great organ. The principal is correspondingly narrow, and the entire principal pyramid is guided by similar considerations. The structural contrast to Klosterneuburg is extreme. In connection with meantone tuning, one must remember that its characteristic is the major third without beats. On a keyboard instrument, this tuning has limitations. A whole set of tonalities is rendered unusable by bad "wolves," but some other tonalities sound very good. The double keys serve the purpose of good intonation in a maximum number of tonalities. The positive of the Franciscan organ offers A-flat major and B major in best quality (in the restoration after the war, the old tuning together with double pitches for certain keys was unfortunately eliminated).

The two extreme types, described by the Klosterneuburg and Franciscan organs, eventually approach each other. Finally the conditions for organ playing and organ building in the tradition of Innsbruck and Klosterneuberg are destroyed by the changed situation of church music, in which the cappella inheritance is spent. The high and late baroque preserves the large organization but weakens the tonal characteristics to the extent that registers are added more easily and thoughtlessly. In this respect, the significant organ of the abbey Herzogenburg, near St. Pölten, offers a good example. It has suffered reconstructions which, however, have not extinguished its essential characteristics. The organ is more than a century younger than the Franciscan and the festive Klosterneuburg instruments. It is a typical instrument and therefore supplies clues for the total musical situation. The builder of the organ, Johann Hencke, a sculptor's son born in Westphalia, became a Vienna citizen and worked himself up to become the leading master in Austria. The Augustinian abbey Herzogenburg gave him a well-paid commission to build a large topflight instrument, in which he invested all his experience and knowledge. Several typical qualities characterize the situation. Great organ and pedal remain related to each other, but the latter forfeits all traditions of the cappella complex. It is reduced to twelve tones serviceable only for the foundation of a nonpolyphonic bass line. Explicit polyphonic textures can be played only on the main work (used manualiter). The relation of the positive to the great organ has not changed. Into the casing of the positive, Hencke places an additional specific thoroughbass positive in octave relation to the positive proper. The spatial arrangement on the choir loft is characteristic. The unity of great organ and pedal is preserved but split into a right and a left half each in the order of wholetones. The large West window so common in the baroque seems to have partly caused this disposition (the advantage of this arrangement for the organ builder lies in his being able to distribute the large pipes better and with more justice to their sonority). Between the right and left large structures, the thus isolated console opens the organist's view toward the high altar and offers him a much better contact with the ensemble. Herzogenburg cultivated church music oriented by thoroughbass. The rich inventory in the abbey of stringed and wind instruments points toward the musical array of Vienna as a model.

Somewhat tighter but related is the organ in the pilgrimage church on the Sonntagberg near Waidhofen an der Ybbs. Daniel Gran painted the glorious ceiling frescoes, other masters of the first order worked here, and also the organ calls for special attention. The year 1763 is painted on the casing. The instrument evinces unspoiled the original intonation, because the contemporary ambitions of organists were not taken too seriously in a remote place. Musicians can profit greatly from acquainting themselves here with the tonal balance and qualities of historic intonation. At the time, each pipe was voiced in respect to its optimum at the initial expense of considerable differences in the sound of single pipes in a register. Two hundred long years of "being blown" finally produced sufficient evenness of the registers while keeping the tone very much alive. One should proceed similarly today when voicing an organ! (Today one can quickly remove the inequalities of intonation by various tricks; but in return the tone of the organ becomes dull, lame, and without stimulating vitality.)

The instrument on the Sonntagberg contains the usual great organ together with the reduced pedal of twelve bass pitches, and moreover a positive suitable for thoroughbass playing. The positive can be coupled to the main work. The bass octave in the manuals lacks the tones C-sharp and D-sharp. The tones F-sharp and G-sharp appear in the double, split upper keys D-F# and E-G#. This arrangement points toward a tuning according to Kirnberger.[125] This was also Bach's tuning and should be reintroduced because its explicit character strongly influences the music. In meantone tuning, the influence on the sonority derived from the beatless major thirds. The sound of a seventeenth-century organ is totally spoiled by the quasi modern, very fast beating of the major third, as we know it from our common mathematical tuning by the twelfth root of two (the term *gleichschwebend*, "equally beating," is nonsense — depending on the range, fifths beat at different speeds; in two adjoining fifths, the tempos of the beats relate as 2 to 3)! Later than meantone tuning, Werckmeister demonstrates a historically significant system.[126] A very special procedure is the tempering daily applied by Bach in person to his harpsichord and then publicized by his pupil Kirnberger. As *Kirnberger III* (there are two other similar tunings by him), it has today been introduced in professional circles. In a later chapter (cf. pp. 163 ff.) I shall set forth the methods of historic tunings including the one by Bach. Keys in the great octave of an organ disposed (in a broken octave) as on the Sonntagberg signify Bach's tuning. It is special, because each tonality sounds a bit different. Some tonalities have thirds free of beats, others are all the more disadvantaged; but no tonality suffers from such a bad "wolf" that it could not be used. The reduction of musical practice to the tuning according to the twelfth root of two has eliminated the character of tonalities! At most one senses at radical transpositions the density of the sound influenced by the major thirds, but this has nothing to do with the character of a tonality! Mozart still judges the character of different tonalities according to the results of the Kirnberger temperament; and if one contemplates the choice of keys in Schubert's *Winterreise* and *Die schöne Müllerin*, one finds there, too, the same approach! Our sterile tuning has become perfectly equalized only in our century. Today one frequently tunes with the help of an electric

gadget. A good harpsichord player should master meantone and Kirnberger III tunings! Instruments of which the intonation is so unstable
must be taken care of by the player!

In conclusion, I wish to discuss organs from the periods of the
Vienna classics and the early romantics. In this connection, the organ
in the Stadtpfarrkirche (now the cathedral) in Eisenstadt is for us musicians of utmost interest. After a highly successful restoration, it is in
optimal condition and presents itself as at the time when Haydn played
it. In one respect, this instrument is the exact opposite of all Austrian
organs discussed above. Most organ builders have a basic attitude with
which they approach any commission. They build, for instance, large
organ types even when small instruments have been ordered, and the
other way around. The good Silesian organ builder Bukow, who more
than a century ago still furnished excellent instruments in the best tradition (the valuable organ in the church of the Piarists in Vienna is his
work), is a master who always had to build large instruments and who
executed the wind chest for a small instrument in a manner so clumsy
and massive that he practically never produced a specific positive. Mallek,
the master of the Haydn organ, does the opposite: even a large organ
is for him only an enlarged positive. This trait extends to the tonal quality
of his organ stops. Joseph Haydn played the instrument himself and
employed it for performances of his Masses (the High Mass in the chapel
of the palace was usually preceded by a "public general rehearsal" at
nine o'clock in the morning in the Stadtpfarrkirche). The great organ
has a wind chest like that of a positive. The channels run in a line with
the keys. All big pipes stand together at one end of the chest and do
not have the best possible articulation! (Old organ builders paid special
attention to a tonally advantageous placement of the pipes. Hence the
pitches were so arranged on the chests that big pipes stand distributed
in several groups. Positives did not participate in this development, for
the simple tracker action by levers does not permit it. Only for a few
large pipes, the wind is detoured to a tonally more advantageous place.)
Mallek's Eisenstadt organ, with its traditional principal structure, adequately fills the large church. Variety of registration is provided by a few
stops from the category of gedackt and flute and moreover by a "stimulant
voice," *fugara*, in 4′ position. The positive in the parapet of the choir
loft possesses in addition to the specific thoroughbass coupler a flute
at the octave. A small principal choir at the octave of the great organ
establishes the relation to the latter. The very modest reduced pedal with

a chromatic octave lies in the tradition of the departing eighteenth century. An expansion of the pedal implemented during the restoration has been placed separately. The old corpus holds the musical and mechanical substance as in Haydn's days. The organ has a pleasant, friendly sound, much charm, and perfect suitability for Haydn's use of the organ, thus also the organ-solo Masses.

Within the first third of the nineteenth century, organs adapt themselves to modern tuning. In that period, however, one must not expect the perfection of our temperament. Certain tonalities were still favored by the way beats in major thirds were measured. Thus a residue of tonality characterization according to Kirnberger III was preserved. An indication of the increasingly more equalized temperament is the fully chromatic great octave. The best example is the organ in Heiligenkreuz, the largest maintained mechanical organ in Austria. There are fifty-two registers on two manuals and a pedal. The transfer of the instrument from the (torn-down) West choir loft to the transept brought about rearrangements. Because the organ suffered, moreover, from catastrophic woodworm blight and tin corrosion, more than one half of the sounding material had to be reproduced! The total general character, however, has been preserved. In this organ, every fundamental and overtone series occurs in the most varied register families, producing a rich gradation. What was said about the Eisenstadt work is valid also here but all broadly expanded. Registers in groups are available for each energy display. The builder, Ignaz Kober, born in Olmütz, had contacts with Silbermann and Stein and was also one of the leading piano manufacturers in Vienna. For acquaintance with an instrument from the classic and early-romantic periods, I recommend the large Heiligenkreuz organ. Yet the organ has also retained many traditional qualities from the late baroque, as particularly evinced by the multi-choir principal structure which dominates the space.

Apart from some brief descriptions of Italian organs, the examples treated thus far, which could be easily extended, have been limited to a few Austrian instruments. Another organ tradition for large halls issues from France and Burgundy. Like many branches of Carolingian art, early organ construction, too, was furthered in the heyday of monasteries, but we have no concrete testimony from that period, only some vague writings on early organs. Even for the era of Machaut, we still depend on speculation. Only from the fifteenth century on are there relics of instruments, pictures, and concrete reports. The positive on the Ghent altar piece is painted with such accuracy that it may serve as evidence for organ construction. The painting shows a *positif de table* enlarged by a substructure. It has no casing; mere side boards limit the course of the pipes (further details remain hypothetical). The angel plays an organ piece, that is, an organ arrangement of a church composition. I consider possible an association with the practice of Paumann and the *Tabulatura nova* by Schlick.[127] Unravelling the practice of very early organ-playing is difficult, for Schlick's evidence appertains to music written two generations later. But his performance practice as exhibited in the *Tabulatura* did not fall from heaven and might well have needed the entire fifteenth century to flourish. In the background of the picture, three more angels holding harp and large fiddle "pause" — they are waiting as a group to take over the next section. If we interpret the music scenes of the Ghent altar concretely, the pictures might represent the performance of a work by Ciconia.[128] An antiphon is first performed by the vocal cappella which sings a structured motet, probably a three-part polyphonic texture (an angel is in the process of counting rests on his fingers). Then the organist plays an arrangement of one section. The third possibility is the partially instrumental execution of a third section by fiddle, harp, and singer (the big fiddle plays the tenor, the harp plays a discant and in addition perhaps a sparse contra). Separation of sections and execution of the music of the sections by varied textures had been a familiar practice for over a century. The alternation of organum sections with Gregorian chant was common already in the Notre Dame period, that is, organa were actually composed in such a manner.

The development of the organ in France has been described by Norbert Dufourcq.[129] Reports on the oldest instruments in France show certain analogies with Italy inasmuch as only large manual works were built in France. From the very beginning, however, pipes of the most diverse timbres were brought into play — principals, gedackts, wide flutes, conical pipes, half-stopped, and reeds. (From personal experience, I know too few French organs and organs in Spain, whereas I have measured hundreds of organs in Austria, Germany, and Italy.)

For thoroughbass playing, the positive organ — whether independent or as rückpositiv — is the suitable instrument. Its tonal balance and energies, that is, mensuration and voicing, must be well adjusted to the demands of the continuo. In Central Europe, the thoroughbass situation was first served by specially built, self-sufficient positives. The Italian organ, as mentioned earlier, did not have to develop a positive, for it

already had one in the smallest organ types. Moreover, one knew well
the construction *di legno* which leads to even gentler tones. The actual
continuo was managed by the *Gedackt in die Musik.* To increase the tone,
a flute at the octave could be added. The organ continuo did not directly participate in the expressiveness and energy investment of soloists.
It never took the wind out of the soloist's sails. *Opus decimum* by Schütz
contains again and again rests for the soloist: now the continuo must
have musical weight, and the alternation must occur quickly and with
a display of the upper-voice lines.[130] I would not insist on rigid four-
part realization. The organ positive can very well control the energy
of the continuo material by alternating thin and full textures. All depends on keeping the continuo improvised. I emphasize once more that
a written-out thoroughbass part creates false standards. Whatever is written assumes the weight of a worked-out composition. This procedure
brought about the continuo parts to the notorious editions by Riemann
of old chamber music (intended, moreover, for the modern piano!); or
in deliberate reaction to the Riemann principle, continuo parts were
written out of which one ought to be ashamed. What seems acceptable
today sounds repulsive after a week. Whoever cannot improvise a continuo should at least vary the printed stuff! Playing a thoroughbass is
a pedagogically superior practice which can reactivate all musical forces
misguided by smooth commercialism and which rouses the hobbled
fantasy!

The cases of obbligato concertizing organ parts present special
problems. They depart from the continuo principle and thus require
a very different approach. Such examples exist in the music of Bach and
Handel as also in Vienna classical church music. In Bach's cantata "Gott
soll allein mein Herze haben," for instance, the organist becomes a soloist
next to the solo alto.[131] It is the same situation as in harpsichord concertos when a two-part keyboard texture displaces the proper continuo
task. I would treat such pieces as if dislodged from the harpsichord and
assign to the organ positive the role of that instrument as required by
the performance. The registration will be different. The 8' copula alone
cannot be counted upon, because its specific thoroughbass character is
too modest and restrained for the reaches demanded by the solo part.
One will need at least the flute at the octave. An additional 2' principal
becomes necessary for Haydn's and Mozart's organ solo Masses (think
of the Agnus in Mozart's Mass XV with still other concertizing instruments plus the soprano).[132] Whether one thereby retains the 4' flute de-

pends on the quality of the positive. The playing of such organ soli with jingling high overtones is a conquered disease. The effect of the registration gains by subtleties of touch. A boring permanent legato must be overcome. Here, too, taste is decisive!

If a harpsichord is available besides the organ, an organ solo, such as in the cited Bach cantata "Gott soll allein mein Herze haben," can well profit from surrendering the continuo to the harpsichord. The classical organ solo Masses simply throw overboard the continuo tasks during the organ soli. Because sacred music is always bound by traditional values, the continuo usage there survives into the middle of the nineteenth century. Mendelssohn still accepts the given conditions.

Surveying the positive continuo, one must consider the involvement which varies according to the conditions of the time. In the first third of the seventeenth century, familiarity with *colla parte* playing repeatedly invited an approach to that practice even in the middle of an improvisation. In that era, there were certainly great qualitative differences depending on the player's skill. The middle of the century, defined by Schütz's *Opus decimum* and the increasing spread of the Monteverdi–Schütz style, is deprived of the élan of the first developmental years by the devastation of Central Europe during the Thirty-Year War. One writes for very few singers and continuo, the *Kleine geistliche Konzerte* are typical. With such modest means, the continuo realization assumes high significance. The organ part must "sound," that is, the range of the continuo, its texture, and the occasionally inserted ritornelli must create a real partnership with the singers. I would not recommend relying solely on registration but rather on "playing out" the situation. Toward the end of the century, display and also layout enlarge. The title *concerto* calls for soloists, whether vocal or instrumental; but the continuo must be ready to meet all conditions. Only in the second quarter of the eighteenth century does the organ positive begin to be used specifically for concertizing. The compositional relationships to the concertizing harpsichord are patent. Whether in such cases the actual thoroughbass task is pushed aside depends also on the acoustics of the hall. When several continuo instruments were available, a second one could meet the challenge of a "space continuo." We have already mentioned the coming to an end of the concertizing use of the positive in the church music by Haydn and Mozart.

One more aspect of the positive must be clarified. The pipes of the fundamental register *gedackt* contain no overtones at any octave (cf.

p. 78). By pulling an octave stop to the *gedackt*, one does not achieve
a symbiosis of the two organ voices; for the octave stop has no way of
joining a pitch contained in the overtone series of the fundamental stop.
The two registers are clearly heard at their distance of an octave. If the
$4'$ register, as usual, is also *gedackt*, these tone characteristics repeat themselves once more at the entrance of, for instance, the $2'$ diapason. This
sound void of octaves which characterizes baroque positives is a compositional determinant. It defines Handel's organ concertos, Bach's introduction of a concertizing positive, Mozart's solos for organ and his
church sonatas, and Haydn's use of the instrument. For such music,
it would be a grave error to judge organ registration according to tone
"color." In all early music, organ registration serves to find for a particular composition the appropriate tone structure derived from the overtone spectrum of the pipes.

3. *The Harpsichord Continuo*

Again we shall first give room to an explanation of the instrument
and its types. Harpsichords were already known in the fifteenth century. They originated from the combination of a psaltery with a keyboard.
Artists like Eyck and Memling painted two types of psaltery. There is
a small instrument for discant range, diatonically tuned. It hangs on
a strap on the chest of Eyck's angels. The right hand plays it with a plectron cut from a bird's feather as for writing. The form of the instrument, defined by the lengths of the strings, is a trapezoid with drawn-in
sides. Curved thin walls are glued to a baseboard, in a manner familiar
from viol construction. The flat soundboard with its two slender bridges
is glued to the reinforced upper rim of the side walls. Psalteries had brass
strings. A soundhole, like that of a lute, is cut into the top. This instrument is mainly a prop for the singer. At best it could be used for single
tones of Gregorian phrases in melody lines à la Dufay or Dunstable.

A larger psaltery lies on the lap of the angel in Luis Dalmau's painting "The Well of Life."[133] Although much bigger than the discant form,
it is called *half psaltery*, for its outline is actually formed from a bisection
of the discant form. *Both* hands play the instrument, making possible
a performance of tenor and discant.

As soon as the strings are "plucked" by means of a keyboard, the
conditions for building a harpsichord are given. The physician Arnaut
von Zwolle describes in 1440 the construction of such an instrument,

adding drawings and plans.[134] The transition to a keyboard instrument was facilitated by the wing-shaped contour, directly present in the half psaltery. An older practice was probably also available for the "jacks" (see below). The echiquier of Machaut's period already has a device like a jack guide.[135] To create the specific tone production of a harpsichord, all that was needed was the invention of the movable tongue with the splinter of a bird's feather at the tip.

The echiquier, well known by Machaut, is today often ignored. Its construction initiates the keyboard adapted to the human hand. Inserted into the body of the half psaltery, a series of levers, an inch or thumb apart, forms a plane playable by separate fingers. Considering that the only variable position was B-flat or B-natural, this solution seems almost obvious. Parallel to the plane of the keyboard, a massive walnut post is glued to the bottom of the resonance board, into which vertical shafts have been sawed. In the shafts lie small wooden pegs which can be propelled against the strings from the rear end of the keys. The wooden projectiles already have a little leather cap to produce a good strike tone. Individual dampers for each string also exist. Later the instrument is improved by the insertion of a small lever (known as *Treiber* or driver) which increases the action. The good organ and piano builder Schmahl in Augsburg still built this type with tangents into the 1760s. All such instruments are "pianofortes." The tangential hammer then becomes superseded by a hammer which is mounted at one end of the lever instead of being propelled in a shaft. It is wrong to associate the development of the modern keyboard with the clavichord. Early instruments have few strings and far-reaching applications of monochord divisions. By way of bends, the key levers were linked to monochord divisions. It was then easy to exchange the shaft construction of the echiquier for the jack guides of the harpsichord.

Our best preserved harpsichords are Italian. Let us begin with the transformation of the psaltery to the spinet because this type circulated most widely. The Italian spinet form is a small psaltery that has lost its symmetry. The strings run at a slight angle from left rear to right front. The two psaltery bridges have been fitted: the right one is now strongly curved, the left one almost straight. In the middle zone of the keyboard, the string lengths follow monochord values. The bass is shortened in a curve of the bridge, the discant is slightly too long. Below the soundboard lies the so-called crossblock, a sustaining wall which divides the soundboard in two fields. The key levers reach to the crossblock and thus vary greatly in length. In the bass zone, the bodies of the keys are

very short; in the discant, they are all the longer. Along the crossblock
runs the row of jacks—the name for the special plucking mechanism,
a little piece of hard wood into a cut of which the movable tongue with
its plectrum is inserted. In harpsichords, the pointed quill is cut from
splinters of a raven feather. It withstands many thousand strokes without
fraying. A spring made from a wild boar's neck bristle keeps the tongue
in the right position. When the jack falls back after plucking, the tip
of the quill escapes backward and slips again under the string. The gentle
touch at the jack's return does not excite a fresh tone because the string
is at the same moment dampened by a felt attached to the jack. In a
spinet, the row of jacks crosses the strings at an angle of about twenty
degrees. One makes room for them by running the strings in pairs and
placing two jacks each in the larger interstices between the strings. Seen
from the keyboard, the tip of the jack to the left faces forward, and the
neighboring one to the right faces backward. Because the jacks can thus
not possibly be all engaged or disengaged by the movement of a jack
guide, the spinet can never be built with more than one string register
to a key. In compensation, the spinet type offers a tonal advantage: both
ends of the strings lie on bridges which relay the tone to a resonating
soundboard. With its light structure, the instrument thus develops a very
intensive, lively sonority and optimal tonal energy, in this respect coun-
tervailing the limitation to single stringing. In Italy, this instrument is
known as spinet, from *spina*, thorn, the tip of the feather quill. In England, it is called virginal, again after the tip (Latin *virga*) which actually
looks like the Gregorian hook neume *virga,* that is, like our modern comma (French *virgule*). In Germany, it is simply called *instrument* for reasons of
its wide popularity and manifold use. The bottom board of Italian spinets is made of poplar wood which, grown in Italy, supplies a very mild
and tolerant material. The wood of the thin, curved sides is cedar or
maple; that of the soundboard, cypress. England and Flanders, where
the production of this type was also intensely pursued, lack the special
Italian wood. One substitutes endemic, resonant, and available wood.
As a result, one has to renounce thin sides and consequently builds rectangular spinet forms. There is no difference in regard to stringing, crossblock, and arrangement of jacks.

   The building conditions summarized below achieve an optimal
lively tone in which the single voice ranges (soprano to bass) stand out
against each other very well and do full justice to the projection of polyphonic structures notwithstanding the unified tonal character:

1. Low string tension and a soundboard optimally vibrating because unencumbered by the single set of strings.
2. Strings plucked by an elastic, smooth, and hard quill at a favorable division point of their total length.
3. Graceful body without "dead wood" (the name in instrument building for massive parts of wood which cannot be excited to resonate genuinely and which swallow vibrating energy).
4. The use of two tone-relaying bridges according to the principle of a psaltery.
5. The use of monochord proportions for string lengths, with only some corrections in bass and discant.
6. Strings of appropriate thickness and historic material (no wound strings — they are stiffer and hence not suitable for tone production by jacks).

The very popular spinet type frequently served to assist in conducting, its intensive tone making it particularly suitable for this task. We have a picture of Lassus sitting at the spinet and directing the ensemble by playing along.[136] From this practice, a continuous tradition reaches throughout the whole baroque to the conducting of operas from a harpsichord. Because of the many possibilities for realizing a thoroughbass, the spinet or harpsichord in the seventeenth century was the preeminent instrument for directing an ensemble. The spinet has the additional advantage of being easily transportable and, moreover, when lying on a table, of permitting a convenient grouping around it. This type of instrument, by the way, has not been frequently copied in our time. In the context of industrialized instrument production, a spinet is not easily built, for it requires genuine artistic craftsmanship.

In the seventeenth century, thoroughbass was properly assigned to the wing-shaped type, which seems to be as old as the spinet if not older. The Book of Hours of the Duke of Berry[137] from the year 1409 contains the oldest picture of a harpsichord. Sachs[138] documents for the year 1514 a harpsichord with two sets of 8' strings. Now the quills all face in the same direction, and the jack racks can thus be engaged and disengaged by a shift of the strings (there is enough room for arranging all quills of one jack rack in the same direction because the distances between keys and between strings are now identical). This fact is utilized by the wing-shaped instruments. Our first disposes two sets of strings of the same pitch next to each other. Used singly or as tutti, they can

be adapted to different musical situations. Real registration on these
old instruments was not possible, for shifting the jack guides was so clumsy as not to permit a change during the playing. The equal key lengths,
too, are advantageous! The wing-shaped instruments, however, have
only one tone-relaying bridge; for the front bridge lies in the massive
pinning table where it cannot utilize the vibration energies reaching the
spot. From this difference probably arises the particularly vital tone of
the small spinet type. Italian wing-shaped instruments have been
preserved. The construction drawings by Arnaut von Zwolle[139] provide
the oldest concrete information.

Because of certain difficulties in the production of the string material and the usual identity of harpsichord and organ builders, experiences
with pipe proportions were transferred to harpsichord construction. An
organ builder makes scale drawings. Good skill was shown in matters
of descriptive geometry — which has something of craftmanship — , the
approach to determining proportions was not mathematical. If one redraws
a scale drawing of organ pipes by placing the abscissas regularly according
to the key divisions, one receives fairly exactly the outline of a wing-
shaped instrument.

Italian harpsichords are built almost as gracefully as spinets. A
side wall only 2 or 3 millimeters thick is glued and nailed on a bottom
board of poplar. The heads of the forged nails are covered by a strip
glued all around the border. The sides of the so-called keybed, that is,
the most forward part of the body which encases keys and mechanism,
are massively reinforced, for they hold the tuning-pin table. The keybed
is closed at the back by the crossblock, which carries the soundboard.
The back of the body, moreover, is encircled by a border onto which
the soundboard has been glued. On the curved side, the hitchpins of
the strings penetrate into that border. Inside the body at an upward angle from the crossblock and from the straight to the curved side wall,
a number of struts prevent deformation of the instrument by the string
tension. The soundboard is of cypress wood and startlingly thin: 2.6 millimeters in the bass region of the bridge, 3.2 millimeters in the discant.
It is gently ribbed, and only *one* rugged rib separates the triangle of the
dead board from the resonating plane. That dividing rib runs from the
middle of the crossblock to about the middle of the straight longitudinal
side wall. The separation of the "dead board" resulted partly from concern for the resistance to deformation of the soundboard and partly from
acoustical necessities. The main bridge on top of the soundboard is very

gracious. In order to keep the soundboard as free as possible, the ribs on its underside are indented where they cross the bridge. The stringing disposes of very few differentiations. In the lowest bass region, the laws of string lengths are negated; the rear end of the bridge breaks away toward the left, and thicker strings originally compensated for the missing length. A covered case with lid into which the graceful harpsichord proper was inserted protects it against damage.

In *Orfeo,* Monteverdi prescribes two gravicembali which indicate a larger wing-shaped type. Harpsichords for continuo tasks have two sets of strings at the same pitch (8′ plus 8′). Limited registration was made possible by lateral pulls (two knobs protrude from the right side of the body to shift the jack guides) and by a short iron lever inside the instrument (the player must get up and seize an iron knob to move the jack guide). It would have been easy to make the racks more accessible, but "registration" by the player of the harpsichord was not desired!

In Flanders, in Antwerp, the residence of the Ruckers family,[140] the most important harpsichord builders in the North, the necessary selection of Italian woods was not readily available. The Ruckers accordingly employed ship-building woods that possessed tonal qualities, fir (*Wassertanne, abies*) and oak. As in virginal construction, one could not make strongly curved sides for harpsichords. A special harpsichord type originates, significantly and basically deviating from the Italian principle. The curve of the bridge always follows that of the side wall. The Ruckers abandon the monochord principle and arrive at their own procedure with a different sound distribution. In the bass region, the instruments of Flanders and Italy are still similar. Then the string lengths in instruments by the Ruckers rise to monochord measures in a curve of their own with nonconstant increments. The energy and fullness of these harpsichords increase toward the discant and meet with this sonority the ambitions toward a soloistic instrument. The Ruckers are the first to build two manuals. The earliest such models, however, are transposing instruments (at the fourth for players unable to do so practically, hence alternation of choir tone — also known as low "Schlick tuning" — and cornett tone).[141] Placement on the second manual of the second 8′ set of strings soon suggested itself. At the same time, one introduces strings at the octave by way of a still lower second bridge. The large two-manual Ruckers instruments finally show the classic harpsichord disposition. Three jack racks and as many sets of strings provide a registration controlled by a lever inside the instrument. The racks are arranged so that one 8′ on the lower manual, as exacted by the mechanism, is plucked far from the front bridge. The position on the string of this point of attack creates a sound favoring the fundamental. The same lower manual logically appropriates the second jack rack with strings at the octave, for here the 4′ has to exercise its function. Still closer to the front bridge lies the third jack rack, the second 8′, and produces a much brighter sound. Mechanical reasons assign this jack rack to the upper manual. The situation is the opposite to that of a seventeenth-century organ where the positive was played from the lower manual. Yet this arrangement was accepted for the harpsichord because the mechanism of the latter does not permit another orientation.

Later harpsichord construction added one more sonority. The upper manual with its 8′ register received one further jack rack placed extremely close to the front bridge. One named this register *guitar stop* or *nasat* (thereby borrowing from the organ the name of a specific timbre, the wide fifth, that is, the twelfth!). This set of jacks serves the musical function *sul ponticello*. One used either the one or the other register, never both together, for they pluck the same strings. Special registers were provided for the highly efficient instruments by Kirkman and by Shudi & Broadwood.[142] Harpsichords all had metal strings of brass (in the bass) and unimproved steel. The historic harpsichord, like the spinet, does not know wound strings; for the plectrum made of a splinter from a common raven feather could agitate only a naked string, unencumbered by any winding and capable of readily vibrating at such a small impact. This condition demanded for all old harpsichords great length of strings and body. For theater conductors, the sonority was exceptionally increased. Albrecht Hass, the most famous German harpsichord builder, aded to 8′ and 4′ on the lower manual a set of 16′ strings.[143] The latter run over a special bridge; the instruments are exceedingly long. The 16′ register did not extend to the lowest range. In the bass of the large instruments, Kirkman and Shudi reach down to contra-C_1. They also invent registration props (a kind of "free combination" as in an organ, permitting by way of a foot lever the addition of registers during the playing) and finally the "Venetian Swell," an organ swellbox with a shutter. With such devices, harpsichord builders tried to meet the competition of the new pianoforte. Such types have lost all contact with classic harpsichord construction.

In most cases, the manual range of harpsichords is oriented on C. This tone delimits bass and discant. The early eighteenth century demanded a range below great C. Harpsichord soundboards tend to crack; here the width of the board is the precarious dimension. One therefore tries to squeeze the bigger bass range into the same instrument width and for this purpose builds peculiar split keys. Harpsichord builders call this analogy to turning lutes into theorbos *ravalement*. Bach's "fourniert Clavecin" which he always serviced himself was such a ravalement instrument. His harpsichord compositions reveal this fact by their typical range (G_1-A_1-B^b_1-B_1-C and then chromatically up to d^3). Bach's harpsichord has been lost. In the disposition of his estate, it was evaluated at eighty gold ducats. We are not likely ever to know whether it was built by Bach's nephew Johann Nicolaus Bach, of Jena, or whether the master was Zacharias Hildebrandt, whom Bach greatly appreciated, or some other organ builder.

What is wanted most of all of a harpsichord as a continuo instrument is a definite kind of tone quality. A harpsichord builder can at will determine the sonority by suitable proportions and optimal building materials (I warn of analogies with "baby grands," similarly of irrelevant, improper requests by harpsichordists!).

The agitation of the tone by the plectrum is in principle such a characteristic method that one has to proceed from it as the given condition. Making quills from raven feathers is today practically impossible. The animal is strictly protected. Feathers lost by a raven pair in the Schönbrunn zoo proved to be useless. Ravens in captivity have changed because of civilized forage — one might as well take crow feathers. Today artificially processed plectra are preferred. Such material is very even, and one has learned to deal with it. In this century, plectra of tanned beef leather have gained wide currency; they are perhaps the most durable.

The modern jack has two regulating screws. One controls the distance of the plectrum to the string above it. The other, a capstan screw at the lower end of the jack, brings it to the right height so that all keys respond at about the same level. Finally the position of the damper felt is also adjustable. The spring which holds the plectrum in the right position can also be bent in place. The difference between a modern and a historic jack is enormous. The old jack was made rather naively into an excellently functioning tool; but the player must be fully familiar with every detail in order to effect corrections, additions, and the replacement of used-up plectra. The historic jack requires the common raven quill because the distance from it to the string must be relatively large;

the old action of the jack provided more "air," for which quills from bird feathers are necessary. A sow's bristle functions as the spring for the tongue. This looks primitive but is more appropriate and better than a modern steel or brass spring. (The efficiency curve of a bristle is such that this "spring" is almost tensionless at the position of rest. Then the efficiency rises quickly to exert gentle pressure. A metal spring has a preliminary tension and exerts equal pressure on the tongue in each position.)

The worst discrepancies between historic and modern harpsichords exist in the construction of the body. Today's builders had to develop backward from the tradition of piano construction around 1900. There was a period when firms like Mendler and Schramm introduced cast-iron pianoforte plates in the belief that they were doing something good. One should again insist on a body closed at the bottom, preferably of lightweight construction. The method of letting a soundboard speak also downward need not be advantageous, for the underside radiates the *counter*phase of the vibration. Aspects of modern life with central heating etc. present the greatest danger for a historic instrument, and also for newly made copies. To meet these difficulties, experiments to try out fresh approaches are overdue. There are old methods of conserving wood against excessive shrinkage. The soundboards of old Flemish harpsichords are all painted, in tempera or gouache, with the typical ornamental flowers, bands with maxims, et cetera. These boards were not immediately painted; they had to be prepared by the classic tempera ground. (The old recipe states: crack an egg in the manner of a housewife; separate the yolk; fill the empty half shell with cold-beaten Dutch linseed oil and mix it well with the yolk. If the emulsion is to penetrate more deeply into the wood to be grounded, add ox gall!) The tempera ground is a marvelous means of sealing the wood cells and safeguarding it against hygroscopic loss. One applies it with a not too moist broad brush or a polishing cloth (bridge and ribs must already be glued, for the "ground" is oily). The ingredients are available in any specialized art store. This practical prescription covers one of the many possible processes. One can follow it to prepare new soundboards instead of using varnish which spoils the sound. Plywood for soundboards is improper. Commercial instrument builders use it, anyway, because they fear visible damages more than tonal shortcomings, which the buyer often cannot recognize. (This book is not a text on building instruments nor a manual for buyers, and hence it limits itself to the given suggestions.)

History has taught us several facts concerning jack racks and stringing:

Spinets and virginals can have only one set of strings. Usually there is a clear tonal difference between the polygonal form stemming from the psaltery and the virginal type inserted into a rectangular case. In the latter, the distance from the left bridge to the placement of the jacks is usually much bigger; many English virginals therefore have a rounder and more fundamental tone. The height of the side walls (the distance between bottom and soundboards) is also greater; this tympanum space produces similar effects. It is an error to associate the rectangular form only with England and Germany; there exist also Italian virginals.

Wing-shaped instruments can be classified according to their stringing.

1. Two 8′ sets probably correspond to a common early type. Possibilities of "registration" were hardly considered, for the early harpsichords had no mechanism to permit shifting during the play. The performer never even reaches the lateral pulls while playing. He chose in *advance* the desired sonority (strings 1, strings 2, strings 1 and 2).

2. The introduction of 4′ strings offered new possibilities. At just about the same time, a second keyboard appeared. Structural necessities place the fundamental 8′ and the 4′ on the lower manual; and the second 8′ with a clearer sound richer in overtones, on the upper manual. These large instruments contained registration mechanisms, usually movable knobs above the keyboards. Because these knobs are not always conveniently handled, and in order to make registration independent of the activity of the hands, Kirkman and Shudi build the so-called machine. This happened only when the harpsichord was displaced by the pianoforte.

3. If a historic harpsichord ever possessed a 16′, it was attached to the lower manual, which then controlled three string sets.

4. Harpsichord construction around 1900 originates in a musical orientation in which "sound and color" were of primary interest. The harpsichord which was reclaimed at that time consequently reflects this attitude in its sonority. Pedals permit registration during the play, and

the performers register timbres rather than structures! From this view of the matter, the firm de Witt, one of the first to enter this field so new to piano builders, reconstructed an old wing-type instrument, the so-called *Bach-Flügel*.[144] It thereby created a standard type not overcome until today (on the lower manual, an 8′ with jacks far from the bridge and a 16′; on the upper manual, an 8′ with jacks close to the bridge and a 4′ — nonsense from the standpoint of classic harpsichord construction). Performers on such harpsichords still serve up timbres, audiences still do not understand the basic difference between the tone character of a harpsichord and of a modern highly efficient grand! In old music, pedals for registering are distracting and point toward harpsichord performances of 1920. Apart from the stylistically dangerous temptation of "too much," also a structural consideration argues against a pedal arrangement for registering. To anchor the pedals in the body, the area of the so-called keybed has to be massively built. The legs of the harpsichord must now be equally robust, and thereby the demand for a lightweight body is annulled. The buyer of a harpsichord should consider these circumstances, for the immoderate demands of players concerning furnishings and size are mostly to blame for the perversions of instrument building.

5. In a historic instrument, manual couplers are a rare exception. Harpsichord builders who in most cases are also organ builders know manual couplers from positive to main work. If such coupling had been essential for harpsichord playing, they would have automatically transferred the mechanism. Civilized harpsichord playing, however, proceeded from a very different standpoint. For reasons of tonal aesthetics, one avoided engaging many jack racks simultaneously! At the moment the quill plucks, the harpsichord tone contains many noisy elements which, if multiplied, would render the entrance of the tone too penetrant. (In such a case, the held tone is much poorer in energy and decays rather quickly. Even so, long note values are not actually realizable on a harpsichord. Compositions for the instrument show that this difficulty was countered by diverse ornamentations of the tone.) Historic harpsichord playing never employed more than two rows of jacks simultaneously! Today one should remember this fact and not expect the harpsichord to assert itself in large halls. Harpsichord playing should be offered only in intimate, acoustically suitable rooms. Similar considerations should govern the use of a manual coupler which is justified only for the simultaneous sound of two 8' voices.

6. An interesting special solution, which we know through Bach, is the so-called lute clavier. Because of the way it is played, a lute, as we said earlier, offers the most severe conditions to a composition, which has to adjust itself entirely. To escape this limitation, Bach applied to the lute the basic idea of a keyboard instrument, making this type suitable for higher musical interests. We know of three lute harpsichords owned by Bach. The first was built by a cabinetmaker in Köthen and probably remained there. His nephew Johann Nicolaus made another one for him, and the organ builder Hildebrandt a third. In each of the three instruments, the lengths of the gut strings obviously corresponded to those of the chitarrone (no wound strings!). The range probably lay between C and a^2. It is further reported that the bridges had notches instead of hitch pins and that the soundboard was as thin as a lute table. The bass zone of the instrument had a "little brass octave" ("messingenes Oktävlein"), that is, a set of $4'$ strings. One sees that Bach as a mature master does not want to bother practicing the lute and investing time in it. He satisfies his love for the sound of gut strings through the lute harpsichord without having to overcome in his compositions the hurdles of lute technique. With this special type, Bach was not alone. His lute clavier does not surprise us if we remember that already Praetorius in his *Syntagma*[145] proposed a combination of hurdy-gurdy principle, wing-shaped stringing, and keyboard.

Questions of the harpsichord continuo cannot be answered without specific references to the composition to be played. The performance situation and acoustical conditions also enter. A theater needs instruments of high efficiency. All threads come together in the hands of the conductor (usually the composer). He not only has to supply the continuo sonority but also must "lead." The singers, soloistically employed instruments, and scenic matters — unification of these three matters demands high qualities of a conductor. Therefore the best large harpsichords went to the theaters. For the quickest possible adjustment to different energy levels, two manuals were in the eighteenth century almost a necessity. In the secco recitatives, all depends on the harpsichordist whether to babble or to vitalize a section. Handel's operas present two big problems: the castrato parts and the secco recitatives. Today one claims that Handel's operas are actually a lyrical species, and one therefore rushes to get past the secco recitatives from one aria to the next. This is an error. The "dry" recitative lives on what the performers make of it. Whatever the conventionalism of a secco recitative, it yet contains the challenge of energizing sketchy formulas by personal invention. Who would dare claim that such a grandiose improvisor and master of diminution as Handel would have left himself open to incompetent abuse? If at a performance of a live work of art we look only for documentary evidence without which we allow nothing, then we declare ourselves to be "scholars-only." In this regard, a true musician proceeds from a different standpoint: nothing worse than lack of imagination! Whoever huddles through secco recitatives in Handel operas should give up his place as conductor. Of the liberties in a secco recitative, only a few appoggiatura rules are left today and some formulas for following the singer, which, moreover, are often negated. In this area, far too little authentic documentation is available. One should investigate cases where true artists and masters operated and remain aware of the presence of sterile people also in early music! For us living musicians, only the masterwork and the best musical accomplishment in historic music fulfill a function and justify its existence!

The concept of the theater secco recitative affected also other areas. Bach employed it all through his sacred music. There is no vocal area in which the recitative does not find a place. We still encounter it in concert arias by Mozart. The category gains its life from the contrast between the freedom in a recitative and the strong tendency toward closed form and ensemble in an aria. Regardless in what context it appears, the secco recitative engages the harpsichord. A musical detail symptomatic of the harpsichord recitative is noteworthy: the jump from the third inversion of the dominant seventh chord to the root position of the tonic. Bach, too, writes this progression in the usual style of his time. In a harpsichord continuo, this faulty progression is hardly audible, because strict voice-leading and real harmonic connections do not assert themselves.

We have documentary information about Bach's vexation with the church harpsichord in St. Thomas. It almost wrecked his performance of the *St. John Passion*. The most important task of the Good Friday liturgy, which occupied the entire afternoon and early evening, was the presentation of the Passion story. Between the first and second parts of the Passion, there was a sermon which the minister considered as a challenge for his most impressive pulpit appearance of the year. Lasting more than two hours, it was an immense Lenten meditation of broad dimensions. During these hours, the many people in the Thomas church raised the temperature in the hall considerably; and for the second part of the Passion, the harpsichord was badly out of tune. Bach blamed the deficient qualities of the instrument, "for it had lost its tuning because of the breath of the people in the church." Whatever the situation at the time, the secco recitatives in the *St. John Passion* require a harpsichord. The instrument in St. Thomas had the usual two sets of 8' strings on one manual. In the *St. Matthew Passion*, Bach avoided any such problems by renouncing the harpsichord and assigning the accompaniment of the secco recitatives to an organ positive. One knows it from one glance at the continuo part which, in the *St. Matthew Passion,* consists mainly of rests. This is an obvious indication of a continuo on a positive. Holding these two cases next to each other, one gains immediate insights and understands which continuo type and which instrument a particular composition requires. For the singer of the Evangelist in Bach's *St. Matthew Passion*, the big, difficult part poses a severe challenge. Bach had no first-class tenor and was forced to consider the limited capability of a young Thomas pupil. The continuo part of the recitative shows it clearly. Whereas the harpsichord with its quickly decaying tone does not burden the singer, the continuo played in the same manner on a positive would force the tenor continuously to assert himself against the sustained and dominating sound of the organ. He would have to give more voice, sacrifice the recitative style by singing with too much intensity, and fatigue far too soon. Bach's treatment of the secco recitatives in the *St. Matthew Passion* with a positive continuo is identical with the performance practice common in the seventeenth century. He writes few, very short accompanying chords and leaves the singer mostly by himself. David Kellner writes in 1732 in his text on thoroughbass playing: "When the bass has to hold very long notes, one sometimes removes the hand and pauses until the chord to make the vocalist more clearly audible and not to disgust anyone by the sustained howling of the pipes."[146] And Türk's textbook states concretely: "The accompanist on an organ does not hold the tones to their full value but soon after hitting the chord he raises the fingers from the keys and pauses until a new harmony enters."[147]

In the cantatas by Bach, which encumber the singers physically far less than the Passions, the precautions against overpowering the singer need not be equally strict. Nothing changes, however, in regard to the principle of using for the continuo either harpsichord or organ positive. For the latter, the *St. Matthew Passion* sets the precedent. The issue in this case is not "timbre," etc. but the right dosage of thoroughbass sonority on either instrument. To accompany the Evangelist in the *St. Matthew Passion* on a harpsichord is simply wrong. Bach's Passions, following in this regard an old and proven convention, may serve as a general model for recitative continuos. If at a performance of Schütz's *Christmas Oratorio* one were to sustain the harmonies above the long note values of the continuo on an organ positive, tradition would be violated.[148] I strongly recommend that every player practice recitative accompaniments in both methods and on both instruments and acquire sufficient skill in improvisation. Patented recipes would be the opposite of correct pedagogy. As a teacher I was always pleasantly surprised to see the practical solutions of good musicians come very close to each other.

In an accompagnato recitative, the continuo must be most cautiously realized. According to the affect, the accompanying strings take care of the main task. Yet the accompanied recitative, too, was "conducted" from the thoroughbass instrument. This circumstance may be used as a gauge for the disposition. In accompanied recitatives, winds are the exception and employed for particular tasks. Thus in the first recitative, for instance, in Bach's beautiful *Esto mihi* cantata, "Du wahrer Gott," the oboes cite the German Agnus, "Christe, du Lamm Gottes" (this is not a chorale arrangement but rather a quotation of the Agnus to elucidate the liturgical situation of this work).[149] In such pieces the question arises as to what extent the concept of recitative is still present in view of a fixed meter in the orchestra parts. Is the concept limited to the given text, or may the singer merely introduce appoggiaturas and recitative formulas, or may he free himself of the meter in a kind of *inégalité*? All three cases are possible. The singer's skill and good taste are decisive. A clumsy singer might serve up the *inégalité* so provocatively as to render it inappropriate. The wide differences of composition show best in the scene of the Lord's Supper in the *St. Matthew Passion*[150] when the meter appears in the part of Jesus and gloriously elevates the sacramental words above all comparable passages. These sections are unfortunately often degraded to sentimentality and pathos by too broad a tempo. This precedent case makes one understand most easily what a recitative is and what it is not.

Whether to use a harpsichord or a positive for Bach's accompanied recitatives must be decided within the context of the total situation. The *St. Matthew Passion* avoids the use of a harpsichord, which is thereby excluded also from the accompagnato. Now there does exist a harpsichord part for the *St. Matthew Passion* written by Philipp Emanuel for the occasion of a performance at St. Jacobi in Hamburg. It concerns the direction of the chorus secundus which at that time was not placed on the main choir loft. From that harpsichord part, the assistant conductor directed the ensemble. The part is inappropriate for our concert activity. Our good choirs of today must not be deprived of the Passions by Bach any more than modern pianists of the *Well-tempered Keyboard*, but an adaptation to entirely changed conditions cannot claim the rank of a valid norm. A performance in the right acoustical milieu, the space on the West choir loft and with the proper cast, will help one balance all parts and gain standards. (A "show" in the presbytery, worse than in a concert hall, is unworthy. To this extent, one must not yield to audience demands and the vanity of conductors and soloists. Here the church authorities have to pronounce a clear no.)

There are no simple rules or teaching devices for the most effective manner of realizing a continuo on the harpsichord. A keyboard is the kind of mechanism that, according to the player's skill, permits a maximal reproduction of the complete texture of a composition. This gain is paid for by one's sacrificing the formation of the individual tone — the real contact with the creation of the tone. Between the finger on the key and the string, a playing machine interferes permitting only limited participation in the tone formation. Part of the task of harpsichordists and organists is to save as much spontaneous tone contact as possible "in spite of" the mechanical intermediary. From this viewpoint, a continuo realization is anything but a mere addition of harmonies. Today the basic teaching instrument for the entire group of keyboard instruments is missing, the clavichord! Once every music student had it before him and knew how to make the instrument "ring" by subtleties of touch. The mere tone duration wanted to be kept alive by pressure on the keys. Sensitivity toward keyboard instruments is best acquired on a clavichord, a training everybody once had. A "beginners' class" for organ and harpsichord ought to be built up from the clavichord, which could be cultivated for a lifetime as counterbalance against motoric fortepianistics. Because one can hardly "perform" on the gentle clavichord for even the smallest audience and because good clavichords are rare, this instrument crucial for a real culture of keyboard playing has almost disappeared. We have thereby lost a pedagogic discipline of highest significance.

In conclusion, a few paragraphs on the harpsichord continuo:

1. The continuo embeds a composition in a spatial harmonic sonority which must produce the "filler quality" of the music in relation to the space in which it is heard. The continuo player finds the right dosage in the frequency ranges capable of fashioning this spatial sonority, that is, he must first of all adjust to such demands the display of the continuo sound.

2. Once the "filler quality" is recognized, the musically best realization of the continuo beyond that primary task depends on the player's musicianship, particularly if his part contains concrete indications or suggestions. While the thoroughbass part must never oppress the soloists or push them in the background, it is a full-fledged member of the ensemble, sharing its affect and expressive amplitude. For every musician, the full investment and enhancement of his capacities is a vital necessity. This has nothing to do with virtuoso vanity. A thoroughbass player can be and remain a musician only by solving his task with the full force of his talent. He will need sharp observation and self-criticism in order always to recognize the overall balance in the texture of a master work and to remain the servant of the work.

3. The continuo has a further fundamental task partly solved according to the composer's intention by the figures below the bass. The thoroughbass decisively elaborates the basic law of motion in a particular piece and thereby fulfills a distinct function in the projection of the music. The event of the motion stamps the character of a work. Errors in this regard are the worst disfigurations. Precise figures in a piece convey the valid principle of motion. When the figures below the bass are rudimentary or missing, a careful examination becomes necessary. We are completely familiar with only a few conventions of historic performance practice. Where once understanding could be assumed, today helplessness or arbitrary insolence rules. An educated musician nevertheless recognizes enough details from which to determine securely the norms of motion. For many masterworks, the continuo parts have not been preserved. The figures in scores are often rudimentary or not notated. The parts on the players' stands were often much more explicit than the score, regardless of whether they were voice, orchestra, or thoroughbass parts. Bach's B-minor Mass shows after the Credo only remnants of figures.[151] The musically valid, fundamental law of motion must be interpreted also by the continuo. One cannot decide without rich knowledge of the literature and many comparisons. These statements are meant to supply criteria and touchstones for the continuo practice.

For music in intimate rooms, Bach can renounce the particular continuo concerns and the demands of spatial sonority. In the six violin sonatas with obbligato harpsichord part, for instance, he pushes this aspect aside. These sonatas are primarily trios between violin, harpsichord upper voice, and harpsichord bass. A marvelous polyphonic lineament absorbs the musical receptivity of both players and hearers so completely that concerns for harmony, space, and sonority play no role. The presupposition is chamber music in an intimate room which needs no "filler mass." Polyphonically structured movements sometimes transfer from a continuo situation to the sphere of high polyphony in which they cast off the harmonic accessory. This is the reason for figures to be realized at the beginning of a movement which disappear when the full trio texture is attained. On a two-manual harpsichord one can confirm this situation by letting the right hand change manuals at the moment the thematic substance enters.

4. For accompanying a recitative, a harpsichordist must be familiar with all manners of arpeggio. They are not likely to be metrically broken chords, for metric orders and recitative get on ill together. Whenever a recitative turns into a metrical section, the arpeggio may follow suit.

5. Finally, an informal suggestion to the player: do not worry about strict voice-leading in a harpsichord continuo. One must grant liberties to give the continuo just as much substance as needed at the moment. Apart from registration, the continuo has a right to adapt itself by full chords or thin texture. The primacy of four-voice harmony has other reasons. One must remember that harmony and some counterpoint were once learned by way of improvised thoroughbass practice! There, clean four-part texture simply belonged to "good behavior!" One also has to bear in mind that the harmonic matter generally does not reach below f^0 and above f^2. If a continuo acompaniment to recorders lies at a high pitch just below them, the harpsichordist's right hand is pulled so far up that the tonal bridge to the bass breaks. It is a characteristic of recorders that one experiences their sound not at the high pitch at which they really play. Inversely, a tenor voice sounds "high" although it seldom exceeds g^1. The harmonic substance of a harpsichord continuo, in short, occupies mainly the space of the one-lined octave, regardless of where the juncture with the soloist might lie.

The exceptional case of a continuo on a regal stems from Monteverdi's idea as a "stage director" at the appearance of Caronte, the ferryman of the underworld, in the third act of *Orfeo*. Here Monteverdi wants his hearers to get goose pimples; any other aesthetic concern is out of place. Accompanying on the regal follows the same rules: the "white notes" are played short; in between, a good player may follow all kinds of ideas and intensify the part — all in Monteverdi's spirit and intent.

CHAPTER VI

The Remaining Historic Instrumentarium

This chapter must remain a compact sketch, for several volumes would be needed to do justice to the subject. We begin with stringed instruments.

In Europe, plucked instruments developed mainly in the lute and harp families. Because of our earlier discussion of the lute in the context of basso continuo (cf. pp. 67 ff.), it need here only be supplemented by comments on the guitar. Guitars seem to originate in Spain and Southern Italy, but they are found also in Germany and the rest of Europe. In Italy they are partners of the mandolin. Single stringing is characteristic, as is the shape of the body. Its typical outline and waisted sides relate it to early fiddle types. It developed chronologically parallel to the lutes. With all their differences of shape, both instruments are played similarly because of details of the fingerboard and principles of stringing. In structure and playing possibilities, the guitar seems like a modest stepsister of the lute. Here, too, one tries to build light. The delicate ribbing of the guitar front, made in various ways, is necessary for mere reasons of solidity; for the very thin belly is of pine whereas the back and sides are made of hard wood (once nut or maple, today exotic wood like palisander, etc.). In size, the guitar closely follows the common lute measurements. A simple pegboard was finally transformed into the pegbox of today, which by way of machine screws permits easy and secure tuning (the cogwheel device was first applied to the double bass at the turn from the seventeenth century to the eighteenth). For a long time, the guitar had a kind of parallel function to the lute and then endured in folk music long after the lute had passed from popularity. In Europe, good guitar builders, like the Vienna workshop Staufer in the nineteenth century, constructed the plain, simple form with pegboard and not too large a body but with a civilized tone. In the early twentieth century, the guitar experienced a noteworthy rise by way of Spanish virtuosos and instrument builders. In its own way, it has undergone the entire renaissance of the lute family and still endures. Today one usually tunes on E (fourths with the third g^0-b^0 in the middle). The notation follows the guitar tradition of the nineteenth century by using the treble clef transposing *in ottava bassa,* but good guitarists know how to cope with lute tablatures. The guitar, too, has developed a few special types. The *chitarra battente* has a gently curved back put together of ribs as in a lute. Some instruments also supply two string courses. Finally, the big bass guitar relates to the theorbo by having a series of bass strings on a second pegbox.

The mandolin need not be discussed in this context, for it is irrelevant to the performance of early music.

The harp dates far back into pre-Christian times. The whole Mediterranean basin knew the most diverse types of harp forms more than two thousand years before our era. Here we shall trace the harp in European music since about 1400. The organ scene on the Ghent altarpiece shows a precisely painted harp. One clearly recognizes in detail the three parts of the harp body—resonator, neck, and pillar. The resonator seems to be made like a fiddle corpus. The neck, meeting the strings in an exactly fitting opposite curve, and the pillar (also known as column) are well joined. The strings lie in one plane at equal distances from each other. A reinforcing board is glued to the middle of the resonator where the string ends are knotted. Diatonic tuning symptomatic for harps may be assumed also for the gothic instrument.

The repeatedly cited instrument collection of the Kunsthistorisches Museum in Vienna possesses an instrument one century younger. The piece stems from Italy[152] and is of high quality. Its twenty-nine strings (embracing four diatonic octaves) reach considerably into the bass region. Compared to the harp in the Ghent painting, this old original instrument is very graceful. The resonating body proper is built in the manner of a trumscheit (tromba marina).[153] Drilling and burning produced a hollow space of an approximately elliptic cross section resulting in a strongly curved harp belly. The strings are attached to single wooden hooks doweled into the resonator. The strings are not equidistant. The bass strings with a much wider amplitude are given more space. The instrument, as a matter of course, had no wound strings.

The next milestone in the history of the harp is the written-out part in the third act of Monteverdi's *Orfeo*.[154] The score prescribes *Un Arpa doppia,* which refers to the big bass range (down to contra A_1). What Monteverdi composed is a genuine, full-fledged harp part! Such treatment of the instrument in 1607 does not fall from the sky. Monteverdi remained within the general situation defined by the technique of the good players of his time. The inertia with which playing methods survive as a kind of craftsmanship permits conclusions backward concerning the use of the harp in the sixteenth and even fifteenth centuries. To credit the harp only with playing the notes of the contratenor in a chanson is not enough. In every musical historic style, an instrument was always used according to its tonal and technical potential. When the possibility of fully realizing its character fades, the instrument vanishes from musical practice. In the history of Western music, such situations frequently recur. Instruments, for a long period carriers of a particular musical attitude, must yield when they cease to meet the demands of a fundamentally new style, of a new principle of musical statement. Think of the disappearance of all harpsichord forms at the turn from the eighteenth to the nineteenth centuries.

In the history of the Western harp, the following stages can be isolated:

1. Purely diatonic harps, unable to alter pitches while being played.
2. Expansion by the insertion of B-flat and B-natural.
3. The hook harp, in which a tuning hook for each string permits single pitch adjustments and thus full chromaticism albeit by bothersome manipulation.
4. The pedal harp (and finally the double-pedal harp), which decisively initiates the modern use of the instrument. The diatonic pitches can be altered by pedals each of which controls all tones of the same name. The older construction allows a half-tone correction. The double-pedal harp doubles this procedure and thereby achieves a series of special tonal, harmonic, and technical formulas characteristic of harp music written in the era of Mahler and Strauss.

A few more words about the hook harp. It is of historic interest and offers us a clue for the performance practice of many an old composition. On the neck of the harp, at one-fifteenth of each string length, separate hooks are fastened which a quick touch can flip up or lay down. Thus each separate tone can be chromatically altered, giving the harp access to all tonalities. The flipping of the single hooks, however, takes time. The harpist at an *Orfeo* performance needs great skill to manage the part on a hook harp correctly and without tempo delay.

The pedal harp is not so young as it seems. Simultaneous alteration by pedals of a whole group of strings carrying the same name was brought about by Tyrolean harp builders as early as about 1720. One century later, the further improvement of twofold alteration follows. The pedals can now be hitched into a first and second catch. An attempt to construct a fully chromatic harp by cross stringing remained unfruitful, because on such an instrument typical harp features would be unplayable (wide-spread chords, glissandi, bisbigliando, and other idiomatic techniques). Neither players nor composers want to give up the typical harp jargon. The instrument is so strongly marked by the manner it is played that it cannot do without it.

We have already reported on psalteries. The briefly mentioned gothic "pianoforte" deserves a few more words. It must have been wing-shaped, otherwise there would have been no adequate room for the "chekker" board (a board with vertical shafts holding small wooden sticks which are shot against the strings from the rear end of the key). A special transmission lever (the driver) assures the reliable upward propulsion of the little stick by the key. This bit of information about Machaut's music necessitates our rethinking the early history of keyboard instruments. The *echiquier*,[155] as the chess or checker board was called in France, could be the starting point for all keyboard instruments.

We shall now outline the pianoforte development since the second half of the eighteenth century.

When Bach paid his famous visit to the King of Prussia, he had to play the improvised three-part fugue on Frederick's C-minor theme on a wing-shaped pianoforte by Silbermann! I saw the instrument before the war in the Potsdam castle (it perished in the Berlin horrors). The stringing reflects the new type, stronger than the contemporary harpsichord stringing. The instrument has a harpsichord body. Bridge, pinning table, and soundboard are arranged as in a one-manual harpsichord with two sets of 8′ strings. The range corresponds to that of the contem-

porary extended wing-shaped instrument. Bach, at first unfavorably in-
clined toward Silbermann's pianoforte (he criticized the heavy action),
reportedly approved of the wing-shaped instruments which Frederick
the Great had bought from Silbermann. One should bear in mind that
the musical ambition of the time rejected the midcentury harpsichord!
The mechanism of the pianoforte is interesting. Into the back end of
the key lever, a wooden hammer bed is doweled (not felt-lined). In it
lies the type of hammer later representative of the so-called Vienna
mechanism. The hammer head is a little parchment roll, the thickness
of about three pieces of parchment. The crown is covered with specially
treated doeskin. The little roller, with a diameter of about 12 millimeters,
is glued into a socket of linden wood; the hammer shank joined to it
is perilously thin. At the short lever end of the hammer one finds a felt-
covered rail as escapement. Still missing are the backchecks on which
the hammers ride when falling back. The weight of the hammer for the
key c^1 is 1.4 grams! The damper is lifted by the key by way of a lever
wire. This pianoforte by Silbermann is still marked by its closeness to
a top-efficiency harpsichord. After familiarizing oneself with the touch,
one can readily transfer from harpsichord to pianoforte (and the other way
around). Yet we know that the king later favored the English superharp-
sichords which once again succeeded in displacing the early pianofortes.

Not only the wing-shaped type changes from jacks to hammers
but also the virginal form. Here the situation is much more critical; the
limited space necessitates grotesquely narrow separations between the
strings which the hammers have to hit exactly. Early experiments with
this type are not usable for superior tasks, yet they led to the second
type of the hammer clavier, the square piano.

One can pursue the development to the full concert grand. There
is a direct line from Gottfried Silbermann to Stein. After the death of
the latter, his daughter Nanette traveled with her workmen and the entire big shop from Augsburg to Vienna where she obtained citizenship
from Emperor Joseph II. She built up her workshop on the Landstrasse
and for several years was Beethoven's pupil. She married the highly gifted
pianist Streicher, under whose name the workshop survived into the twentieth century. In early piano construction, the role of Vienna was decisive. The old monarchy drew from its cultural confines a series of talents
like the Stein daughter. Anton Walter, the piano builder favored by
Mozart, arrived from Swabia; the brothers Schantz, from Chladrup in

Bohemia. Conrad Graf immigrated from South Germany; the excellent organ and pianoforte builder Ignaz Kober, from Olmütz. Josef and Ignaz Hofmann came from Bavaria. All were experienced journeymen when they moved to Vienna, a cultural center of the time. Walter's apprentice Brodmann eventually became a very good master, whose apprentice, in turn, was the first Bösendorfer.

Walter's pianoforte is oriented on F (ranging from contra F_1 up to f^3). For a while, this remains the norm. A pianoforte by Hofmann in the Technical Museum of Vienna appears to me superior in regard to optimal construction, exquisite workmanship, and tonal quality. During the decades of the classical style, this type of instrument derives its outstanding quality and significance from the graceful execution of the mechanism. A change made by Nanette Stein-Streicher for Beethoven is very revealing. At a time when his hearing was still halfway intact, Beethoven possessed a pianoforte by Sebastian Erard, who had given it to him as a present. He played it at all occasions. The instrument has the so-called Erard mechanism. This is another, fundamentally different piano mechanism in which the hammer is mounted not on the key lever but on a separate rail. From the back of the key lever, a kind of jack known as *Stosszunge* leads to the hammer and propels it upward. Beethoven lets this mechanism be altered. Nanette moves the pivot of the key lever forward by 52 millimeters (the upper keys by 47 millimeters), lengthens the lower keys at the front end by almost 1 inch, and thereby changes the tone intensity of the instrument. The path of the *Stosszunge* is now lengthened by 1½ millimeters. The elements of the mechanism are gracious; but after the alteration, the touch was considerably harder and the dynamics louder by at least one-third. These facts can be read off the instrument. After Beethoven's death, it went to his brother Johann, an apothecary in Linz, and stands today on loan from the City of Linz as one of the most important objects in the music instrument collection of the Vienna Kunsthistorisches Museum. One cannot make Beethoven's increasing deafness responsible for the alteration of the pianoforte. In a letter of 1809, Reichardt writes: "On Beethoven's advice and request, Streicher has made his instruments more resistant, more elastic...He has thereby given his instruments a greater and more varied character so that they must satisfy, more than any other instrument, any virtuoso concerned with more than just superficial sparkle."

This development, in which the Streicher workshop decisively participated, led in the second half of the nineteenth century to an increased heaviness of the so-called Vienna mechanism. The *Prell-* or rebound hammer cannot be used in piano construction aiming at ever larger sounds. Now a second kind of pianoforte mechanism outstrips the Viennese action. All "improvements" occur within the development from the Erard mechanism to the double escapement action, today usually referred to as English mechanism. Consider the differences: the fall of the key on the Potsdam instrument is barely 4 millimeters; on the pianofortes of the period around Mozart and Haydn, it is about the same; then it grows slowly to 11 millimeters. The energy needed for playing is now multiplied. Proper performance practice of the piano music from Haydn to Schubert, and even Mendelssohn, requires the historic instruments. Too few playable old pianofortes exist to meet this factual demand. I wish to report a typical case. Konrad Graf placed a specially constructed hammer pianoforte at the disposal of Beethoven during the last years of his life. This instrument had quadruple stringing so that Beethoven could not break the strings too easily. Toward the front, there is a kind of "prompter's box" to focus the tone. Beethoven probably never used it, for his deafness made playing impossible. In a roundabout way, the pianoforte reached the Beethoven house in Bonn. Graf offered the twin instrument to the young pianist Clara Wieck who in Vienna gave on it a spectacular performance of the Hammerklavier Sonata. Graf made her a present of the pianoforte, which then became the instrument of Robert Schumann, her husband. After his death, she gave the instrument once more to a friend. The new owner was Brahms who bequeathed it to the Vienna Gesellschaft der Musikfreunde. During the last war, the music instruments of the Musikverein were moved to the collections of the State, that is, to the Kunsthistorisches Museum. There, next to Beethoven's Erard pianoforte, this instrument is the piece richest in tradition. One must realize that a specific instrument of the Beethoven era still had validity for Brahms! Today we are caught in the belief that pianistic activity has to depend exclusively on the modern top-efficiency action, on the accomplishments of a Steinway. The modern pianoforte obviously possesses a multitude of useful qualities, but it is not the sole salvation. It does not do justice to links of tradition. Unfortunately, modern piano construction is exclusively conditioned by principles of commercial production. A few well-preserved historic instruments stand in museums and are thus removed from practical music-making.

The type of the square pianoforte either proceeds from the construction principles of the unfretted clavichord, in which case the pegs are placed along the right flank (a very revealing, exact drawing with mechanical details of this type can be found in the great compendium on organ building by Dom Bedos);[156] or it relates back to a special spinet type, in which case the pegs are placed parallel to the front of the keys. This other kind of spinet is actually a bent wing-shaped instrument. The otherwise straight course of the left side turns right at the crossblock at an angle of about sixty degrees. The result is diagonal stringing as in virginals. The same difficulty that burdened the virginal type now also affects the table pianoforte: under the work conditions of the time, an action adjusted to the minimal distances between the strings cost troublesome labor. Anyway, this type was a very popular form of the intimate pianoforte and was built with sundry "improvements" into the last quarter of the nineteenth century before the so-called pianino, or upright pianoforte, displaced it.

Upright keyboard instruments were already introduced among harpsichords. They both suffer from the same weakness that the plucking or striking mechanism must be retrieved to its initial position by a spring (and not by gravity as in all wing-shaped forms). This deficiency is somehow noticeable and reduces the value of all "giraffe" keyboard instruments, uprights, etc. Because of the limited space in modern apartments (and because one expects a pianoforte to be a proper-size piece of furniture), the upright has today become the household instrument. Musical viewpoints and tonal quality are displaced by dubious advertisements. Here intelligent buyers should set aright the commercial attitude of the producers.

Finally we turn to a discussion of the clavichord. I wish it would rise to a properly appreciated position. In the music education of children, it deserves preference over any other keyboard instrument. It forces players consciously to shape the duration of the tone, which sounds only as long as the key bears the vitalizing pressure of the finger. The player thereby experiences metric and rhythmic structures much more clearly. A tone of longer duration can be revitalized by a rocking motion of the finger on the key; this, too, serves to sensitize the player to the experience of temporal duration. I consider the minimal tonal energy of the clavichord a further advantage. It is the mildest and gentlest instrument of all. In our world which disregards reasonable limits also for hearing and mercilessly flays our ears, making music on intimate, sensitive levels helps us not to lose all aesthetic standards amidst the orgies of noise.

The key has the simplest possible transmission to the production of the tone. At the end of the key sits a tangent, that is, an edge formed like a screwdriver blade, which is hit against the string where it adheres with gentle pressure. The left ends of the clavichord strings are braided with felt so that only the string portion to the right of the tangent can sound (until the bridge). In this manner, one string can produce several tones depending on the spot where it is agitated and delimited. The result was a fretted clavichord (that is, an instrument on which certain tone combinations were impossible). With an increase in the number of lines to be played and the resulting denser texture, the frets had to be reduced and eventually eliminated to bring about the unfretted clavichord. Because the tone is initiated quasi at the end of the string (the tangent setting the limit), the amplitude of the vibrating string is small. Relatively thick strings (to counter the risk of breaking when hit) under rather high tension do not allow intensive vibrations. The clavichord, to be sure, has the simplest action which keeps the finger in the best contact with the tone, but these advantages do not really assert themselves vis-à-vis the soft small sound. The clavichord is therefore an instrument for the player alone. The page turner might just hear enough to be satisfied!

Early clavichords are often found in pictures. They developed directly out of the monochord and, like other stringed instruments with keys, demonstrate a particular method of producing tones by way of a keyboard. The symbiosis of keyboard and monochord or clavichord is apparently not the first of its kind. A relatively small number of strings produces many tones. The creation of tones by the tangent must take into account the greatly varying distances between the points touched on a particular string, but here the ideal equidistance of the keys on the keyboard and the division canon of the string do not coincide. Toward the discant, the differences of the string lengths shrink to fractions of the differences in the bass region. Even if we assume for early instruments a small range, perhaps three octaves, the distances between the lengths relate as 1:4. To meet these difficulties, the key levers had to be led in an extreme radial arrangement. This feature does not fit the notion of an early encounter between key and string. A revealing image of an early instrument can be seen in a wood carving by Adriaen van Wesel.[157] A group of angels making music still shows the clavichord type with hardly a soundboard. At the ends of the strings, one sees, respectively, tuning pins and hitch pins. The key bodies show the profile expediently cut to prevent deformation by finger pressure. The building of clavichords soon becomes more refined. The arrangement of the strings and the growth of a small soundboard relate to the spinet. To do justice to the principle of hexachordic, modal diatonism, the number of strings increases. Chromatic halftones are gained by fretting the string of the same pitch name. Because the clavichord was expected to render the entire lofty, that is, polyphonically demanding music playable *per tasto,* the double functions of strings were ever more reduced. This process runs parallel to the concretization of the thoroughbass. The end product is a fully chromatic clavichord now designated unfretted. This is the *Well-tempered Keyboard!* From this viewpoint, one understands the variety of textures and structures. In the *Well-tempered Keyboard,* one senses lute music, there are many harpsichord pieces, and some movements point toward the organ positive. Just as today the modern piano has to submit to impossible demands (Mahler's Eighth Symphony *à quatre mains!*), so similarly everything was expected of a clavichord. With its extremely delicate sound which needs to find resonance in the player's musical imagination, the instrument was ideal for such vicarious use. The larger the number of strings, the thinner they must be. In the unfretted instruments, there is not much difference in this respect from the spinets. In order not to keep breaking the discant strings, they usually occur in double courses.

The clavichord was in use for a long time. It was *the* instrument of Philipp Emanuel Bach, corresponding fully in sensitivity to his efforts toward intensifying the galant style. Mozart still played it. New instruments ought to be more careful in obeying the laws of string length; reliance solely on string tension is inappropriate for an unfretted clavichord.

We have reached the bowed stringed instruments. The species originates with fiddle forms. The resonating body is at first a variation of an adequately large wooden spoon covered by a flat top which is the actual resonating plane. As a relic of St. Catherine of Siena, the fiddle she played has been preserved intact under a glass bell in the sacristy of the church in Siena where she is buried. The Kunsthistorisches Museum in Vienna owns a similar instrument; it has survived because of an exceptionally beautiful carving (a nude woman) on the spoon body. Besides the more or less modified spoon body and the flat top (often shaped toward the neck which developed out of the spoon handle), the earliest fiddle also had a fingerboard and pegboard. The number of strings was minimal; three seems to have been an early norm.

The spoon corpus is soon superseded by the chipbox form. The body now consists of a thin back, a sliver encircling the sides, and a belly. The latter soon becomes curved by the joining of two little boards cut like cask staves. Driven-in braces secure the glued seem. A flat vault originates. This shape can be further forced by raising the height of the sides at the neck and the tailpin. To give the bow enough freedom of motion with an increased number of strings, the width of the body has to be drawn in; soon the typical middle bouts appear at the waist (as the inward curves of the sides are called). This detail transforms the specific fiddle form into the viol form. The larger bowed instruments share with the lute types the position of the fingering hand. In smaller fiddle types, the left hand, while holding the instrument, embraces the neck. The fingerboard receives lute frets (mandolin types, as also the cister [citole] of Archduke Ferdinand of Tyrol, have metal frets firmly inserted into the fingerboard, like the ones common in modern guitars).[158]

All fiddle types have soundholes fitting precisely the particular type. First they are half-moons cut around the area of the bridge. Later (as in the viol in the organ picture of the Ghent altar) they move away from the bridge toward the middle of the body creating ever new resonant potentials of the fiddle and viol bellies and eventually turning into the "flames" of the gamba and the F-holes of the violin. The soundholes, regardless of form or placement, are cuts through a resonating plane which according to their execution produce characteristic modes of vibration. Think of the figures on Chladni plates.[159] Whether flat top and soundhole (lute principle) or vaulted top and paired slits — the cuts "soften" the resonating planes in a very particular manner and enable them to resonate with the specific vibrations of the strings. The F-holes on a violin, for instance, make a break in the otherwise rigid, tight arch of the belly between the two curves of the waist; and this elasticized zone carries the bridge. Violin makers knew a special method of execution. They strung the unvarnished "white" violin and made it playable. Then they strewed the belly evenly with puffball spores or clubmoss seeds and played the instrument in this condition. Chladni figures appeared in the dust which served knowledgeable and experienced builders as a criterion for quality. Portions of the belly too thick and inert showed inadequate movement of the dust particles. In such a case, the instrument maker took his familiar egg-shaped scraperblade and from the outside shaved the critical zones of the top thinner. This was a well-known procedure in historic instrument-building, proven by the old tools! Only after the violin or viola had suffered the last application of the scraper was it appropriately varnished (even here one could still differentiate by filling the pores and thereby regulating the extent to which the varnish was permitted to penetrate and harden the top).

The instrument types may be classified more exactly:

1. Fiddle types with spoon corpus, three strings, stepped flat top, and pegboard.

2. Fiddle forms with box corpus, incipient vault in the manner of cask staves.

3. Early viol forms developing the preceding type by solid incorporation of the neck, improved quality of the top, slowly increasing number of strings, introduction of middle bouts, occasional pegbox as in a lute, first bassbar forms, and soundpost.

4. Further improved viol forms in which incidentals might become typical. Arched tops gouged by a chisel prevail. Outline, neck plate, stringing, F-hole form, execution of the bassbar, placement of the soundpost, and the pegbox develop into specific characteristics of the viol da gamba. Compared to *da braccio* forms (held freely by the hands), viols played *da gamba* have considerably higher sides. Viols da gamba remain without tailpin because the continuously changing angle at which the instrument is held while played can be controlled exclusively by the knees (the change of angle avoids excessive demands of the bow arm threatened by the large number of strings).

The viol family possesses very graceful bodies, relatively thin gut strings, and hence a somewhat thin tone particularly suited for melodic design. At the turn to the eighteenth century, the viol advances to the role of a virtuoso instrument with the character of a leading top voice regardless of its actual pitch range. In the sixteenth century, gambas appear in three sizes: two extremes one octave apart and a medium size between them. These types cover the entire tonal space of the music of the time (the highest discant range eventually becomes the property of the violin). At the turn to the seventeenth century, a consort of viols da gamba consists of five instruments. In analogy to the vocal madrigal, the instrumental gamba ricercar, too, becomes typical. This practice lasts throughout the century but is modified in the performance of, let us say, a cantata where we may find a mixture of violins, viols, gambas, violoncello, bassoon, and perhaps other winds. In the eighteenth century, the bass gamba predominates. Players become ever more skillful in mastering finger positions. The high string register increasingly calls exclusively for violins. The large gamba survives longest.

Precondition for the development of the violin family was the changed musical situation at the turn to the seventeenth century. In the thoroughbass style, the lines of the upper voices carrying the affect and intensified expression become increasingly important. Among the stringed instruments, a top-efficiency type becomes essential. One knows very well that the tension of the strings has to be significantly increased and therefore secures the form of the instrument against deforming forces. To the vault of the belly now corresponds the countervault of the back. The outline develops in curves approaching circles (see the monograph by Hans Kayser, *Die Form der Geige*, which attempts to derive the outlines of the violin from monochord laws and the overtone series expressed in terms of vector quantities).[160] The compactness of the overall form, the anchoring of the neck on the body, the jutting-out of belly and back beyond the sides, the new F-holes, the new angle of the bridge, the slowly evolving forms of the bridge, these and many other details yield a much denser overtone constellation in which the first partials massively developed determine the sonority. By comparison, the overtone constellation of gambas reaches much higher while the lowest partials are essentially more discreet than in the violin group. A larger instrument developed according to the stated principles of the violin form is the violoncello, a specific bass type with a strong harmonic function. For a long time, it remains exclusively a bass for the harmony, declared to be the thoroughbass instrument *kat' exochen* and forced to remain satisfied with this function. One senses this quality a little even in Beethoven's Sonatas for Pianoforte and Violoncello! Only in the course of the nineteenth century does the violoncello advance to become a melody instrument, often at the expense of the quality of the music. (In France there is a kind of hybrid violoncello, called *basse de viole*. A gamba body is tuned like a cello with an additional highest string d^1 or e^1. This instrument is most suited for the solo cello sonatas by Bach, which were probably played on it.)

Violin, viola, and violoncello of the modern orchestra submitted to one more adaptation. Since about the middle of the last century, old instruments are being rebuilt and receive a far more massive bassbar. The neck is removed and replaced by a usually much longer one at a different angle. The original pegbox and scroll are then dovetailed back onto the new neck by a sophisticated procedure of craftsmanship. The angle between string and bridge is steeper. If necessary, the belly is reinforced by a lining in the soundpost region. The result is the modern violin, viola, and violoncello with more than tripled string tension! The reason lies primarily in the change of ensemble formations of the closing nineteenth and the twentieth centuries. Twelve first-violin stands are not rare today. To let this accumulation produce a real intensification of the sound, the sonority of the string section had to be whipped up. Electric technical measurements yield a whole set of revealing data (for a while I worked at the Hertz Institute in Berlin where such questions were investigated in the context of acoustical research). The old violin, as described above, possesses an overtone constellation of fairly exact values. The modern violin loses the balance of the tonal elements, and also the overtone positions are variedly distorted. The violin choir produces beats between the overtone positions which create the iridescent, exciting tone of the violin section in, for instance, the orchestra of Gustav Mahler. One must beware of using this violin type in small numbers. Two first violins alone sound out of tune with the best intonation of the players. Their overtone series are discrepant. For the present performance practice of early music, the question is urgent. Should such music be played only on old violins, or is the modern musician at liberty to play also old music on the instrument and with the technique familiar to him? This problem afffects many aspects and must therefore not be solved by one-sided intolerance! In the case of the modern violin, an overall balance must be achieved. The players ought to be thoroughly informed about all musical and structural qualities of the particular composition to be able to concentrate their personal share on the essential tasks of interpretation. With such good insights into the composition, they may under some circumstances be preferable to performers with old instruments, the more so as exclusive concern with the peculiarity of an old instrument often turns into purism.

The bow is part of the stringed instruments. In this area the problems appear even more complex. Very old, relatively short round bows are known only from pictures. All traditions concerning the use of the bow are extinguished. We have reasonably good information, however, about the so-called baroque bow. What matters is concentration on drawing the bow, effected by a relatively light stick of minimal elasticity with a broad tip and also broader frog. Legato qualities are the main issue. The up-and-down change of the bow with all its modifications becomes paramount. The old bow fits the old violin, not the modernized one. For the top-efficiency violin, the Tourte bow, a modern type, is appropriate.[161] When playing old chamber music, it helps to grasp the stick of the modern bow at the ornamental wrapping. Leopold

Mozart held it there. In this position, the weight of the bow shifts slightly; and the hand carries the bow better across the strings rather than pressing it. Once a player has understood this principle of guiding the bow, he will also, as is customary, manage the thumb at the frog. String players adapt more easily to the old ways of playing than pianists, but one must beware of a certain one-sidedness. Advanced knowledge of styles ought to be a required course in every serious music school, taught by an expert in theory and practice.

All we have said of the violin is valid, with small differences, also for the viola and violoncello. The latter, today played from a sitting position, has become a full-fledged partner of the other instruments in a string quartet. The technical demands are similar.

The situation of the bass viol varies according to the type used. In the course of the sixteenth century, a subbass joined the gamba trio, just as other instrument families produced large bass forms. The historically built basses still common today are a gamba type enlarged to string lengths at *ottava bassa*. They have five strings with contra-C_1 below the sequence of fourths rising above contra-E_1. Basses of this type remain related to the sound of gambas. As late as 1920, only the low C_1 and E_1 strings had silver winding around the gut kernel. In the seventeenth century, only pure gut strings were employed. In the last one and one-half centuries, the players' left hand has marvelously developed and transferred from the violoncello the technique of separate fingering. In the chapter on thoroughbass, I have already mentioned the necessity of arranging the thoroughbass part for the bass viol by removing all coloration. Modern double-bass players certainly manage agile passages; but thereby a characteristic of the old practice, namely a real subbass effect, is lost.

The new double basses are hybrids of gamba form and a kind of large violoncello. Significantly they have a vaulted back. The walls in all parts, moreover, are much stronger. Compared to preserved original basses, they are coarse. New basses usually do without the lowest string because a four-string instrument is easier to play. Its bridge is less curved, and the bow arm tires less.

A separate little family is formed by instruments with resonating strings: viola d'amour and baryton. The former is in every detail a viola da braccio (with flat back). Thin resonating brass strings, about five or six, are guided through separate holes in a mezzanine level of the bridge. These strings, which cannot be stopped, vibrate softly along with the melody strings depending on the resonance relationship. Usually they were tuned pentatonically fitting the tonality of the piece. The resonating strings run in a kind of tunnel in the hollow neck below the fingerboard. The extremely large pegbox required for so many strings determines the typical appearance of this instrument group. The melody strings are numerous. The late-baroque form of the viola d'amour is tuned in a big D-major chord (seven pitches from d^0 to d^2).

Here there exists a cross-relation to a family of specific renaissance instruments, the liras, which I shall mention only briefly. The range of the large instruments reaches down to the great octave. They have many strings with an almost flat bridge. There are some similarities to the lute. The liras are solo instruments. The actual melodic line was played on the highest and perhaps the next strings. As often as possible, the bow takes along an arpeggio accompaniment, to the extent the left hand can finger it. The instrument disappears already in the seventeenth century because it could not adapt itself to the compositional demands of the full-blown thoroughbass era.

The large bass instrument of the gamba family, too, produced a separate species with resonating strings, the baryton. It was a genuine virtuoso instrument, permitting under certain circumstances also cheap effects like a thumb arpeggio of the left hand on the resonating strings which lay open at the beginning of the neck. Joseph Haydn's patron, Prince Nikolaus Esterházy, was a baryton virtuoso. For this instrument, Haydn composed over one hundred trios, six octets, further duets, trios, cassations, quintets, and concertos. This linkage justifies the existence of the baryton until today. There are very few gamba performers, however, capable of playing it.

One more type has to be treated. It lives more than seven centuries and dies as a beggar's instrument: the rotte, the hurdy-gurdy. Intelligent reasoning led to the formation of this type, which probably existed in an earlier version as a wind instrument, the bagpipe. The special principle of making music develops most naturally from the disposition of the instrument. The hurdy-gurdy imitates the bagpipe as a stringed instrument. A fiddle body built in the manner of a box and already with a vaulted top accommodates two (and later three) strings. One thin string carries the melody, the other supplies a drone. The melody string is not fingered above a fingerboard but stopped by clamps through a kind of keyboard mechanism. The player holds the hurdy-gurdy in his lap, the left hand lifts the little levers of the clamping machine—a procedure for musical dilettantes even if kings have played this instrument! The strings are agitated by a stroking wheel of which the axis passing through the length of the body ends outside in a crank. The Anglo-Saxon crwth may have been the ancestor of this idea although it employed a bow for stroking the melody and drone strings. Here the wheel does it. (One of the tricks of playing the rotte consists in always pressing the wheel against the strings. Because the bearing at the bottom of the shaft is far too wide, a special swing is needed to avoid the creation of a penetrating dynamic wave with each turn of the crank.) The rotte is always and exclusively the carrier of a special type of burden polyphony! Compositions for the hurdy-gurdy do not exist. A spooky scene, in Schubert's "Leiermann," renders a completely correct demonstration of the instrument: burden sounds, then melody snatches. Schubert has realistically transmitted the texture and sound of the beggar's hurdy-gurdy. Today the rotte is a stage curiosity and hardly of any serious use in performance practice restricted to master works.

We shall discuss the historic wind instruments only summarily. Many of the original instruments are lost. It is practical to group these instruments, too, according to principles of tone generation.

Flutes date back very far. Their variety is so great that we shall here restrict ourselves to Western music. Straight beaked flutes occur in very early illustrations. They are all upper-voice instruments in the size of about the later soprano or alto type. For our narrower concern with the performance of a concrete instrumental task, one needs a part appropriately written out for the flute. Flute participation is sometimes mentioned in connection with Notre Dame organa, but not until Machaut's time does one find upper voices requiring the recorder. For the periods of Burgundian and Netherlands music, one thinks repeatedly of flute participation, particularly in the realm of the chanson. In all these cases, the recorder sounds *in ottava*, if not sometimes even two octaves above the notated line. In the sixteenth century, the octave doubling above the *chiavi naturali* is taken for granted. When the name *flautino* occurs, then the double octave is intended. In the *Orfeo* score, the extreme case of "Un Flautino alla Vigesima seconda" is specially marked. In 1535 appears the very important book on recorder playing by Silvestro Ganassi, to which I keep referring.[162] This text on the art of appropriate instrumental diminution is of greatest practical value.

All early flute types seem to share a fruitful relationship to basic problems. All flutes necessarily develop within the constraints set by the human breath. In beaked flutes, regardless of size, the width of the lip is bound to it. In proportion to their size, discant instruments have therefore very wide lips; tenor, bass, and subbass flutes, extremely narrow ones. In the latter group, the energy mustered at the lip just suffices to bring about in the flute body the resonance coupling to the air and to generate a tone. Because of the extreme relation of lip width to inner space, large flutes carry relatively well (cf. the discussion of this problem in connection with organ flue pipes, pp. 78 f.). Before the development of the big flute family, relatively wide discant recorders predominate. The situation we have described for recorders then repeats itself for transverse flutes. Here, as well, the amount of human breath fits only high-pitched instruments. The development of large transverse flutes in analogy to large recorders proved inexpedient. An extremely large transverse flute has a deficient energy balance compared to the high-pitched types, the more so as it also lacks the advantages of the marked buildup process (like that of a flue pipe and recorder). The size of the blowhole of transverse flutes plays the same role as the width of the lip of recorders. Because this measurement greatly influences the tone formation, playing historic music on old transverse flutes with their typical tone quality has its justification. Even with the best playing technique, modern flutes do not reproduce this quality.

Except for the largest types, old recorders are made of one piece of wood. In the course of the sixteenth century, the steadily increasing trend toward homogeneous sonority brought about different sizes. In the *Syntagma*, Praetorius classifies the flutes in correspondence with the human voice ranges but in ottava. He further distinguishes the small flautini forms (in quintadecima) and, if need be, the smallest discants above. But also the bass is enlarged with flutes in loco notation (large tenor and large bass).

Important in the baroque is the change of flute measurements. The instrument becomes considerably narrower, hence overblows more easily, has a larger discant range, but drastically loses carrying power. The widely deployed flute choir is replaced by the tonally optimal type, the alto flute, which before the disappearance of the recorder family soars once more into favor and gains a place in high-baroque concertizing.

The baroque recorder is now notated loco in the French violin clef. The specific tonal charm of the recorder stems from the embouchure system. The flue-pipe lip initiates typical buildup processes and overtone formations. Because the height of the mouth, that is, the distance from the lower to the upper lip, remains unchanged, and because the different pitch ranges can only be reached by differentiation of the breath pressure and of the modifiable opening of the thumb hole for overblowing, the recorder possesses a characteristic manner of expression and of dynamic possibilities. Further subtle differentiation is accomplished by the application of different articulation syllables. Finally, the manner of breathing itself—and with it the whole complex known to singers by the catchword "breath support"—bears significantly on the characteristic, personal tone of a player. Uncultured flute playing can often be heard. The recorder, too, must be conquered by empathy.

In Western music, transverse flutes had to struggle for acceptance in serious music. For a long time, they were burdened by certain military aspects: a gang of mercenary soldiers marched to the sound of transverse flutes and barrel drums. Those flutes corresponded approximately to the modern piccolo. Lassus employs transverse flutes in his ensemble. All the oldest transverse flutes are either naturally hollow or cylindrically bored. The particular feature of transverse flutes as compared to recorders is the adjustability of the embouchure. The windway—formed by the player's lips—and the mouth position at the blowhole are changeable. One half of the hole is covered by the lower lip. Then the air stream flows against the remaining half of the hole where it creates the typical conditions (discussed above in connection with the organ, pp. 77 ff.). By the application of experiences with the recorder, cylindrical transverse pipes—known as "Swiss pipes" because of their association with Swiss mercenary gangs—undergo a civilizing procedure at the beginning of the eighteenth century, which elevates them to the standard of the other concertizing instruments. The bore becomes conical; the diameter at the open end is about one-half of that at the blowhole. Now the transverse flute loses its penetrant sauciness and finds its place in the ensemble. Yet it retains a considerable advantage over the recorder which is also its specific virtue: it can blow piano as well as forte in each register (changeable conditions of the embouchure!). The elegant restraint of the recorder is foreign to it. In the second third of the eighteenth century, it surpasses the recorder as the specific virtuoso instrument, also because of its much wider range. Transverse flutes then become increasingly equipped with keys. Böhm's system of ring keys finally brings about the last improvement. To profit ultimately from the application of these new principles, the flute returns to a cylindrical bore. The last stage in the development is encumbered by the numerical disproportion between transverse flutes and swarms of strings in the modern symphony orchestra. A relatively too large mouth hole, it is true, produces a well-carrying flute tone, but it is accompanied by ugly blowing noises. The typical transverse flute of the orchestra is not usable in chamber music. For such tasks, players today usually resort to a second head-joint with a smaller mouth hole.

The so-called piccolo, the transverse flute in ottava, is scaled to half of the orchestra flute. All tone qualities of the latter are even more penetrating. The personality of the player of the transverse flute declares itself strongly. A flutist with a beautiful expressive tone is a rarity.

All flutes develop their wide range by overblowing. The consequences for the sound, particularly in multiple overblowing, have been discussed in the section on the organ (cf. pp. 77 ff.).

The flute family comprises one other instrument, once popular in the Alps, the gemshorn. A recorder lip at the thick end of a chamois horn and several tone holes created a flute-like instrument. Closely related to it is the family of "vessel" flutes, vulgar types common in the Far East, in China, in Japan, and introduced into Europe as ocarina.

For a whole group of wind instruments, a double reed provides another principle of tone generation. Today this type is represented by oboe, oboe d'amore, English horn, bassoon, and double bassoon. In early music practice, the intrumentarium of this branch was much richer. We shall deal first with the group of capped instruments. A whole series of instruments, prominently the krummhorn, was blown by a method, today no longer in use, by which the reeds vibrate freely. The reeds are covered by a cap; through a slit in the cap, the player presses his breath. The tone qualities of a freely vibrating reed are quite different from a reed stuck between the player's compressed lips. Capped instruments, moreover, cannot overblow and thus have a very limited range.

Visiting the Musée Mahillon[163] in Brussels thirty years ago, I still found some reeds that had been made for instruments at the beginning of the sixteenth century. A cassette belonging to seven krummhorns (Correr, Venice, 1506) also contained a large number of old reeds of which some were still usable. After softening them in my mouth, I could blow an alto and a tenor instrument. The tone of the old instruments is clear, firm, cool, and singularly apt for designing a line in polyphony. The breath pressure needed to agitate the old reeds is slightly less than for our modern oboe. The preparation of the reeds is very different from that of our oboe reeds, etc.; the old reeds are about twice as wide, and the extent of the scraping and shaving is shortened by about one-third.

The body of the krummhorn has a cylindrical bore, which becomes conical only at the spot where the body begins to curve. There two tone holes are drilled. In relation to the narrow bore, the tone holes are rather large. In the Brussels collection, the seven instruments of different sizes lie together in an original case. This shows with what consistent logic instruments were built in families to conform to musical practice. Because krummhorns could not overblow, such a large number of instruments was needed to accommodate a specific historic standard of registers, church-mode ranges, and contemporary compositional procedures. Thomas Stoltzer, whom I consider the superior German composer of the Josquin era, mentions specifically in the dedication of his 37th Psalm to Margrave Albrecht of Brandenburg that, for a performance of the work, he had deliberately counted on a krummhorn ensemble (in addition to the voices)![164] For decades now, imitations of krummhorns are being offered and assiduously bought. I am always distressed to see in what superficial and claptrap manner early music has become an object of commercial exploitation. The imitations are more or less poor. The real double reed is mostly replaced by a piece of plastic tube squeezed together by a primitive clamp. Whoever wants to become honestly engaged with a krummhorn — and I consider the krummhorn a key instrument of sixteenth-century music — must learn to make his own reeds, like oboists and bassoonists for whom it is (or should be) a matter of course. Here a whole group of historic instruments must be met with greater seriousness. The krummhorns one encounters everywhere around 1500 do not appertain to a single generation of musicians! They must already have existed around 1450, and their family structure was probably already perfected around 1500. To be sure, they leave the stage very soon (in the pavanes by Hermann Schein of 1612 they make a late appearance) because their limited range could not be extended and because compositional ambitions do not let themselves be impeded by the inadequacy of an instrument.[165] The original krummhorn sound is best rendered by certain old organ stops of the same name, which are relatively narrow organ krummhorns. The wide cromorne has a very different sound. (In the last ten years, the situation has improved. One finds good krummhorn players who have mastered the old instrument.)

Like the krummhorns, other double-reed instruments, too, utilized the cap system. The bagpipe comes first to mind. We may repeat what we said about the hurdy-gurdy: the bagpipe is not an ensemble instrument. With its bourdon, it has a one-sided duty to a *single* kind of polyphony and thus stands isolated against all other compositional events. It has remained alive in Ireland and England, where whole groups of bagpipers march to the music. The sound of the bagpipe is outdoor music!

Here we must mention the so-called bladder pipe. There is no clear proof that it was a pommer with a freely vibrating reed. It may have been an early relative of the clarinet. Its reed is covered by a pig's bladder. This elastic cap was perhaps its essential feature.

Of real significance are instruments with a conic bore. Here again we find families.

The pommers (shawms) all have a conic bore of which the angle is wider than that of the oboe today. Although the type existed in the twelfth century, the family originated only in the sixteenth century when instrumental choirs developed everywhere in analogy to voices. Pommers were blown like krummhorns. The players stuck the reed so deeply into the mouth that the cavity of the plate acted as a cap. To avoid injury to the palate and, moreover, ruining the reed, the "thorn" (the brass tube to which the reeds are tied; the Viennese term is *Stift*) was invested with the so-called pirouette, a ring to be placed in the indentation of the chin.

We do not know whether the small pommers could be overblown. Not before the seventeenth century was the instrument, first of all the discant pommer, transformed to be blown by lip pressure. The discant pommer becomes known as "haut bois," misnamed *oboe* by German players. Pommers have a hearty, copious tone, which one can hear on preserved instruments. The tone character is strongly influenced by the specific way the reeds are prepared—light or heavy. All players of the pommer are oboists or bassoonists; they retain the reeds in the lip area, thereby altering the pommer tone. The involvement of wind players, on the other hand, who as members of first-class orchestras are used to a standard of impeccable music-making and thus automatically maintain a high artistic level is a great advantage, for they protect against the abuse common with krummhorn and zink. The use of pommers today makes sense, particularly in the realm of the French oboe. Particularly recommended are discant, alto, and tenor pommers. Bass pommers always had difficulties. The tone holes are drilled not where they proportionately belong but where they are reachable by the fingers. Only the most distant positions were made accessible by keys. For bass pommers, caution is required, particularly when for the sake of "historic correctness" situations are provoked with which the players cannot properly cope.

The baroque oboe is closely related to the so-called Vienna oboe, which grew directly out of it. The baroque oboe has the dryer, clear tone and the high capacity for "design." Like recorder, pommer, dulcian, etc., it is a diatonic music instrument. Chromaticism is accomplished by cross fingering (in which the player covers the second nearest hole and thereby lowers the pitch by a semitone; the exact adjustment of these tone values depends on the player's quality). Some pitches received a special double hole; but on every old oboe, $f^1\#$ is more or less out of tune.

Next to the oboe, the oboe d'amore was much in use during the baroque period. The choice between these two instruments depends more often on the tonality of a particular piece than on a decision for reasons of timbre. (The oboe d'amore has a "love foot," a ball-shaped extension with a small hole for the outlet of the tone, in contrast to the rather trumpet-like end of the oboe. The English horn ends in a "pear.") The oboe d'amore is based on a^0 and thus contains three sharps in its natural substance. Hence Bach uses it only in sharp keys. The situation is similar to that of the English horn and its variants: the oboe da caccia and the type referred to as taille. Here the range is foremost decisive, paralleling that of the oboe a fifth below.

In this "Viennese" book, the differences between the Vienna and French oboes must be discussed. The contrast derives from their different origins. The Vienna oboe, as mentioned above, came directly out of the baroque type without having to experience big leaps in its development. It steadily improved the key system but always retained its relation to diatonism. Its specific qualities are tied to overblowing. Yet all these facts do not suffice to define the contrast of the two types. The playing of the Vienna oboe manifests also a principle of embouchure, a tonal aesthetics, a particular breath control, and a deliberate restraint of expression. The French oboe is a child of the second half of the nineteenth century, aesthetically bound to the French music of Saint-Saëns, Ravel, and the impressionists. It never denies these contacts. The distinction is based on facts: each music has its own appropriate oboe type which participates in shaping the character of the style.

Tenor and bass regions are entrusted, contemporarily with the pommers, to the family of dulcians. In order to bring distant finger holes closer, a body made of fruitwood (plum, hard pear, maple, also nut) has two internal bores, leading up and down and connected at the lower end. At first, the bores were burned out; for at such length, the old

spoon drill runs away. Later one bored conically, most widely at the
open end. The thorn familiar from the oboe curves increasingly and
becomes the predecessor of the S-crook of the bassoon. The dulcian looks
from the outside like a bassoon made of one piece and sounds much
like it. Again the preparation of the reed and the embouchure of the
player are of the greatest influence on the development of a specific tone.
One approaches the tone function of old instruments more closely by
pushing the reed further in between the pressed lips.

Out of practical considerations, the large dulcian was put together
of separate parts. The result was the fagotto (= bundle) or bassoon. The
course of the bore also changes because the conicalness can now be better distributed. In many areas, the historic bassoon played a leading
role, thus as a thoroughbass instrument for the execution of the actual
bass line. If one cannot burden the singer of a solo cantata in a resonating room by a hesitantly articulating 16' bass viol, then one certainly
prefers the bassoon.

There is an old engraving in the Vienna Albertina.[166] Emperor
Joseph I (an excellent musician) sits in the nave of the Vienna Burgkapelle at the Walter positive organ, which today stands next door in
the museum, and plays the thoroughbass. On the music stand lies a Mass
of his father's, the Emperor Leopold I. To his left are castrato, alto, tenor,
and bass; and on the right, two violinists. The bassoonist stands behind
the emperor, looks into his music, and plays the bass line. Cast and all
details are typical. Wherever a good local bassoonist could be found,
he was preferred to a violoncellist or bass-viol player. We find the same
situation at the northern end of Europe, in Husum, where Bruhns was
active. If one thinks of the multi-choir compositions which the seventeenth century favors in many timbre combinations, then the common
practice of involving double-reed instruments appears plausible. They
provide an excellent balance to each other as well as to the old trombones, regals, positives, and properly cast vocal choirs.

The modern bassoon is conditioned by the late nineteenth and
early twentieth centuries. The tone qualities are changed not so much
by the instrument as by the embouchure method. One demands of the
modern bassoon not so much the design of the bass line as the subtlest
dynamic insertion even in the most outlandish timbre mixtures. The
bassoon now serves sonority and color. This fact has marked the education of more than two generations of bassoonists. For the performance
of old music, a modern player would have to acquire a special attack

and blowing technique. One cannot possibly cope with "Quoniam tu solus sanctus" from Bach's B-minor Mass if the bassoonists concentrate on beautiful tone and "accompaniment" of the singer. Here an optimum of design is needed, because four parts move within the same tonal space of the small octave — precisely where lines blur easily. In this case, two old bassoons are recommended; they have the most advantageous proportions. But the decision is made in the player's head! All depends on his proper embouchure, his sense for style, and his awareness of historic compositional structures. The historic bassoon alone does not suffice! The S-crooks, too, have an amazing influence on the character of the sound. Many little mosaic pieces produce the picture.

An old bass instrument, of which we possess too few precise reports and preserved pieces, is the sordun. It was apparently the earliest type built according to the bassoon principle (separation into many single tubes). The mensuration is so arranged that a cone shape in the first first quarter of the bore is followed by cylindrical tubes. The organ stop of the same name corresponds in its bell mensuration exactly to the same principle but has considerably wider dimensions. The lost sound is perhaps best preserved by the cool, clear tone of an organ dulcian or sordun.

Another group of historic double-reed instruments has practically disappeared, the group of rankets. The difficulty of reaching distant holes on straight tubes apparently led to the attempt of inserting a coiled-snake bore into a fitting body. One of the most beautiful instruments of this kind in the Vienna Museum is made of a piece of elephant's or mammoth's tusk. The familiar brass thorn leads into the cylindrical mantle, in which the bore goes up and down, adjoining bores always connected by a tight joint. On the cylindrical mantle, the finger holes now lie close together. Italian painters placed the ranket in the hands of ladies. Today we cannot tell in how many sizes the instrument was built. Because the rankets are contemporary with other instrument families which paralleled the four voice categories, they may well have been governed by the same principle. The organ stop of the same name typically uses a mounted cap as resonator. There is also some correspondence of timbre.

The art collection from Ambras castle of the dukes of the Tyrol, now in the Vienna Kunsthistorisches Museum, contains one other quaint group of instruments certainly built for some mummery. The underlying principle is that of the ranket; but the actual sounding body is a tube wound around a cylinder, the whole thing enclosed in a cover in the shape of a dragon. The sounding tube is arranged so that the finger holes lie next to each other on the dragon's back. The tube ends in the dragon's mouth. The grouping by family and the size of the instruments remind one of the case with krummhorns in the Mahillon Museum.

What was the music played by such instruments? The ricercar repertory is appropriate, beginning with Stoltzer's *Octo tonorum melodiae*.[167] One may further include instrumental performance of the madrigal and chanson literature. Although dance music has been transmitted on a broad basis only since 1600, it was certainly cultivated for a long time in the manner demonstrated by the early variation suites. Monteverdi's *Orfeo*, which I keep quoting, contains enough instrumental examples; the moresca at the end is a well-known type. The Innsbruck *Tartölten*, as those strange Tyrolean instruments are called, can be easily imagined in processions and parades. Wind families like pommers (or the Tyrolean rankets) fit very well the neatly composed five-part dance movements, shortly after 1600, by Isaac Posch.[168] For music to be actually danced, winds have always provided the decisively sweeping sonority. Old performance practice does not employ strings "in a swarm." For such occasions, only winds could carry the sound assertively.

The use of a *single* reed is also very old. As a kind of primitive clarinet, for instance, the chalumeau is still today popular for dance music in the French Pyrenees. The name of the clarinet indicates that it first appeared as a substitute for the clarin trumpet in the second half of the eighteenth century. It soon became a favorite of traveling Bohemian virtuosos. The decisive step toward serious use of the instrument was made by Denner, who installed the overblowing key named after him and secured the intonation.[169] Whenever clarinetists happened to be in Eisenstadt, Haydn employed them in his early symphonic music. Their proximity to trumpets can still be recognized in Haydn's great Masses. Three large clarinets are common in the early nineteenth century. Typically, they are notated in a normal G-clef to be read as a tablature in B-flat and A. Clarinets are transposing instruments. Therefore a note indicates only a particular fingering and an embouchure which produce different pitches according to the chosen instrument. Even the modern bass clarinets accomplish the downward transpositions by large intervals according to the same principle of notation. At the end of the eighteenth century, the clarinets in C, B-flat, and A were joined by a still larger form, the basset horn, at a fifth below the C clarinet.

Mozart's *Requiem* sets one of the precedents. The man commissioning the Mass for the Dead probably had such instruments at his disposal (in modern performances of the *Requiem*, the basset horns are submersed because far too many strings and, in relation to the practice of Mozart's time, an overlarge chorus cover the single players of the "alto clarinets"; here, too, correction of the balance is urgently needed!). Finally, several small clarinets (in E-flat and A-flat) came into being in order to enrich the discant instruments in military march music. The large bass clarinets have become fully established in our century. The clarinet of the Vienna classics still had very few mechanical keys. The tuning of clarinets in C, B-flat, or A served primarily the access to the tonality of the piece to be played. The individual tonal character of each type of clarinet was consciously utilized by Carl Maria von Weber. It comes fully to life in the relatively small orchestra in the first third of the nineteenth century. Today, when a superperfect mechanical key system permits everything, clarinetists have regrettably retreated to the medium-sized instrument in B-flat (for they are experts in transposing). In chamber music, where the tonal character becomes distinctly manifested, the clarinet type prescribed by the composer must be demanded.

In our century, the penetration of the bass clarinets (and double-bass clarinet) into the lowest pitch regions has gained this instrument family a much greater share in the modern orchestra. These types are of no further concern to the performance of historic music.

In another large family of diverse wind instruments, the player's lips function as the immediate tone producers. Of great influence are variously formed mouthpieces, which basically regulate the lip action, and the "mensuration" of the instrument, the particular course of the tone tube. From these points of view, groups are formed. (Here I cannot deal with exotic instruments and early types of Antiquity; information will be found in Curt Sachs's book.[170] We shall only consider the instrumentarium directly related to the great Western music tradition.)

Our first group contains the trumpet forms and related instruments.

A military trumpet, the signal instrument of a commander, is implied by the behavior of the trumpets, mentioned earlier, in Dufay's festive Christmas music, "Gloria ad modum tubae."[171] Here a large trumpet tone is desired. Because a field captain generally was not a musician (Binchois is the exception) and trumpets were restricted to the military, such fanfares made no technically difficult demands. The tonal range limited itself to the three or four lowest positions of the tonal supply. The tones produced by the trumpets are exclusively overtones, beginning with the interval of twelfth above the fundamental. The trumpets of that period are made of silver, perhaps also of gold; the precious metal underlines the importance of the carrier of the trumpet. Because of their artistic value, large silver trumpets embellished with gold and precious stones have been preserved until today. Empress Maria Theresa still commissioned the famous Vienna wind-instrument maker Leichnamschneider to build a large trumpet set, preciously executed for the Hofburgkapelle, the Imperial Chapel, on the occasion of a Corpus Christi procession.

These instruments stand fully in the tradition of the sixteenth-century trumpet. They are all large D-trumpets, that is, almost twice the size of the instruments used in a modern orchestra. They are "natural" trumpets, yielding only the tones of the harmonic series. Increased pressure of breath and lips chases the trumpet into ever higher positions. In the baroque period, players specialized in certain embouchures for the upper pitch regions. "Field" blowing is the rough, strong tone production of the military command instrument. "Clarin" blowing is the other method with a narrower mouthpiece and special lip and breath technique for explicitly artful heights. The old trumpets speak amazingly easily at extremely high pitches. We repeatedly received permission to use the silver trumpets of the Imperial Chapel; after a very brief practice period, the students of the Vienna Academy could play up to f^3-sharp. This readiness for the highest zones results from an extremely large ratio between the length of the trumpet tube and its diameter: the big old D-trumpets have the same diameter as the modern B-flat type. The old trumpets, to be sure, were not tuned in D but according to the cornet pitch discussed earlier, that is, high C. When the high tuning lost its predominance, the trumpet "in ut" became the D-trumpet.

During the seventeenth century, the superiority of trumpeters based on their aristocratic background disappeared. (The services of an aristocratic "field captain" in the sixteenth century could be secured by holding his kinsmen as bail.)

The instrument is now of brass. Although the trumpeters belong to a guild, they no longer enjoy a socially elevated status. What now counts is only the musician's ability. In this period, wind players of high excellence and skill in the special clarin technique came to the fore. We can no longer with certainty understand the special "advantages" of the instruments. The trumpeters themselves do not discuss their methods. We believe to have caught on somewhat to the tricks of Gottlieb Reiche, Bach's star trumpeter.[172] The coiling of the clarin trumpets was circular and covered by the usual leather bandages. Pictures of Reiche show him holding the instrument with spread-out fingers; apparently the fingers close several small holes. The problem was to select from the thicket of the highest overtone positions of the trumpet those that were musically usable; and, for this purpose, small holes would be of great help. Reiche died of ruptured lungs on the steps of the choir loft after a Bach performance. Blowing such soloistic parts was obviously a bad physical strain. The extremely high pitches demanded the trumpeter's full exertion.

Another historic trumpet type to be considered is the slide trumpet. We have enough illustrations and also a special composition for it, Josquin's Royal Fanfare.[173] This music presupposes a wholetone slide. The trumpet was pushed back and forth against the mouthpiece which was attached to a shorter trumpet tube. Transposition by a wholetone was probably the usual procedure, and the slide itself limited to one move. *Trombe da tirarsi* are mostly formed so that the course of the tube is similar to that of a trombone, except that tubes and bell lie in one plane. The musical attitude and blowing technique for the Royal Fanfare are no different from those for Dufay's Gloria. The trumpet continues to move in this track for the remainder of the century. A good example of the use of different trumpet types is the fanfare at the beginning of Monteverdi's *Orfeo*. The top part is marked *Clarino*, probably an early model for actual clarin blowing. The part calls for scale passages across a fifth in the two-lined octave. Below this Clarino trumpet, there are military types of almost shocking primitiveness down to the *Vulgano* in the lowest region.[174]

Concertos by Schütz also show clarin parts. In his German Magnificat from *Opus decimum*, the text passage, "Er übet Gewalt mit seinem Arm" ("He has shown strength with his arm") involves two real clarin lines.[175] This section in the "Deutsches Concert" from the *Symphoniae sacrae secunda pars* permits an inference concerning the absolute pitch at the time of Schütz. The trumpets used were certainly in *ut*, hence the concerto sounds on cornett pitch. Consequently all such compositions can be brought to this pitch. In relation to our modern a^1 at 442 Hz, the piece must be transposed up by a good halftone.

The great difference between top trumpeters and musicians modestly equipped for prior choirs, municipal bands, etc. manifests itself in the way the instrument is used and the special skill it requires. The grand Serenada à 8 by J. J. Fux summons in the intrada a solo trumpet which exhibits both the artistry of clarin blowing and the big festive sound of the instrument.[176] The movement begins with a trumpet solo (in which the player must be released of all metric obligations, blowing his solemn fanfare in full freedom). Later in the movement, the special technique of clarin blowing is required. A very similar situation exists in Fux's solo cantata "Plaudite" for tenor and solo trumpeter.[177] Apparently the early clarinet really displaced the clarin trumpeter. The trumpet parts in the Masses of Haydn and Mozart belong to the artistically more modest, but tonally intensive, trumpet type below the actual clarin zones. From this practice ensues the conversion of the trumpet by means of diverse valve systems. There even existed a trumpet with keys, which had a shabby tone. Finally, Sax's pump valves and the rotary valves can instantly lower the tuning of the trumpet by, respectively, a halftone, wholetone, and minor third. For this purpose, tubular crooks of the necessary length are hitched to the main trumpet tube. Difficulties arise when more than one crook is used at a time, for the length of each separate crook is proportioned to the original length of the trumpet. Thus the halftone crook, for instance, is too short for a trumpet already lowered by the minor-third crook. All three crooks at the same time produce an even worse intonation. Such deficiencies of any valve system must be corrected by the player's embouchure.

For extremely high clarin parts, we use today very small trumpets (in D-alto or even F-alto). Here, too, many obstacles must be overcome in order to present a civilized tone and some balance of sound. A blowing technique once burdened by secretiveness concerns different syllables of articulation which lend the tone production a certain precision.

The choice of appropriate mouthpieces for definite tasks is limited today, for each good trumpeter carries his mouthpiece in his coat pocket. The security of his embouchure stands and falls with the mouthpiece intimately known to him. Old field trumpets had big wide mouthpieces, almost the size of a modern trombone mouthpiece. "First" trumpeters, always responsible for high pitches, blow on relatively narrower mouthpieces. One must never forget that the trumpet is first of all an eminently rhythmic instrument! Therefore, trumpets combine with timpani to form a unit!

Because of this constant bond, I want to make in this connection a few essential comments about the timpani. As instruments in Western civilization, they gain their main significance after the sixteenth century. Musically they serve not as soloists but always as bass of the trumpet group. This orientation determines pitch registers, construction, and musical use. Their occurrence as a pair was already fixed during their purely military employment. Two relatively small timpani hang from the right and left sides of the horse's neck. Their alliance with the trumpets settles the tuning on tonic and dominant.

A kettledrum always consists of a copper kettle covered by a calf's skin tanned like parchment. Proceeding from simple tension cords, one eventually tightens the skins by more than a half dozen tuning handles. The timpani mounted on horses could not be large. The timpani joining the old trumpets were also smaller than commonly assumed today.

To achieve the specific old timpani sound, several conditions must be met. The kettle form must be correct (somewhat flat bottom, the circular kettle pulled up — the sound wave must bounce back from the copper bottom; the conical kettles of the modern machine timpani do not accomplish this end). The skins must be properly tanned. The timpani must be hit by proper sticks. The latter were originally lathed from a cattle bone, but soon one used tough, hard wood. The naked heads of the sticks render a very clear sound which, however, could be minimally differentiated (neither pianissimo nor a rough forte could be produced). Such sticks, on the other hand, educe from the timpani very clear pitch experiences (for ceremonies of mourning, the skins and stick heads were covered with cloth). For old music involving timpani, it is relatively easy to follow historic performance practices. One will try to borrow the smallest possible timpani, perhaps from a church. Appropriate sticks can be turned on a lathe. Correct tanning of the skins might encounter difficulties, because tanneries have today become industrialized and hardly accept specialized orders. The right stick remains the most decisive factor. The modern felt head, even the hardest available, has a different tone. Size and tension of the skin determine whether to place the dominant a fifth above or a fourth below the tonic. Often one will have to compose the kettledrum part, because in the seventeenth and eighteenth centuries it was improvised following the trumpet parts. Three trumpets are practically always joined by timpani, even when not specifically mentioned in the score.

After this detour to the historic timpani, we now turn to the trombone family as one of the most important in old music.

There is a link from the open slide trumpet to the trombone. The essential feature of the "invention" consisted in doubling the small extension of the slide trumpet by letting it slide simultaneously along two sections of the tube. This type developed probably soon after 1400. The problem was solved by a U-shaped slide pulled over two open legs of the slide trumpet. The trombone has now been in use for half a millennium and it has basically not changed.

Certain tone characteristics, however, were adjusted to the style of any period. In the fifteenth and sixteenth centuries, the trombone is a tenor instrument. In this register, the trombone functions at its best. The size of the slide fits the mobility and length of the player's arm; and the length of the tubes pulled above each other is just right to keep them tight and operating well. The embouchure, the mouthpiece — all factors favor the tenor trombone. Soon the bass trombone was developed and an alto instrument promptly introduced. For the lowest regions one finally constructed a *trombone doppio* which adds the interval of a fourth at the bottom. A second slide in the direction of the bell is supplied with an auxiliary metal bar which hooks into notches a half-tone apart. The large path to be traversed by the slide of the bass trombone is shortened by a lever, a quasi-prolongation of the trombonist's right arm. A discant trombone did not stand the test of performance practice; for in a small trombone, the often barely overlapping tubes do not close tightly. The open legs of old trombones have no "shoe" (the name for the reinforcement of the end of the tube which is ground into the slide proper). Great knowledge and care were needed to form the brass sheet into a tube, to "solder it hard," mold it most carefully on the iron thorn, hammer the tone-defining bell properly, and solder all parts absolutely tightly. The old instruments have thin walls. In spite of machines, instrument builders of today are not capable of reproducing the quality of the *trombone doppio* with the coat of arms of Bishop Paris Lodron of Salzburg.[178] The conicalness of the bell as well as the proportions of the tube and the mouthpiece influence the tone greatly. The most decisive factor, however, is the stylistic knowledge of the trombonist. If one wishes to produce copies of old trombones, one must realize the limitations of modern production methods. Many thousand hammer strokes hit every point of the historic trombone before a brass plate became a trombone. Hammering significantly alters the acoustical qualities of the brass. Modern copies consist of a drawn brass tube and have much thicker walls. The bell is "pressed" on a turning lathe, as the process is called of adjusting the metal to a form while rotating it. The trombone barefuly suffers a hammer stroke.

Let us summarize the observations concerning the historic trombone. The particular qualities of these instruments and the great musical tasks encounter each other in cappella music, the sacred music of the Burgundian and Netherlands periods. This alliance forms a type so concrete that it endures for a long time. The voices of a sacred composition and the trombone trio are so attuned to each other that this symbiosis persists at a time when the style has apparently lost all contact with the original situation as it existed during Josquin's life. In Mozart's Salzburg Masses, for instance, the three trombones go with the voices. Today one usually omits the trombones, particularly as one would be forced to employ modern instruments. If old trombones, or at least well used, sensitively made copies, are at one's disposal, they certainly should become involved! How different is the sound of the end of the Kyrie in the Coronation Mass with trombones![179] The farther back one turns, the more intimate is the unity of realized sound and compositional intent. Because a trombone ensemble was anchored in all halfway capable municipal music organizations, it was available in many places for the performance of church music. In the sixteenth century, doubling of the almost soloistic vocal cappella by trombones (and zinks for the uppermost part) was a matter of course in large halls. I recall once more Bach's arrangement of a Palestrina Mass for the Protestant liturgy at the Thomaskirche with a trombone trio and zinks added to the boys and young men of the Thomas School.[180] Bach was following a clear, precise tradition.

To the trombone group belong the zinks (cornetti), as closely related to it as trumpets and timpani. Zinks are very old. One sees a zink illustrated in Compostela.[181] Its essence is a self-contradictory union of *two* kinds of musical instruments, trumpets and woodwinds. Narrow conical horn types have long been known. The Jewish shofar (a ram's horn with a strange cry blown on the High Holidays) is an ancient zink. There is a linkage to the horn with finger holes. A white (mute) zink (turned on a lathe out of one piece of wood) consists of mouthpiece and corpus all in one. The mouthpiece has a noticeably small diameter and some similarity to the modern French-horn mouthpiece. The cone of the bore is much wider than in an oboe. The tone holes conform to experiences with tone holes on the pommer. What happens here is that an air column, a "resonator" as we know it from woodwind instruments, enters into forced coupling with the agitating lips. As in all brass instruments, the lip frequency is thereby determined by the resonator — again a coupled system.

With its finger holes, the zink becomes an instrument with optimally developed intonation adjustments. The two white (mute) zinks which in the cappella lie above the trombone trio are standard in a five-part chorus.

Larger zinks, corresponding to alto, tenor, and bass registers, were built curved so that the fingers could reach the holes more easily. The bass size even had to be made with several curves (known as serpent; of all zinks, it lasted longest and still occurs in military music of the nineteenth century; it was displaced only by the valve trombones). Black zinks were made of at least two layers glued together, in which the hollow space was scooped out with a gouge. To protect the glued joint against being dissolved by humidity, these zinks were bandaged with leather dyed black; hence the name. All zinks would be of utmost importance for old music if only there were not such difficulties of intonation! Modern copies are almost without exception unreliable.

The zink builders were once also good players. Old zinks show how much they had been worked over and how the profile of the bore had been rasped again and again. Historic zinks are museum pieces and thus removed from performance practice. Copies are not satisfactory. The special advantages of the attack are no longer known, therefore a broadly based methodical foundation has not been established. Under such circumstances, the zink has to be replaced by other instruments. Performing early music with out-of-tune zinks is musical mischief. The substitution, in any case, is difficult. Experimentally we have substituted small clarinets for white zinks, blown by intelligent musicians who understood the special situation and eliminated the juicy clarinet attack by a hard embouchure. Occasionally we have also used the cornet à piston of military bands. Because on the choir loft of the Vienna Burgkapelle we were invisible to the audience, to our amusement the "falsification" always succeeded. One can hope for an elevation of the zink in our time from a stage curiosity to an honest musical instrument only after creating a serious base for methodical instruction in blowing the zink and persuading instrument makers to become involved in a long, difficult training period.

The horns, too, cause problems. The starting point was the hunting horn. At the beginning of the eighteenth century, it was already used soloistically. Performances today with a baroque horn introduce a difficulty hitherto deliberately overlooked: the old horns were blown with a trumpet mouthpiece, and trumpeters instructed the players how to blow. The proportions of the horn, too, were different. The conicalness becomes tonally effective only at the bell. With sets of crooks or tuning slides, the horn was readily adapted to the tonality required by a composition. The so-called inventions horn furthermore has an easily adjustable extra crook. Only at the beginning of the nineteenth century does the shift occur toward the attack and sonority of the horn as we know it today. As *waldhorn*, this type has been marked by the music of Carl Maria von Weber. The kettle mouthpiece of the baroque horn has turned into a conical tube, and the embouchure has departed from the principle characteristic of trumpets. The new horn type controls wide dynamic differentiation and tonal energy, as the result of which the baroque horn was quickly eliminated. Today we are exclusively fixed on this type! Chamber music and symphonies of the nineteenth century have brought to the fore the dominating role of the waldhorn. In this prototype, mouthpiece, embouchure, mensuration, and musical situation all came together. Horn players now cover an extraordinarily large tonal range. The lowest pitches can be brought out by pedal tones (as on the trombone by slackening the lips), the highest can be achieved up to the twenty-fourth overtone and even above. A skillful player can produce a whole set of usable pitches by correcting the pitch of ekmelic tone positions through "stopping" (the horn player puts his appropriately cupped hand into the bell and thereby significantly influences the intonation).[182] The invention by Sax of pump valves and the introduction of rotary valves made the crooks almost unnecessary and rendered the horn capable of meeting any challenge of a composition. The successive horn types are: hunting horn, natural horn, inventions horn, waldhorn, and valve horn.

For much early music, such as the first Brandenburg Concerto by Bach, the correct approach is still missing and has to be worked out to achieve the right sound. For the high registers, historic, small hip horns blown at the hunt with a kettle mouthpiece could provide a usable type. Many arguments have been caused by the instrumentation of Bach's funeral motet for the governor of Leipzig, "O Jesu Christ, mein's Lebens Licht."[183] Some claim that *lituus primus* and *secundus* are those little horns. We have tried original instruments from the Vienna Museum. Their sound is so penetrating that they are unusable for parts functioning as an accompaniment placed at the top. The score specifies also

a white zink (cornetto) and the three traditional trombones. For this outdoor music at the grave, the ensemble of the municipal pipers of Leipzig and the Thomas School were engaged.

Historic percussion instruments remain to be discussed (we an-
ticipated kettledrums together with the trumpets). One must first ask
whether the given musical situation demands emphatic profiling of meters
or rhythmic elements.

The "bells" in Notre Dame organa are today difficult to realize.
Bell types are now quite different. Special research has supplied the following example. In the Scaligeri castle in Verona there hangs an eighth-
century bell, originally from San Zeno, which offers a precedent. The
bell has the form of a hemisphere. It was hung by its somewhat large
suspension ring and struck by a hammer on the outside. It was never
"rung," that is, swung so as to be hit by a clapper. Today this bell might
be called the prototype of an octave bell. This definition is insufficient,
for the Verona bell does not emit the confusingly complex sonority of
later bells. The pitch lies at the border of the two-lined octave. It gives
only this one pitch and a few incidental overtones. With this bell as a
norm, one would have to cast more than a half dozen for practical use.

Next to the bells of the gothic era, percussion instruments appear
particularly in dance music and related areas. Small cymbals were taken
over from the Moorish civilization. Castanets were played by the dancing girl herself and belong to the historic percussion group. One sees
triangles on painted scenes depicting even church-music situations (for
the reproduction of the original sounds, a few rings must be hung on
the horizontal bar; they add an intensive jingle to the sound).

Percussion instruments in the performance of early music must be
strictly judged as to whether they conform to the serious intent of a good
program or simply offer the audience one more element of distraction.
They belong to old dance music. The melody of an estampie on a fiddle
alone is insufficient. Here a musical percussionist can be active by supporting the harmonic foundation, marking metric contours, and diver-
sifying details of interpretation. Nowhere does one need more sensitive
taste for finding the right degree and manner of participation.

Principles of Singing

I want to submit some thoughts concerning the human voice,
for singing is a highly important feature of performance practice.

Tradition has given primacy to the male voice. Boys' voices are included as male voices *in spe*. This one-track approach is artificial; but when monks report on singing, the result is necessarily one-sided!

For the evaluation of singing habits in the music of the ancient West, one must render an account of the very different premises. Certain monasteries were said not to manage cultivated singing because of the lack of suitable voices; others enjoyed a high reputation. The monastic choir schools began musical education in early childhood, as children of five and six years were apportioned to monasteries. In a monastery with a good teacher, talents exposed to such a long training period achieved a high standard. The art of plainchant *cantores* therefore deserves respect. A kind of ornamented singing probably existed in some monasteries at an early period. As stated before: in elevated vocal art, the concepts of artful and artificial are inseparable. Contacts with the East, with Byzantium, led in some places to an exaggerated singing skill, the falsetto. As an explanation, I must discuss fundamentals of singing methods.

The human voice, considered unsentimentally, is a wind instrument. The vocal lips (we are used to calling them vocal *cords*; they are, however, fleshy organs, best comparable to a trumpeter's lips, but more differentiated and subtle) and their function defy in their fineness the observation feasible for other instruments. In place of the metal ring of the trumpet mouthpiece, the cartilaginous larynx provides the firm anchorage. The two vocal lips are grown in right and left (no need to include here the Morgagni pocket and the "false" vocal cords). The fixed points are the thyroid, cricoid, and arytenoid cartilages. On the rear border of the cricoid cartilage sit the arytenoid cartilages to each of which, respectively, an end of the vocal lips is attached. During the breathing process, the vocal lips are separated to form a triangular opening, closed toward the thyroid cartilage and opening according to the changing distance between the arytenoid cartilages. One may assume that direct coupling to the brain causes the particular position of the arytenoid cartilages. Most important for a tone to be sung is its being preceded by an *audiation* [a term introduced by Professor Edwin E. Gordon, of Temple University, to replace the visual and thus unsatisfactory *imagination*]. It produces a precise positioning and tension of the vocal lips (which are a very complicated network of muscles, coated with a fine mucous membrane). The contraction of the vocal lips and hence the closure of the triangular glottis fissure, the relevant position of the larynx in the neck (where it hangs highly movable from the horns of the hyoid bone) — all this happens without the direct participation of our will. The position of the larynx is automatically coupled to the realization of the vocal sound, which also involves the shaping of the nose-throat area, placing of the tongue, and positioning of the lips. Further included in this complex are breathing and posture. All these connections are thoroughly formed in a long training period beginning in childhood.

It would be very dangerous for a voice teacher to proceed from an exact anatomic definition of all these details and from an abstract development of single, perhaps trainable features; for the difficult coordination of so many partial aspects cannot be treated by way of a system, a typification, or some generalizations. Each man is a "subject," determined by pre-birth conditions and most individually developed later in life. He escapes every generalization. In the sphere of art, these circumstances demand that the teacher shape the decisive development "out of" and "with" the forces of the learner, liberate his gifts as much as possible, and guide them toward the appropriately optimal goal.

Historically there is no steady evaluation of all aspects of singing. Temporal styles favored very different aesthetics and with it an art of singing often oriented toward diverse aims. Every clearly developed musical style has its own vocal aesthetics, technique, and schooling. We cannot trace the traditions far back; they soon turn into utopias. But one firm condition applies also to the art of singing: thorough knowledge of the compositional structures, intimate and high-level study of style.

As a method, a good teacher will use a minimum of abstract training and rather proceed from the spontaneous experience of music. Teaching material, pedagogically appropriate and simultaneously appealing to the student's best potential, can be excerpted from traditional vocal music. If the voice is formed by genuine music, the singer's spontaneous musical powers are equally addressed. He moves on a terrain appearing to him accessible because of his experience. I shall not expound methods of singing. For a general understanding, one must first comprehend the basis from which to proceed. Developing a voice, one might begin with a method of breathing. If in this regard the pupil's experience is underdeveloped or misformed, then, of course, he is initially not open to a differentiated education. If, on the other hand, this is the one area where the student's ability is really at home, then this approach, readily affirmed by his willingness, permits a control of the functions. Breathing, which indeed can suffer from a thousand habits of misbehavior, offers the most direct, but perhaps also the most brutal, advance. This method yields the quickest results, but it can also lead to a complete derailment. Only very experienced teachers can apply it safely.

The second method proceeds from the other end and tries to build up the voice from the resonating complex. In many cases, this detour has proven fruitful. The activation of resonance indirectly also stimulates the directly creative forces. Yet this method, too, may not overcome some blockage of the vocal disposition. Constant pottering in this field sometimes arrests the student's free initiative. Much one-sidedness may thus originate, from "pebbles in one's mouth" to a suffocated voice.

The center of it all, the activity in the larynx, is fortunately inaccessible to the voice teacher. Success is anchored in the desire to imitate, in the realm of experience, and thus in music. Here the teacher-student relation must be optimal. Here the teacher, demonstrating for immediate contact, must stimulate imitation of his singing. The function of the larynx offers the possibility of using the tonal attack as a methodical principle, as a key to the old art of singing. The event can be described in terms of anatomic physics. In a healthy voice, the glottis is closed before the attack. The tonal attack, the pushing-through of air, opens it. There are countless ways of doing it, from faulty explosion to equally faulty aspiration. Baroque vocal education knew a kind of gargling gymnastics in the so-called *trillo* (not to be confused with the ornamental trill). It was the hacking into pieces of a tone by many attacks. We have reports on how students in training became more and more exact, how the tempo of the attacks increased, how a deliberately involved diaphragm participated (anatomic nonsense, for the diaphragm cannot contribute anything to the exhaling phase, during which it remains a passive muscle; exhaling is an activity of the epigastric muscles). The greatest confusion reigns in the definition of "support," including the pertinent breath control and cultivation. Anatomically certain is that the lungs in regard to their volume consist almost exclusively of air. Through the bronchial system and with the speed of sound, the tone of the vocal cords reaches the pulmonary space where it finds its resonance. The air then flowing into the throat is thus "sounding" air. The agents mutually uphold each other. Voice training therefore aims at a good balance between air transmission and simultaneous preservation of resonating space. Physically, anatomically, and also nervously, each student is differently equipped and must be properly judged concerning his capabilities and limitations. For efficient breathing, the optimal posture must be found for each individual singer. (The lung apices are not of much use in singing. Filling and emptying them would severely curb other important actions.) A posture entirely appropriate to an individual leads without further difficulties to a correct breathing technique. The old singing masters elaborated on this complex in connection with the trillo.

These comments do not intend to ignore the tendency toward the training of the most diverse vocal characters, as demanded also by musical styles. The human voice can be guided toward any desired temporal style, and each musical style is receptive to special vocal qualities. Bohemia, Poland, and the Hungarian-Slavic region, for example, provide voices best suited to conquer the large opera houses. The situation in Italy is similar; old singing traditions offer orientation. Italians, moreover, meet the vocal experience with full vitality and relish the sensuality of sound. All these attitudes participate in the development and cultivation of operatic singing and the aesthetics determined by it. For performing early music, one must free oneself from such preconceptions.

In historic vocal art, one encounters over and over again the castrato. Notwithstanding the goose pimples this complex evokes, it provides a key to renaissance and baroque music. Phonograph recordings of castrato voices exist (for instance, in the archives of the Vienna Musik-hochschule). They come from the Sistine Chapel (where in the 1930s Perosi still had at least two in his ensemble).[184] What one hears is the sound of a beautiful boy soprano who securely, skillfully, and with boundless breath sings pseudo-religious junk. A castrato's range extends from a^0 to d^3. Such castrato voices set the standard of singing toward which all vocal training was oriented. The castrato voice possesses an optimal capacity for linear design. By way of this relic one sees how compositional technique, aesthetic conviction, and musical practice mutually enhanced each other to accomplish a full unity of style, as in the days of Josquin or the high baroque of the operas by Handel. The castrato roles in the latter are an obstacle to modern performances. From experience I recommend not substituting trousered women but tenors. The tenor is a high-voice category. He conveys in his singing the experience of height and is therefore best suited to do aesthetic justice to such roles. We even have a historic "excuse": whenever castratos were not available, in opera they were replaced by tenors.

All voice problems finally resolve in one's understanding the relation to voice range. Like recorders, like woodwind instruments, the human voice is also capable of a kind of overblowing. Compared to instruments, however, there is a fundamental difference. Wind instruments are coupled systems of which the resonant part assumes the function of defining the frequency. In other words, in an oboe the reed is highly tolerant, subordinating itself at any moment to coupling with the resonator. In the case of the human voice, however, the resonator, being far too small and adjustable, has little influence on the primary pitch produced by the vocal cords. The situation is the same as that of the reed-stop regal of the organ. A small resonator decisively participates in defining the timbre of a tone; but on the frequency, the resonator in the regal has no bearing. Each musician knows the strangely squeaking glissandi when the oboist tries his reed before attaching it to the body of the instrument. This is exactly the physical situation of the human voice. It took thousands of years of education and crystallization before the voice obeyed and, like strings, produced tones of constant pitch. It was the voice which rather late tied the concept *melos* to fixed pitches. The whole differentiated creation of tone thus becomes really intelligible only from the aspect of singing. The function of the vocal lips is now comparable to pitch correction on the organ regal: the movable tuning wire changes the length of the vibrating reed to accomplish the desired tuning. The pitch can slide around within a fifth and more. The vocal lips act similarly. They lie slack in the lowest regions (cf. the pedal tones of a trombonist). The higher one ascends, the more they tighten from the border, where they are attached to the cartilaginous structure of the larynx. Then comes the zone of falsetto. With the help of the stroboscope, I made a typical observation on myself. In the morning, the vocal lips are not free of mucus. If at that time one sings falsetto, a mucous thread remains lying in the middle of the length of the vocal lips, an indication that there is a still, inactive zone (these observations can now be filmed in slow motion). After this division (into front and back sections of each vocal lip), the fastening occurs a second time, ending again in a vibration of the outermost border zone. This phenomenon underlies the Austrian yodel, which consists in a quick shift from one vibration principle to the other. Falsettists cultivate the zone of overblowing. Historically, the alto register was sung in this manner. Each of the two vibration processes has a limited range. By the eighteenth century, composers were demanding an extensive range attainable only through *both* registers together. The modern recipe for singers wishing to master this difficulty is an optimal equalization of registers! Cleanly isolated chest voice and similarly head voice (the common terms today for the vocal phenomena described) have to be bound together and equalized. The low voice register must already contain the high one, and inversely the top must remain joined to the bottom. The realization of this balance, which must carefully consider the personal disposition of each singer, forms the alpha and omega of modern voice training.

The facts discussed above concerning the instrument "human voice" offer a kind of key for each historic style. In order: the restricted ranges of traditional vocal parts, on the one hand, and the abundance of elevated falsetto features, on the other, suggest that one worked for a long time with the separate registers of chest and head voice. A variety of ornamental techniques, moreover, shows that throat agility was practiced almost out of context and that tone formation by head resonance etc. did not greatly matter. It was a throat technique driven to extreme virtuosity unencumbered by other complexes such as observation of resonance above the throat, et cetera. Modern research could profitably investigate hitherto neglected manners of folk music where many older performance practices and former conditions of artful execution have been preserved. Confirmation has repeatedly come from discoveries made in regions not yet commercially exploited.

One must remember that, in regard to throat agility, vocal art at the beginning of the sixteenth century had already reached a peak. From Ganassi's[185] referring to singing in his textbook on recorder playing as the best possible model for the performance of bravura recorder passages, we may infer the style of singing, the kind of artistic statement, and even the method of voice training.

This chapter on the education of singers is obviously not to be understood as a concrete method. Many music examples would be necessary, for the musician and the singer must be educated as one. Actually there are as many methods as students.

CHAPTER VII

The Historic Tunings

The fundamental tuning problem derives from the consonant value of the pure major third. One knows thirds as the sex determinators of major and minor; their tonal sensuousness is overwhelming. If one inverts the beatfree major third c^1-e^1 into the sixth e^1-c^2, the latter can again be divided into two thirds, e^1-$g\#^1$ and ab^1-c^2, whereby $g\#^1$ and ab^1 are two very different tones. Proceeding from the beatfree major third as the strongest formant of harmonic relations, one cannot possibly contain all these fine and manifold differentiations in one keyboard. Each pure major third generates in the middle of the space of the minor sixth a pitch that can be materialized only by two different tones, and tuning nuances affect the melodic quality of each tone.

The problem is particularly acute on keyboard instruments on which each pitch is rigidly fixed beyond the player's control. A practical solution is somewhat easier to achieve on all instruments which permit the player to adjust a pitch by his finger or breath, but the theoretic difficulty remains. A violinist, for example, guides the leading tone very close to its resolution (that is, the major third to the fourth, and the major seventh to the octave). He will also distinguish between the major and minor wholetones, perhaps without intellectual control. Equally strong is the impact on a stable sound, which to us means the triad. The main issue in the major triad is the consonance of the third, of which the relations to root and fifth are precisely regulated. A major triad achieves stability only when the third reaches its highest degree of consonance. The minor triad has a different problem. In spite of a carefully "felt"

163

third, there is no harmonic unity because the structural qualities do not exist in the overtone series. A minor triad can even sound terribly false if, for example, one pulls a reed stop in the pedal, let us say a 16' fagotto, for Bach's Dorian Organ Toccata.[186] The contra-D_1 in the final chord contains in its overtone series a powerful major third (f^0-sharp), which clashes badly with the minor third played on the manual. An organist must choose his registers in conformity with the sound and not spoil that final chord by a basic musical blunder. This example should serve to call attention to the many genuine existing problems of sound.

In an ensemble, each player strives toward intonation that produces the best possible total sound, whereby he constantly corrects himself. Strong modulatory deviations must again and again be directed toward the overall tuning. If in traditional music one wants to rely on the modern piano temperament, the piano ought to be present. Otherwise this standard is not applicable, for the directional powers furnished a musician by his feeling and his tonal experience bear no relation whatsoever to a mechanistic tonal principle. The special manner of tuning keyboard instruments relates them exactly to the style of a period.

Let us proceed from modern temperament. The piano of about 1910 offered an equilibrium which, on the one hand, left to the piano sound sufficient tonal charm to remain of aesthetic value and to relate to "music," and which, on the other hand, opened up the development of modern piano music because of the completely equalized temperament. In the course of the nineteenth century, the piano sound had changed to the extent that the old characteristic elements of "wood," rich in overtones, were superseded by a sound marked almost exclusively by octaves. The more or less false intonation in modern tuning of all intervals except the octave fits into the total picture of modern music. From a temperament based on the twelfth root of two and its tonal legalization on the piano, there is a straight and compelling road to the piano pieces by Arnold Schönberg.[187] The borderline lies precisely there: on one side modern music, on the other side early music.

The balance of twelve pitches within an octave commonly used today ignores the relations to the actual norms of consonance. On a keyboard instrument, this is the last waystation in the approach toward a serviceable and practicable compromise for both the player and instrument builder. Because of the impossibility of realizing by way of a keyboard the highly difficult relationships of harmonically refined compositions full of sophisticated modulations, the sterilizing mechanical procedure of evenly dividing the octave offered the last expedient appropriate to the situation. The amorphous material of the twelve pitches was smuggled into musical thought by way of the piano. Most musicians were not even aware of the consequences.

Farther back in the Romantic era, the piano was less competent as regulator. Already the music of Schumann and Brahms is so open to sentiment that a mechanistic tonal experience à la "twelfth root of two" is inadmissible as foundation of music-making. The farther we reach back in the nineteenth century, the more that sterile tuning deteriorates from compromise to inappropriateness. The very name *equally beating temperament* is symptomatic. In the 1830s, Nannette Stein-Streicher, a pupil of Beethoven, added tuning instructions to the pianos built by her company for setting a temperament across the circle of fifths with the help of equally fast beats. This is not the mechanical division of the octave common today! Compared to the fifth a^0-e^1, for instance, the fifth e^1-b^1 beats half as fast again in modern tuning whereas neighboring fifths in equally beating temperament ought to beat in the relation 2:3. This mathematically inexact tuning contained residues of an older practice. Such approximate tunings were intended solely for the pianoforte. The organ no longer participated.

Reaching farther back into the past, we find a typical tuning principle at the end of the eighteenth century. The music of that period absolutely demanded a consistent sound, adequate for the form and texture of the composition. Keyboard instruments, by nature incapable of responding to these desired conditions, were shunted into a practice of variedly qualified keys, some of which for reasons of physics contain noticeably and sometimes even acutely distorted intervals. This specification caused by keyboard instruments also serves characterization and marks keys also in ensemble forms. As the result of all these conditions, the tuning that prevailed (meantone) was a compromise based on some distribution (not always a subtle one) of the syntonic comma within the space of the major third C to E. The procedure yields several strongly favored keys but also a set of more or less distorted keys. No key is absolutely unbearable, but many improvements remained desirable. Well documented by Bach's pupil Kirnberger, this kind of tuning still shows in the manner in which Mozart assigned characterizations to the various keys according to their tonal qualities. Schubert's sensitive choice of keys is best attested to by his song cycles, which move within the inherited aesthetic norms.

Kirnberger reports several tuning procedures popular in the first half of the eighteenth century. The so-called Kirnberger III formulation allegedly presents Bach's system in the last years of his life.[188] In these areas, opinions clashed. Bach's repeated arguments with Gottfried Silbermann are known. The latter clung to certain meantone chords which prompted Bach always to play some real "wolves," thus feeding Silbermann's irritation. ("Wolves" are chords with reversely disposed thirds. The worst of all wolves is the triad F#-B♭-C#, in which B-flat lies intolerably high, having originated in meantone temperament where it was tuned as the lower third of D. An A-sharp was never tuned.) Kirnberger III is important for us because it is intimately connected with Bach's music practice, thus exhibiting a regulation valid also for us. In all such minimally differentiated procedures, each key has a particular character.

Slightly earlier than the Kirnberger tuning is one by Werckmeister. Kepler, as a mathematician, also developed a temperament. One pushed the badly sounding keys back and forth like an Old Maid or Black Peter in a card game, knowing full well that a keyboard instrument had to pay for the mitigation of a bad sound in one key by turbidity in other keys. The entire eighteenth century experimented with various recipes for such very subtle balancing. From this viewpoint, one understands that Bach permitted nobody to tune his personal harpsichord.

The first two thirds of the seventeenth century and the entire sixteenth century were dominated by meantone tuning. This temperament expresses a different attitude. One aimed at beatless major thirds, for which purpose the tonal field of action of keyboard instruments was radically reduced. When such restriction becomes unfeasible for the instrument and its use, one resorts to auxiliary construction devices rather than sacrificing the principle of the beat-free third. Double key positions are introduced. Ambitious thoroughbass positives of that period all have at least two key positions in double arrangement. One constructed double upper keys for D#-E♭ and G#-A♭, and for increased precision sometimes also for A#-B♭ and even C#-D♭. The acceptance in return of distorted fifths, worse than in our modern temperament, shows the primary concern for the third. One century earlier, the third had still been a kind of half-consonance; and, earlier still, it had taken its place among the dissonances! One must remember these facts to appreciate properly the arrival of meantone tuning. A little swindle occurs already around 1640. When there was no way of building double keys (or double pipes, channels, and tracker elements), one tuned a pitch halfway between G#-A♭ and D#-E♭. These relative thirds rattle worse than the ones in modern temperament. By adjusting on the f^1 key the discrepancy of the fifths between b^0-flat and c^2, the solution does not destroy the general character of meantone temperament.

For the proper understanding of this whole musical era, one must think of the tonal radius of action of the compositions. The cappella is engaged in church modes and their transpositions, including chiavette. To these conditions, positives and regals and also the spinet types had had to subordinate themselves (and when the discrepancies became intolerable, the organist simply omitted the third). For such reasons, a keyboard instrument cannot establish any contact with works like the fifth and sixth volumes of the Gesualdo madrigals.[189] One did not count on the participation of such instruments. Here gambas, recorders, and lutes played along.

The introduction of meantone tuning on keyboard instruments is difficult to date. Investigating Palestrina's motets in regard to their harmonic content, one finds that this music adheres to meantone temperament. In Josquin's works, too, many compositions treat the third in an advanced fashion. Time always passes before a principle of composition is recognized, understood, and applied by a craft like tuning a keyboard.

I have no data covering the change in instrument construction away from the still older Pythagorean tuning. The musical situation makes one recognize the start of new viewpoints. As long as the keyboard shows exclusively diatonic positions with only one variable pitch — the upper key B-flat — one can manage well with a beatfree circle of fifths. This is Pythagorean tuning given for the portative and also the early *positif de table*.[190] It served as a first method in the development of leading-tone material in the Church modes. The tuning is simple: one proceeded from *ut* (c^1) in beatfree fifths in both directions, occasionally favoring the sharp side.

All these historic tunings discussed thus far have a bearing on keyboard construction. The layout of the low octave is especially illuminating, for it permits one to draw conclusions concerning the tuning procedure on a particular instrument. If the great bass octave is "short," that is, traditionally diatonic with B and B-flat as the only variables, then we identify tuning in pure fifths. Split keys at G#-A♭ and D#-E♭ confirm the fact. If, however, the bass octave increases its capacity by splitting the upper keys D-F# and E-G# (the principle of ravalement), then one of the Kirnberger tunings is in order. The appearance of the tones c^0#, d^0#, f^0#, and g^0# only in the small octave indicates that one did not count on these four pitches as roots. The "broken" octave shows a gradual move toward full chromaticism in the great octave, a contemporary practice with the Kirnberger tunings. A fully chromatic bass octave in the original organ proves that the principle of contracting fifths to avoid the syntonic comma (C-E or F-A) has been abandoned.

The discant end of the keyboard also obeys certain norms. An organ with a^2 as its highest tone points to the sixteenth century. For a long period, c^3 then sets the upper limit. Only after 1800 does d^3 assert itself. The rich aliquot sonority of the organ is missing in harpsichords and hammer pianofortes. At the turn toward the nineteenth century, hammer pianofortes in particular then drastically break through the long-accustomed upper confines.

Tuning problems pertaining to a musical style are tied to keyboard instruments. All efforts concerning historic tunings implicate the favored sonorities of the major third. One must bear in mind that thirds exhibit penetrant tonal relationships: they represent the sex (major or minor) and act as dynamic carriers of leading-tone tendencies. Did organ and harpsichord builders consider the particular structure of the triad and hence the exact ratio of the major third before music theory (which generally limps behind) recognized and defined the phenomenon?

The presence of double keys for G-sharp and A-flat as early as 1470 in the frequently mentioned rood-loft organ in San Petronio demonstrates the crux of all tuning procedures — the optimal tuning of the major third. Instruments playing with the cappella needed this double disposition and, at an early time, also the differentiation of D-sharp and E-flat. (Raise A-flat below C, and adjust D-sharp to B.) Sometimes the keys B-flat and A-sharp were also split. The complication of double keys (and double mechanical elements, channels, and pipes) affected only positives, that is choir organs playing along with the cappella. Organs in large halls had only C-sharp, E-flat, F-sharp, G-sharp, B-flat; the organist knew which harmonic risks he could take. This arrangement was followed until the death of Schütz.

Harpsichords were tuned analogously to organs. One tried to keep the resonating soundboards as narrow as possible, for excessive width causes warps and cracks. The extension or *ravalement* of harpsichords results from crowding too many tone positions into a width too tight for it. On harpsichords, meantone temperament could be handled much more easily than on organs: harpsichord players know how to use the tuning key, and critical pitches could be retuned in a few minutes. The instrument could therefore dispense with split keys. (For split keys on *ravalement* instruments, see pp. 96 and 109 above.)

The problem of split keys was a burden to instrument builders. Consequently, one obtained a halfway tolerable interpretation from a one-sidedly oriented scale. All subsequent temperaments dilute the sonority of the third. Modern keyboard instruments adjust the intervals by falsifying all except the octave. Tuners discuss the varying practices of distributing beats in the circle of fifths but cannot reconcile the results with the sound of a pure third. The current compromise of equal temperament has extinguished the individual character of tonalities while also making all tonalities accessible by way of a keyboard.

In one other regard, meantone tuning differs drastically from modern tuning. It can afford to supply organ pipes with much more wind, thereby considerably strengthening their tonal character. The windways of the organ pipes in Klosterneuburg (1642), to give an example, are almost three times as wide as those in Heiligenkreuz (1803). Kober, the organ builder of Heiligenkreuz, had to reduce rigorously the tonal energy of his pipes. He was one of the first masters to give his organ balanced contracted fifths. Although the tuning was not absolutely levelled and some keys had purer thirds than others, he yet had to diminish the energy level radically. The third remains the central problem. In 1947, the organ in Klosterneuburg received a modern temperament; the thirds have an ugly rattle, and the instrument sounds brutal. (A current restoration has set itself the central task of regaining meantone temperament.) It was in order to mitigate the harshness of the thirds that Kober mercilessly throttled the air in the windways. Harpsichords, too, suffer from modern temperament. Tonal blend and structured sonority demand pure intervals.

Absolute pitch has been sufficiently documented. We know well the pitch standard of the recorder groups in the Este collection and from Ambras Castle in the Vienna Kunsthistorisches Museum (the largest unified collection of historic instruments, besides the original music). The collection establishes the cornett tone. The low French pitch is equally determined. Bach's organ in St. Thomas stood at 415 Hz; in St. Nicolai, a wholetone higher. The organs of the Vienna classical period were just slightly lower than the cornett tone (in Eisenstadt, the cathedral once offered 452 Hz, similarly the Barmherzige Brüder and the Esterházy palace). Until the First World War, the Paris a^2 at 435 Hz was generally valid; since then the pitch has been raised to 440 Hz and today even to 443 Hz. Because absolute pitch greatly affects the sound of strings, the higher pitch promotes a sensuous, overly excited, radiant tone. For more about it, see p. 134.

Practically one learns tuning best at a harpsichord, for one deals with only single strings. The pegs, moreover, are not so tight as to require much force. The tuning key must be put in place with great care in order not to dull the edges of the pegs. It is advisable to tune first the $8'$ which lies far from the bridge; follow with the second $8'$ and the $4'$.

To learn historic tunings, begin with meantone temperament. It is the easiest to achieve and produces poignant sonorities. Tune a^1 and then all other A pitches (it is good always to have something ready for comparison in case the initial a^1 swims away). Then pull up f^1 until the third is free of beats. Next tune f^0 (pure) and then two fifths upward, c^1 and g^1, which retain beats (of the fifths, both too small, the lower beats to the higher in the ratio 2:3). From g^1 one takes the lower octave g^0 (pure) and then again two narrow fifths upward as before (g^0-d^1-a^1). The result has to agree with the initial a^1 (the syntonic comma is thus divided among four fifths). Once this circle of fifths has been well distributed, one proceeds by beatless major thirds: g^0-b^0, a^0-c^1#, d^1 down to b^0-flat, up again c^1-e^1, d^1-f^1#, e^1-g^1#, and g^1 down to eb^1. If a^1-flat is used instead of g^1-sharp, one tunes it as a lower major third of c^2; similarly, an occasional d^1-sharp as upper major third of b^0. Finally one tunes pure octaves across the whole keyboard.

We have already mentioned the method of balancing D$^\#$-E^b and G$^\#$-A^b. (The division of the ninth b^0-flat to c^2 by f^1 follows the general division procedure according to which the upper interval always beats more quickly. For fifths, the relation is 2:3; for thirds, about 5:6.)

The Kirnberger III temperament is also based on a circle of four meantone fifths, here compressed into the beatless third C-E. The syntonic comma is distributed among c^1-g^1-d^2 (then a pure octave down to d^1)-a^1-e^2.

With Kirnberger, one begins with the meantone fifth a^1-e^2 (it helps to have acquired some experience with the circle of four fifths in meantone temperament). From that e^2 one finds a pure e^1 and then, equally without beats, c^1. There begins the strongly beating sequence of fifths as described. Then follow beatless fifths: E-B-F$^\#$ and downward C-F-B^b-

E^b-A^b-D^b. The return with the insertion of exactly pure octaves is not especially mentioned. One must try to execute the tuning within the space of one and one-half octaves, otherwise the discrepancies from getting our ears adjusted to the setting of compressed fifths become too noticeable. Practically one remains within the tonal space g^0 to e^2. Here, too, our ears function with optimal acuteness. This temperament yields sharp characterization of keys! One has to realize this fact when choosing this tuning.

From experience I recommend one other tuning more easily mastered and offering a résumé of the tonal specifics of historic tunings. Proceeding from a^1 (in accordance with the participating instruments varying from an occasional 416 Hz of old recorders to 455 Hz of the *cornett* pitch), one pulls f^1 up to a consonant major third without beats before letting it drop slightly to about one and one-half beats per second. This cautious dilution of the purity leaves the character of the third intact. Now distribute the syntonic comma as well as possible in the circle of fifths f^0-c^1-g^0-d^1-a^1 (neighboring fifths beat as 2:3!). Then set upper thirds enlarged by approximately one and one-half beats: e^1 to c^1, b^0 to g^0; and the lower third b^0-flat to d^1. Then turn the thirds bb^0-d^1, c^1-e^1, f^1-a^1 and g^0-b^0 downward into sixth and divide these into two major thirds (spoiling by beats to a lesser degree the musically more important third). In tuning a harpsichord, a reorientation of G-sharp, for instance, up to A-flat (as lower third from C) is possible for brief periods. One adjusts to the pieces to be played. Acquaintance with this summarily practiced tuning procedure will facilitate the mastery of special tunings required by a particular musical style.

CHAPTER VIII

Bach's *Magnificat* Ad Exemplum

The following comments concerning a superior masterwork of old music, Bach's *Magnificat*, address narrowly circumscribed style problems. Anyone submerging himself in a master work, analyzing its structures, studying the performance practice, and knowing the instrumentarium is likely to arrive at a realization of the music not much different from the plan here submitted. Each concerned conductor who prospects deeply and honestly has the right to devise an optimal plan based on his own insight. There is greater satisfaction in exploring the terrain by oneself and arriving at a goal than in observing a dictated schedule. In this sense, the following suggestions should be read. They merely want to show what has to be known and thought through *before* the decision to start rehearsals for a work.

We have two versions of Bach's *Magnificat*. The one in E-flat provides between the Latin verses of the canticum a series of inserts which fashion the situation of Christmas in German and with the usual means of Bach cantatas. (The choice of this version is extremely attractive for a Christmas performance of the *Magnificat*, particularly in a liturgical setting.) The second version restricts itself to the Latin verses and exists in a careful score (the same watermarks in the paper as in the B-minor Mass, an intimate kindred of the *Magnificat*). The marvelous compactness of the work reveals itself fully in this version, which is almost always preferred. It underlies our discussion.

173

The twelve sections follow an overall plan. At the beginning, there is a concerto of all summoned means. It corresponds to the big first allegro of Bach concertos. Five-part vocal chorus, strings, woodwinds, and the trumpet-timpani unit compete with each other in a brilliant "concertare" of the single groups. This fact alone stresses the importance of good tonal balance between the groups! They must be correctly sized in advance. It would be improper simply to engage a symphony orchestra and a large choir, accept the usual distribution, and rehearse the ensemble according to the conventions of about 1920. One must rather carefully select the smallest possible vocal ensemble from a larger chorus; one tries out the number of flutes, oboes, and bassoons to balance the chorus; and one chooses the number of strings accordingly. The three trumpets will always produce the effect of emphatic prominence (a graphic comparison, as in a charcoal drawing on tinted paper, where the lights are rendered prominent by chalk; this graphic technique seems to me analogous to problems of performance technique!). If the trumpets sting too badly, one has to think of a solution. We once hung strips of rugs from the trumpet stands down to the floor—they helped. With such devices one can build a whole tub around the trumpeters! They nevertheless deserve to be resplendent. The energy quotient of trumpets and timpani just is very high. Old, preferably small kettledrums must be found, otherwise the trumpets hang in the air. Beaten with the classic bare wooden stick, the timpani supply the trumpets with the real "bass" sound. Once the arrangements for the first movement have been properly made, the decisions for the other movements fall into place. Optimal in my experience are four singers to each choral part; they provide all the necessary transparency and cleanliness of the lines. This vocal ensemble (including the soloists) stands at the edge of the podium or at the choir parapet in a performance in church (which should actually be a matter of course). To this core of the *Magnificat* ensemble we added doubled transverse flutes, doubled oboes and bassoons, two stands each of first and second violins, two violas, two violoncelli, a five-string bass viol perhaps joined by a small bass, and finally an organ positive. In the absence of secco recitatives, harpsichord participation is not directly required but attractive in some pieces like "Esurientes." These details define the total cast. We shall confront just one vocal difficulty in "Et misericordia" (see below).

Back to the first movement. Jubilant scales, heavily accented exclamations, continuous motion in an everpresent triple meter constitute the instrumental opening, just as if an instrumental concerto were to begin. This explicitly "splendid" music-making is joined by the voices, always in clear arrays to be carefully observed by the conductor: first two sopranos, then alto plus tenor (cf. also "Esurientes"), and finally in addition the bass. At the very entrance of alto and tenor, one wishes for a male alto in justice to the given pitch range. Low female altos misrepresent the range, for they must appear "above" the tenor with an extremely high pitch character. The best disposition involves mezzosopranos and a falsetto tenor. This situation is constantly present throughout the first movement and therefore requires a fundamental, genuine solution. Later the voices withdraw to let an instrumental postlude close the movement. With the D-trumpets, Bach accepts a tonal handicap into the bargain. Considering that the trumpets supply him only the diatonic material of D major, one is amused to watch him nevertheless accomplish the modulations necessary for the generation of the form. The counterplay of the various groups — voices and instrumental choirs — must be lively, for then only does the movement become realized through vital music-making. The bassoons must guarantee the very active bass line. The part for the five-string bass viol must be written out deprived of coloration. The bass-viol players do not eliminate anything on their own, for their present superior technique permits them to play all notes of this movement; but it does not sound, a busy rasping dominates! The conductor must therefore prepare a well thought-through, concrete bass part. The tempo of the piece is determined by the trumpeters whose difficult part sounds natural and festive only at a tempo exactly adapted to the embouchure of the trumpets. Depending on the trumpeters' skill, the quarter lies around M.M.90 or a bit higher. Resonance conditions will also influence the tempo.

After the initial "concerto," one needs a pause of a few heartbeats, no more. If one tears the *Magnificat* apart by cesuras, the relations from movement to movement disappear and the composition loses the dimension of the large form (one can truly dispense with the exercise "chorus get up — chorus sit down"). As in the B-minor Mass, five soloists are needed in the *Magnificat*. At one time, the section leaders concertized and sang the solo parts. In addition to the alto, anyway, two solo sopranos are required in "Suscepit Israel." To set up a solo quartet in which soprano and alto conveniently divide up the mezzosoprano sections — this should no longer happen, for the attitudes of the two vocal parts differ and demand the variety prescribed by Bach.

The following aria, "Et exultavit," is in 3/8 meter, which signifies *proportio tripla* notated in tablature tradition. To keep the movement from running away, a few subtle details of phrasing in the first-violin part in measures 3 and 4 prevent hustling. I call attention to the hemiola of measures 10-11 (count quarters), all the more so as it involves all parts. The instrumental ritornello must receive its proper tutti weight and exhibit the joyfulness of the music. I further recommend a return to the old convention of interpreting Bach's indications of *forte* and *piano* not so much as a modern dynamic command but rather as a sign for the ripieno players to participate or to pause. The clarity of the lines would suffer badly if three stands of violinists (or even more) are sentenced to tickling their instruments in order to avoid covering a soloist. The old practice of letting the ripieno players pause at *piano* is more effective. This procedure, moreover, clarifies the outline of the form! If the concertmaster (or his stand) remains alone, the musical situation of the solo episodes thus created can be fully realized in the manner of a Vivaldi concerto with the spirit of chamber music yet with full force of the performers.

"Et exultavit" is a motto aria like most arias by Bach of that period. The bass line requires special attention. For the ripieno sections, the conductor must again write out a bass-viol part deprived of coloration (this concerns only the ritonelli!). The complete text as notated by Bach may be given to the violoncello and perhaps one bassoon. I preferred to restrict myself to the bassoon in the solo episodes and to add the bass viol in the ritornelli. Such organization of the musical substance projects almost by itself the form and delivery. (At the end of the aria, the solo soprano is not to be granted a special ritardando. A moderate tenuto suffices but not a ritardando foreign to the style and inimical to the form; otherwise the final ritornello becomes separated from the main structure.)

After a pause as long as at the beginning of the aria, one of the subtlest and most difficult movements of the *Magnificat* follows, which conductors must liberate from a wrong tradition. "Quia respexit" with "Omnes generationes" attached to it are comparable to a "prelude and fugue." These two sections form a whole! The movement begins with a kind of ritornello without tutti character. Thoroughbass and the first oboe d'amore alone carry the formal element. The choice of meter and tempo is decisive. It is not the oboe part that helps one find the tempo, but the bass line! The latter shows absolutely without doubt only two accents per measure. In this adagio, the *half* note is the value on which the meter is built! Mary's text relates entirely to her person, "for He has seen the humility of His maid." This text can be shared only by *one* solo instrument, given to only *one* oboe d'amore. The oboist has to adjust himself to not more than two accents, two stresses within each measure — and even these swim away in ties. The oboe begins the movement with fully notated diminutions. To give an intelligible analogy: the deep bow from d^2 to e^1 in the first phrase is repeated again and again, bending down and rising up, until the ritornello ends within a^2 and b^0, the last bow with the following humble rise. Somebody will say that this is thick, sentimental romanticism! In our intellectually dehumanized time, I shall gladly pocket this criticism and claim that such a declarative gesture dwells in every note written by a master. The whole baroque doctrine of affections is exclusively directed at the intensification of a characteristic expression. Precisely the success or failure of such expression distances a masterwork from convention. Not that such attempts at a "speaking" expression alone could account for the quality of a superior composition! The greatness appears in the unification of all artistic dimensions. The comments stemming from my analogy seem appropriate because they help liberate a piece by Bach from a faulty tradition of yesteryear. The tempo seems right at the old *tactus integer valor* (half note = M.M. 52). The bassoon joins the continuo positive for the bass line in a most carefully apportioned *stile francese*. Then the soprano enters, presenting the first text phrase according to the principle of a motto aria. Voice, oboe, and thoroughbass make the music flow in intent coordination and without any painful counting (this aria is usually offered in an 8/8 count and thereby becomes isolated from the following big tutti!). In measure 18, this section ends. With "Ecce enim" a thematic counterfigure begins, and in the eighth measure the closing word of the soprano gives way to "omnes generationes." Here there is no change of tempo, no trace of a cesura, no ritardando, but only the shift from counting halves to counting quarters (quarternote = M.M. 104). A grand tutti (without the trumpets which would not fit the affect) broadly fills the measures, climbing up the scale on "omnes" until the big concentration on C-sharp, the brief organpoint, and the fermata (mm. 21-24). The exalted voices then cannot get away from their quasi C-sharp major. While they persist, the bass group enters one measure too soon, as it were, calling the tutti back to the tonic F-sharp minor. After this movement, the cesura may be a bit longer.

Again in the spirit of baroque affection theory, "Quia fecit" is given to a bass (as is "Quoniam" in the doxology of the B-minor Mass). This aria begins with a two-voice organ ritornello. A rugged thrumming by all violoncelli, bassoons, and bass viol, together with a lost, cheap harmonization on the organ, would be out of place. Every aria in Vivaldi concerto form sets in the ritornello a musically satisfying situation. Therefore my organists have always tried to turn this aria into a small improvised organ concerto. The old positives and the brief pauses make it easy to eliminate a 4′ register and even a 2′ diapason before the entrance of the solo bass; the handles for the stops lie directly next to the keyboard, permitting an elegant change. The thoroughbass line is best entrusted to a bassoon. The bass soloist must not rattle single sixteenth notes (an Ochs von Lerchenau is here unwanted!). It is again a motto aria; the solo bass should attempt to leave his calling card in measure 5 in the most civilized manner. The tempo of the bass aria is the same as that of "Omnes generationes."

The sonority of the next movement, "Et misericordia," changes totally to an almost sophisticated modern mixture of muted strings and deep gentle transverse flutes. The pause between "Quia fecit" and this movement should be just long enough to let the pathos of the A-major aria die away before beginning the siciliano quietly on the minor dominant. The corresponding movement in the B-minor Mass is "Et in spiritum." One may set only the four mild accents and certainly not beat out twelve eights. If this duet has been well rehearsed, minimal conducting signs will be required. All the conductor need do is concentrate at the beginning on the establishment of the exactly fitting tempo and then to maintain the flow of the movement! Rhythm and meter in this piece deserve a few comments. The tie from the first to second measures robs both voices in the second measure of the initial stress (no false squeezing in the tie!). The situation in the next measure is the same. Bach's notation calls for very cautious accentuation. The strings must merely surrender to Bach's phrasing in order to obtain the desired result. The entry of the voices introduces a difficulty. If a low female voice sings the alto part, the tenor sounds like an "upper voice," and the pitch registers become doubtful. In the *Magnificat*, an overbred "perfumed" male alto is unbearable; but a fine, loose tenor with a high falsetto fits as upper part and contrast much better to the more rugged lower tenor. All participants must be warned in rehearsals never to squeeze the syncopations. After the first "timentibus," the closing tone b^1 of the first violin

(m. 17) turns in the next instance in the alto into the minor ninth b^1-flat (in the dominant chord), arriving a dotted quarter too early. The harmonic event is weighty. At this and corresponding places, exaggerated vocal engagement is inappropriate. For all such situations of a madrigalesque affect, Bach's genius spontaneously finds the proper musical means. This duet, too, remains in the schematic form of a Vivaldi concerto.

"Fecit potentiam" requires the full involvement of all means. The piece is carried by a characteristic moving bass which metrically never changes until the general pause at the end. Its course leads in each case across four measures, always from the tonic descending through a passing seventh to the sixth as the tonic relative. The exactness of the four-measure ostinato is not absolute and adjusts itself to the overall occurrences. A performance must project this foundation very clearly, otherwise a structural element is lost, as if the ostinato bass in a chaconne were ignored. For this bass line, I always utilized all means. The five-string bass viol plays only the eighth notes; the violoncelli and bassoons, everything. To the bass-viol entrance, I also added the organ pedal, not to manifest "pedal playing" but to mark the first and third quarters. It suits the bass to play this music *grave* in a kind of *stile francese*. The underlying pulse is M.M. 52 for the halfnote. Above this foundation, always clearly present as carrier, as norm, as motor impulse, lies a tutti entrance after the beat, out of which the tenor extricates its fugue entry. Each subsequent entry is accompanied by a fresh strong accent of the tutti. When all voices have entered after twenty measures, trumpet and transverse flutes play a last *comes*. Then follows a dissolution of the fugue theme into metric motion with the grandiose interpretation of "dispersit," everything carried by the bass foundation until "superbos," which breaks off abruptly (let only a little tenuto flow into the general pause), and onward to "mente cordis sui." Now count only halves! The notes, however, retain their value! Already the first syncopation shows that only halves can act as units of the motion. In this sole main meter, the movement ends with the descending trumpet fanfare, shifting to the large meter of the two wholenotes in the penultimate and last measures. By observing this organization, one projects the large form and the particular quality of the movement in which ostinato arrangement and fugue join.

Unfortunately, most performances let the fugue whir through its course, approaching caricature with choirs that are too large. Then follows often a bombastically stretched ending in bad theatrics. After this piece, a brief pause is permissible.

A notated *stile francese* prevails in "Deposuit." One best leans only on the main accent of the downbeat. The bowed thoroughbass must not lapse into a mechanistic motor drive of continuous nonlegato. The dotted quarter in the second measure must in no case be separated from the following sixteenth notes. The dotted value of the note must be treated analogously to that of the first violins in the first measure, of which the descending détaché run is tightly joined to $f\#^2$. The energetic bows carry the affect contents of this tenor aria. In measures 9, 10, and 11, the continuo shows that it is structured by whole measures. If in the initial ritornello one has clarified this feature in the violin unison, the tenor adjusts more easily to the model. At the entry of the singer, the concertmaster's stand should again be by itself. The violin of the concertmaster and possibly also of the player beside him are then capable of continuing the full intensity of the energetic violin entrance without covering the singer. One cannot bend the material of the violin scales in piano punctiliousness without derailing its expression. From beginning to end, "Deposuit" is a piece under high tension with forte behavior. One achieves balance with the singer by letting the ripieno pause. The legato formulas of the ascending "exaltavit" supply the contrast. As in the initial ritornello, themes of precipitation and of sudden falls are combined with climbs up to heights that cannot be maintained, until a kind of violin glissando brushes away the last remnant of resistance.

After a brief exhaling in the wake of the excitement of this energy-charged tenor aria, a singularly joyful piece follows, the flutes spreading a special basic quality generally reserved for a siciliano. "Esurientes" thus provides steep contrast to the tenor aria, with a charm it must never lose. The pizzicato contra-E_1 at the very end must be like a smile. The piece must never be degraded by roughness, the characteristic syncopations at the very beginning of the flute parts must be performed without squeezing the tie. The sixteenth note after each dot is best slurred. In this graceful alto aria with transverse flutes, we used several times a harpsichord as continuo instrument because it puts the sound of the flutes in better relief. The rests in the thoroughbass after each beat, in particular, lose the problem of their actual length. Sustained quarter-note chords on the positive produce a tough dough; eighth notes on the positive followed by a rest result in the extreme rendition of a dance piece.

With a harpsichord, one escapes these problems. For the thoroughbass the two flutes demand a violoncello and, if available, the small bass viol. The latter is needed only for the ritornelli in order to lend them their own dimension. *Tempo ordinario* is appropriate (the quarter note at M.M. 72). It permits the flutes to exhibit the subtlest differentiations of legato and all the art of embouchure. A handsome mezzosoprano with some low notes is preferable to a ponderous alto. Similarly, the movement can gain much from a clever harpsichordist. At the end of the voice part, a kind of tenuto or ritardando is realized by the composition. Here one might permit the singer to take leave with a discreet tenuto before the joyful ritornello reappears and then vanishes in the bass pizzicato. (Letting the singer of an aria end his part with a broad cadence has always appeared to me as exaggerating the value of the vocal part. Occasionally one senses Bach's approval. The stereotyped closing ritardandi by singers, who thereby sever the final ritornello, indicate bad behavior arising from insufficient reflection.)

The following chorale arrangement is burdened by an erroneous tradition which does not recognize the orientation of the piece by whole measures! In a sense, the end of the work is here prefigured by the quotation of the Luther version of the Magnificat for congregational singing. The oboes blow victoriously the "German Magnificat" in the *tonus peregrinus*. Every Protestant knew this melody. Bach needed only to expose the cantus firmus in order to evoke in every listener the association: "My soul magnifies the Lord, and my spirit rejoices in God, my Savior." Consider the rest of the cast: three boys' voices; bassoons and bass viol tacent! The violoncelli lie in the small octave and the one above it, reaching as high as a^1! Each bass function, each bass weight is eliminated. There is no ritornello, hence formally a "chorale arrangement." The boys begin ascending and descending, "Suscepit Israel puerum suum." Then the oboes enter in the tutti with the cantus firmus. The meter of the piece derives from the cantus firmus. Bach chose not a 3/8 meter, the sign of *proportio tripla*, but the 3/4 meter. Hence one must move at the lowest limit of a metric whole, here facilitated by the cantus firmus. The dotted halfnote at M.M. 50 should work. A careful positive continuo joins. Inspecting the facts, anybody knowing the Bible notices that Bach here composed a particular scene of significant relation to the *Magnificat*. It is the visit of three youths in Abraham's tent. He recognizes them as angels and receives from them the promise of the Messiah. The chorale arrangement concludes completely outside the tonality compass of the *Magnificat* in B major! An unreal picture vanishes. These details suffice for the performance of this movement.

And now the finale of the *Magnificat* is built up. In the main key of D major, the cappella fugue begins, "Sicut locutus est ad patres nostros, Abraham et semini ejus in saecula." The large meter is retained, transformed from *proportio sesquialtera* into duple measure. The bass, eliminated in the preceding piece to dispossess it of all earthly heaviness, is now pronouncedly present. It would be best if one could conduct whole measures! One will have to resort to alla-breve beats (I have heard this fugue with quarters beaten out!). The soprano ties at the end of the fugue show clearly that *whole* notes set the pulse of the motion.

I consider the fugue the beginning of the finale because of the reappearance of the tonic. The finale consists quasi of several movements. The last words of the *Magnificat* are subito followed by the lesser doxology, "Gloria Patri." Again the tempo is the same; one must merely shift at 1:2. The glory of the Trinity is again grandly set to music. The tutti beginning has no trumpets (as if the music of earthly emperors and kings meant nothing). In performances, we have always coated the note values of the first measure in the "French" manner; thus the eighth-note triplets are easily conjoined. These triplets ascend, not clumsily and laboriously, but arising from the *tasto solo A*, gaining ever greater heights, stretching (again French) the cadential tension above the temporarily concluding five-six chord of the second dominant, and closing on the dominant. The second section of the doxology follows subito: "Gloria Filio." The music proceeds from the dominant (again the *tasto solo* organpoint) and spreads in this E-major space, aiming at a tonic position driven still farther by modulation. The tonic appears in minor in the relative of the main key of the *Magnificat*. In the second section of the doxology, the same triplet scales interweave at different pitch ranges. The third section, "Gloria et Spiritui sancto," comes from high pitches and reverses the triplet theme in contrary motion, sinking down from soprano to bass. The complete trumpet-timpani group is drawn into the last tutti entrance. The cadence lands on the fermata on the dominant, followed closely by a reminiscence of the *Magnificat* beginning. In the third measure, the first voice pair enters, alto and tenor. To the two initial four-measure groups (same bass), eight further measures are attached in which the basses, descending a wide space by thirds, arrive at the final tonic. The seven measures of the actual close quote at first the beginning of the *Magnificat*. Then the bustling tumult catches the bass group and reaches the end with amassed strength. The final stretto on "Sicut erat" is not a da capo but a compact intensified reprise ingeniously compressed into the smallest space.

This abbreviated reprise stands in a kind of *proportio sesquialtera* relation to the "Gloria Patri" sections. These sections, in turn, derive their tempo relations from the chorale arrangement. The tempo at the beginning of the *Magnificat* obviously corresponds exactly to that of the closing section. A metric order is therewith encoded which embraces a large portion of the work. I am not suggesting a mechanical computing of tempi by precise metronome numbers. What always matters are large-scale orders which do not tolerate millimeter measuring tapes, neither in the rhythms of the music nor in the interrelationship of the tempi.

Looking at the whole work, one recognizes the many connections and also the compactness of the form. In the arias, Vivaldi concerto form dominates exclusively. This formal scheme is also valid for the overall structure of the *Magnificat*. Tutti and solo sections alternate. In this sense one can also understand the closing reprise. (Anyone denying an overall structure to the B-minor Mass ignores Bach's recovery of the central passage of the doxology: "Gratias" and "Dona nobis" are identical. In the *Magnificat* the cohesive frame is produced by the abbreviated reprise of the beginning. The High Mass and the *Magnificat* are deeply related!)

These comments on the *Magnificat* obviously offer only a rough survey. A conductor must pursue many further investigations, extending from the cast, the phrasing, past the continuo (which, after all, sets new problems for each performance) up to a harmonic analysis, the determination of the "fall" of the events, and the actual analysis of each compositional feature. This cannot be done within the framework of this book.

Perhaps, however, this book may cause one or the other conductor to become thoughtful, to begin an investigation on his own, and to repudiate false conventions. If one must witness over and again how the study of a work begins with the playing of a more or less good phonograph record, and how such prepackaged solutions of challenges to be personally mastered are tolerated (such a phonograph model can be falsified by a few tricks to fake a "personal note"), then a musician recognizes all the more clearly the absolute necessity of studying a masterwork thoroughly. Only devotion entitles a conductor to think of performing a work!

APPENDIX

Summary of Historic
Consonance Theory

All musical material, all musical relations, considered from the standpoint of physics, are mathematical phenomena. They can be defined by numbers. The sense of hearing enables man to experience quantities spontaneously as qualities.

We know that the ancient Greeks tried to clarify musical phenomena. In their search for a system and for recognition of an underlying principle, they found an experimental tool in the monochord. Here we have a unique precedent: tone experiences become measurable and controllable as string lengths and extensions. Mathematical proportions become spontaneously experienced sound. This transfer between the categories of quality and quantity occurs through no other sense organ with such direct precision and insistence. The concept of quantity does not lie in a continuum of values; its nature is not linear but rather develops as a discontinuum, as a "structure." If the musical relations and orders are replaced by a sliding method and changed into a continuum, the quality of musical experience disappears.

Musical activity, spontaneous experience, and quality existed before experimental confirmation; and therefore a significant investigation succeeds in revealing a fundamental insight. Thinning the continuum of multiples, known to us as the overtone series, by eliminating ekmelic tones, one reaches in a mathematical system known to the ancients the actual order of phenomena acceptable to the senses. The order contains the fundamental values 1, 2, and 3; growth by the sums of these numbers yields 4, 5, and 6; then the next principle of growth by products and powers establishes the mathematical positions 8, 9, 10, 12, 15, and 16. This has been the musical limit of the mathematical order. How it sounds can be read off Table I at the end of this chapter. (Erwin Schrödinger, thoroughly acquainted with ancient Greek culture, said in an Alpbach seminar to my students: "This is Planck's quantum jump.") The ancient Greek knowledge offers a clue to consonance concepts in zones and categories. In "mutation jumps," special areas of consonance become widened. Until today we call intervals derived from 1, 2, and 3 *perfect*; and those derived from the sum, products, and powers of these numbers we designate as major or minor. Stretching or shrinking these imperfect values, we think, respectively, of augmented and diminished intervals.

The starting point in the melodic dimension is the event of rise and fall in tonal space, that is, of pitch. An early aesthetic melodic law is based on the norm of the sine curve, which balances spatial up and down. (Tone as a physical phenomenon presents itself as a sine curve!) With the smallest of the perfect intervals, structures crystallize which govern all scale formations. Center, upper fourth, and lower fourth delimit the melodic sine motion. The fourth subdivided in minor third and wholetone results in anhemitonic pentatonism. By finally securely placing the halftone value, one arrives at Western diatonism. The stations of this development can still be observed today, for the clock indicating cultural phases shows different times everywhere and can be millennia late. Islamic civilization, for instance, has preserved an early condition in glissando, gliding tones which precede the crystallization of our familiar interval concepts. Here the Greek *diastema* means exclusively *tension*. The term assumes its other meaning, *distance*, with the establishment of fixed positions within the various scale systems.

In regard to degree and rank order of consonances, physical-mathematical laws and musical experience fully coincide. With the number 15 (the product of 3 and 5, that is, fifth and third), one reaches the most sensitive position of diatonism. The immediate neighbor is the simplest consonance of the transposed concept 2 (octave). Thereby the dominating law of musical dynamism comes into being, the diatonic leading-tone progression from the most complex to the simplest sounding relationship, the generating force of musical cadence. The law appears anew when related to the scale of the sine curve: it rules the step from the major third to the perfect fourth. Out of these facts arise the old basic scales. Depending on the position of the halftone, the scale is falling, rising, or neutral (named, respectively, dorian, lydian, and phrygian—not to be confused with the Church modes).

It is a fundamental musical procedure of all times to differentiate a few prototypes, archetypes, in countless variations. Musical fantasy alters the types and creates ever new particular cases. Because of preoccupation with that capacity for creative variation within structural musical laws, knowledge of the actual fundamental relationships is often pushed so far into the background and forgotten as to be covered and replaced by technical procedures grown out of a temporal situation. The specialization of today is burdened by its concern with most subtly differentiated details. One glance at the recipes of various kinds of modern music reveals the terribly short life of attempted procedures, whereby honest search and effort are evident. We face such a spread of experimental methods and compositional results that no claims can be made beyond a single case or for a future period. It will be necessary to clarify which contacts and correspondences exist with true human experience. Similar situations existed at moments when, for instance, the traditional culture of antiquity was replaced by early Western music practice. By selection, many beginnings dried up. Periods of cumulative mutation jumps are followed by periods of relentless selection. This natural selection process gives hope for an unperverted future of music.

Harmony, the third musical dimension, is governed by the same laws of physics and of human experience. Harmonic phenomena appear in order: organum consonance, major and minor triads, cadential laws, development of ever more differentiated sounds. They all are phases of the encounter with the fundamental phenomenon. Diverse problems push effectively forward depending on temporal conditions and musical consciousness, and yet a great prevalent tendency characterizes the whole development of Western music. Harmonic cadence draws its energy from the same leading-tone law that brought about scale formations. Even the subtlest particular appearances result from it. The potential of tonal relationships sounding simultaneously is far from exhausted (see Table II with the classical Greek arrangements). In a sense, even the concept of the major seventh is a consonance! As an active organ builder, I am steadily confronted with the task of expressing musical matters in numbers and descriptive geometry. The leading-tone seventh has long been used as a harmonic register (for example, in the restoration in 1942 of the West organ in St. Florian with the seventh 8/15). A genuine tonal law can be realized even with the third of the third (5 × 5 = 25). The ekmelic tone positions in the harmonic series, on the other hand, are of an entirely different nature and can destroy the sound (i.e., the partial tones corresponding to the numbers 7, 11, 13, 14, 17, 19, etc.). Their proximity to consonant points is so close that they make them indistinct. Relating solely to the fundamental, their consonant function is too meager to compensate for their incompetence to create a real contact with the other pitches. The ekmelic tones are the primary dissonance in an absolute negative sense. Writing them with the notes of our system is misleading! Tonal laws as arche-phenomena demand utmost precision. Notating the tone corresponding to the number 7 (a bit below b^1-flat in relation to C) as B-flat, or 11 with F-sharp, is simply wrong. Correcting one's auditory impression of these tones toward the written pitch is impossible, for it would deny their very existence. Ever since the development of various methods for simplifying on a keyboard the playing of pitches actually not realizable on it, one has become accustomed to approximations and commits grave errors in judging fundamental tonal phenomena. Here lie difficult tasks for a future music theory. The historic systems are sketched in the following pages.

In the scales of the music of antiquity, restricted to the two dimensions of rhythm and melos, the "falling" tetrachord prevailed in the dorian mode (on E). The lydian mode (on C) with the ascending leading tone from major third to perfect fourth then easily absorbed the new harmonic dimension and merged with the major mode. The triadic sounding of the tonal relationships here coincides with their gravitational tendencies. The major mode properly marks the cadential positions by its initial point, the two turning points of the curve, and the leading-tone discharge.

The hellenistic period replaces the sine-curve scales by tone rows. The tradition of gliding in the tonal space and the attempt to transcend diatonism by still subtler differentiations lead to experiments with chromatic and enharmonic minimal progressions and to a new systematism. The logic of the ancient scales becomes ever more invisible. The Church modes then establish octave scales; the authentic versions present rows with the fundamental (the finalis) setting a frame. In the plagal versions, one can still recognize the ancient modes with the fundamental in the center, although the octave frame of their range deprives them, too, of the classical logic. Hellenistic and Church modes arose under the growing influence of the slowly developing polyphony. Any harmonic structure presupposes the simultaneity of different yet connected tones and therefore builds in principle an ascending order. This process extinguishes the ancient characterization. The octave scales of the medieval Church modes (rows within an octave frame) jointly with simple harmonies not exceeding the triad lead to the Church modes of the fourteenth to sixteenth centuries (very well characterized in the ricercar collection by Stoltzer around 1520).

The breakthrough to the modern major and minor modes occurs in the works of the great seventeenth-century masters, where it emerges from the logical and exact use of cadential laws. The concept of major manifests itself optimally, because scalar and harmonic forces, uniting in the primacy of "upward" energy, promote each other mutually. The concept of minor remains ambiguous. Zarlino calls the triad *C durum*: C-E-G. Forming *C molle* downward as C-A♭-F, he considers the tone genders in ancient tradition as reciprocal. (Here Riemann hooked up his theory of harmony.) Zarlino ignores the fact that a harmonic downward sound does not exist. The fifth c^1-f^0 formed downward creates as three-dimensional phenomenon a fundamental tone F, thereby directing minor, parallel to major, from the fifth upward. What minor retains is the downward leading-tone tendency of the third, contrary to major. From the compactness of its leading-tone and harmonic structures, the major mode gains absolute superiority from which the minor-mode systems have suffered. The straightening of minor by the logic of major creates, on the other hand, a counterforce and an influx of minor into major (the minor subdominant in major as counterpart to the major dominant in minor).

As early as in the fifteenth century, the significance of the chordal third was notably explored (as in Dunstable's important music). Compared to the fifth 2:3, a third 4:5 or 5:6 shows a much subtler consonance relationship. Later the triad is no longer necessarily treated as a subdivided fifth but constructed of two thirds one above the other. Harmonic laws become ignored as the result of a certain manipulative skill with harmonic elements tolerated by the paper-conditioned, shorthand sloppiness of thoroughbass procedures. The lack of logic stipulates a misbegotten "triad on the seventh degree," which is sheer harmonic nonsense. Common modern harmony texts with cookbook character still have not freed themselves from the grammatically absurd thoroughbass notation. Theories like that by Riemann, on the other hand, remain caught in basic errors and therefore could not prevent a merely mechanical treatment of the difficult problems.

From the beginning of notation we find that musical instinct has time and again used the leading-tone progression, the smallest possible step, as a cadential force. As *subsemitonium modi*, it haunts the music of the fourteenth to sixteenth centuries, where it became the impromptu responsibility of the performer. The stronger the harmonic engagement in developing all possibilities, the more definite the composer's commitment to the former *subsemitonium modi*. The imagination of composers increasingly attempts to involve additional leading-tone energies. In evaluating harmonic tones, composers soon shift the center of gravity to points admitting such intensification. Their instinct and fantasy are greater and more significant than their concern for an exhaustive system of harmonic events. They do not care how their insights may be clarified and taught to outsiders. Music theory developed and treated as instruction on "how to do it" limps hopelessly behind the musical events, and no light shows on the horizon. Hindemith was a composer concerned with questions of music theory, but his method does not do justice to his artistic creativity. The only purpose of my comments on harmony in the last few centuries is to render more visible the prototypes contained in harmonic formulations and to help recognize phenomena as variants of simplest, original cadential laws effective since antiquity. By inventing new names for every differentiation of harmonic events, illogically formulated, moreover, on the basis of thoroughbass notation, one has arrived at harmony instruction that has nothing to offer, for it does not see the forest for the trees. A musician free to find better insights into the nature of harmonic events might be helped by my suggestions.

Counterpoint instruction shows similar defaults. With Fux, one barely reaches back to Palestrina, let alone Josquin or Dufay. Each Netherlands master and each musical category would deserve a special textbook. Yet Fux, Bellermann, and Jeppesen point to so much logic of voice-leading that a student will learn more from them than from most harmony texts.

In voice-leading, rules governing parallel motion play a big but natural part. The reason lies in the high blend of fundamental consonances. We shall consider them in order. Parallel unisons are monophonic and thus not usable in a texture of independent voices (deliberate unisons are not polyphonic and hence outside our discussion). Parallel octaves sound almost like unisons and weaken the vocal balance. We have the same pitch names for octaves, after all, and distinguish them only by range. Two voices proceeding in octaves destroy the equilibrium of the texture by momentarily becoming an overpowering pair. Parallel octaves are very noticeable. Concern with full equilibrium of the polyphonic texture eventually produces an allergy to parallels. Any conspicuous approach to an octave (coming from the same direction) is then prohibited. Depending on style, these hidden octaves are regulated by more or less strict observation of rules. To a beginning student, strict counterpoint will appear to exist exclusively of prohibitions, and the instruction comparable to an obstacle course. But all pedagogues know the eventual rewards for a pupil from cultivating sensitivity for voice-leading.

Parallel fifths are in a similar situation as parallel octaves. On one hand, the tones of the fifth have a much more independent relationship but, on the other hand, they are acoustically more sensitive. The fifth 2:3 relates to the fundamental value of 1 and in parallel motion produces the effect of a conspicuous base, which skillful voice-leading should avoid. An organ builder is intimately familiar with the acoustical consequences of the sound of the fifth of which he makes ample use to intensify pitch positions related to it (*duodecima!*). He can even save himself the trouble of building actual pipes for the lowest zone if he employs for that fundamental value real pipes at the octave and twelfth. In such a case, one speaks of an "acoustical 32'." One must remember these facts of physics when judging parallel fifths.

From a harmonic standpoint, it is essential to determine whether an occurring progression of parallel fifths is actually experienced as such by our hearing. The so-called Mozart fifths originate from alteration. (The augmented five-six chord lowers the fifth of the dominant ninth chord, from which it derives, so that the original diminished fifth between fifth and ninth becomes perfect, in which form Mozart leads it in parallel motion to the fundamental and the fifth of the tonic.) The perfect fifth created by alteration does not exist and is not experienced as a true harmonic position. Mozart's resolution is explained in harmony textbooks as a "tolerated exception." Leading-tone currents influence all other considerations and necessarily produce the resolution which is in no way an arbitrary exception sanctioned by Mozart. The special case sustained by Mozart's genius should teach us to judge musical phenomena not by their superficial appearance but by deeper reasons.

Counterpoint should cover all methods of melodic voice-leading, that is, all specific manners of *contrapuntus floridus* as much as the opposite cases of imitation. For the acquisition of real knowledge in these areas, the best method is to study live music history by copying many examples from different style periods (cf. p. xiv). This book has no room for details, which can be probed only by the most intensive personal instruction.

A bad discrepancy is carried into a twelve-tone texture by a perfect and pure interval. Traditional consonances must here be painstakingly avoided, for they will be spontaneously recognized. Building stones gained from the twelfth root of 2 necessitate a radical separation from the traditional consonances, which had to be brought about. Comparing exemplary compositions in traditional and twelve-tone styles, one realizes the tremendous labor yet to be done to find a structure permitting modern music to rise from an arbitrary, incidental, amorphous condition to one in which humanly experienced norms will leave freedom to the particulars of artistic life.

TABLE I

* = ekmelic positions.

Comments to Table I

For the ascending tone series, the numbers indicate frequency relations. For the descending tone series, the numbers indicate string lengths. Minor is the logical reciprocal of major. The minor triad at 10:12:15 is not a function of the fundamental C = 1.

TABLE II

Frame   Anhemitonic Pentatonic (3 perfect fourths)

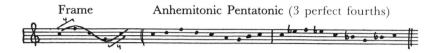

SCALE PROTOTYPES, WITH ADDED CADENTIAL TRIADS

Falling (Greek dorian, leading tone at bottom of tetrachord):

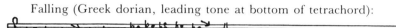

Rising (Green lydian, leading tone at top of tetrachord):

Neutral (Greek phrygian, leading tone in center of tetrachord):

or:

Comments to Table II

    The Greek phrygian mode contains semitone progressions but without leading-tone currents. The step from the major second to the minor third does not change the basic quality of the intervals as in the major and minor modes (the rising or falling sine scales) where the sums or products of the tones effect a transfer to perfect intervals.

    Triads on the three main points of the ascending sine-curve scale produce cadential obligations. (The third of the tonic resolves to the root of the critical point at the top; the third of the critical point at the bottom resolves to the tonic.) In both cases, the phenomenon is the same, even if we call only the dominant-tonic ending *authentic.* The current from the third of the tonic to the root of the upper critical point (which we usually call the subdominant) sets the action of the scalar cadence in motion. The return from the upper to the lower critical point includes the same halftone steps but without energetic charge (root becomes third, i.e., a perfect interval is exchanged for a major interval). These are the prototypes of authentic and plagal harmonic progressions.

One other specific harmonic method, increasingly distancing itself in its logic from stricter diatonism, appears in the so-called deceptive cadence. If the root of the dominant aiming at the center acts like a third, the typical, familiar formula of escaping from the cadential mechanism originates in analogy to the progression principle of the triad tones.

The composer Hugo Kauder called the octave scales *open*. They end on a tone different from the starting tone although its closest relative. He called the sine forms *closed*. Returning to the initial point, they are the prototype of the concept of melody.

From scale material and interaction of major and minor, the cadential positions develop further triadic structures. The major third is retained and complemented by a lower fifth, thereby creating three relative chords which primarily act as substitutes for the cadential triads.

Seventh chords have their prototype in the dominant seventh chord. If the three cadential positions of center and two outside points (commonly called *dominant* and *subdominant*) are replaced by the simplified concept of center and a common outside, then the two outside positions join forces. (The Vienna classical style restricts itself mainly to the positions of the tonic triad and the dominant seventh chord while noticeably pushing back the subdominant.) The dominant seventh chord is framed by the outer points of the sine scale, between which the dominant harmony spreads, flowing toward the middle, the tonic. The third of the subdominant can still be caught in the current (the dominant ninth chord). The fifth of the subdominant has to remain outside. It is the position into which the accumulated dominants should resolve; its inclusion would interfere with any kind of cadential resolution. In analogy to the prototype of the dominant seventh chord, seventh chords occur also on other steps. They are usually treated like the prototype, even when leading-tone currents might demand a different resolution. In the many kinds of seventh chords, the sonority of thirds abundantly outweighs all others. From such an attitude stems the mechanical chord production by way of superimposed thirds.

A schematic representation of minor is more difficult than one of major. The reason lies in the ambivalence of the entire concept of minor. If one builds cadences on the basis of the Greek dorian minor mode, one arrives at the concept of *natural minor*. The descending semitones create currents toward the fifth of the triads while leaving untouched the more important harmonic roots. Octave scales produce the melodic minor. The space of the tonic triad is filled out upward by a tetrachord appropriate to the motion. The approach to the upper tonic by a major tetrachord and the return via a descending (Greek dorian) tetrachord signify genuine scale substances. Harmonic minor is no scale but rather the accounting for all tones of the major-minor cadence, strung up within an octave space. Voice-leading objects: the sixth of the scale leads downward, the seventh upward. These two tones are melodically disjunct because of their leading-tone currents and the separating augmented second. As basis for a systematic explanation of the minor mode, harmonic minor constantly creates nonsense, starting with the "triad on the third degree." Musicians have here always made the right decision. The mirror analogy to the dominant seventh chord in major contains in minor a perfect minor triad with a seventh below the actual harmonic root. This seventh placed on top forms an upper sixth to the harmonic chord material, clearly defined by Rameau as *accord de la sixte ajoutée* (minor subdominant with added sixth). Look at the second movement of the *German Requiem* by Brahms for a wholly correct cadential resolution of the *sixte ajoutée*.

TABLE III: CHORDS

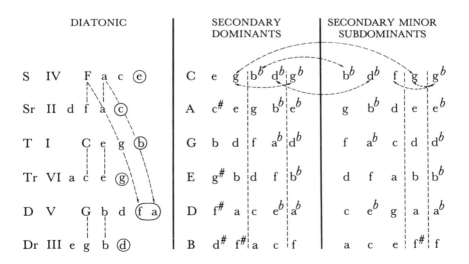

Comments to Table III

The arrangement relates to the main points of the cadential sine curve. The left column shows the cadential symbols and chords together with the commonly used degree designations.

To the dominant formations in the middle column, the chord before each in the left column functions as a kind of tonic. These secondary dominants spring from the enrichment of the semitone currents, at first extending into the substance of the minor-ninth chord. (The supplementary tones are supplied by the corresponding line in the right column.) Roots, being without leading-tone obligations, are often omitted. What remains of the minor-ninth chord is the familiar diminished seventh chord, of which the orthography is secured if the student supplements the missing root (a major third below the pseudo seventh chord).

A last possibility of establishing one more leading tone is offered by a chromatic lowering of the fifth, the sole genuinely alterable tone. (Roots cannot be altered, for all chord tones would lose their perspective. Thirds are either major or minor; alteration of their tonal gender would completely change the cadential function of the chord. Sevenths and ninths are already leading tones. The descent of the seventh is quasi plagal; the step from the minor seventh — absent from the overtone series — to the major third of the tonic leads to an increased value and hence justifies the downward resolution.) The lowered fifth produces the leading tone from above, derived from minor, to the root of the arrival chord. This chromatic lowering of the dominant fifth occurs frequently in a segment of the diminished seventh chord. The special attraction of this material with the familiar modulation to mediant keys stems from its chameleonic behavior. Depending on the arrangement of the chord ingredients, harmony texts burden the student with terminology derived from thoroughbass (such as augmented five-six chord); but the real event is always the intensification of a secondary dominant by a leading tone.

It is permitted to speak of secondary minor subdominants, as listed in the third column. One's instincts accept the minor subdominant in major as fair exchange for the major dominant in minor. The chords shown in the right column appropriately involve the *sixte ajoutée*. To increase leading-tone tension also in this situation, fifth and sixth are replaced by the descending semitone as in the harmonies shown in the middle column. We are used to calling the result a *Neapolitan sixth*. It looks like a sixth chord, which hides behind a simple appearance its origin as "exalted alteration material." There being no Neapolitan triad, explaining this tonal material as a sixth chord veils its real function. All such definitions come from the thoroughbass tradition and lack the logic of a harmonic system.

Footnotes

[1] Johannes Wolf, *Handbuch der Notationskunde* (Leipzig: Breitkopf and Härtel, 1913-1919); Willi Apel, *The Notation of Polyphonic Music, 900-1600,* 5th ed. (Cambridge, Mass.: Mediaeval Academy of America, 1961).

[2] Numerous "inventions" have been attributed to this Benedictine monk who died around 1050 — whether corrrectly so remains doubtful. This book summarizes the main facts in the development of our notation generally associated with his name.

[3] Ligature: a notational sign combining in a single graph melodically connected tones (in vocal music, tones on *one* syllable). The metric value of the notes is determined by their respective positions within the complex. Ligatures disappear with the advent of music printing because of the difficulty of producing appropriate type faces.

[4] The name *bilingua* derives from the presence of *two* notations above the text in the Montpellier tonarium (in which the pieces are arranged according to their modes or tones). Both notations concern the same melody: Carolingian neumes, which indicate only the melodic direction, and a Boethian letter notation, which permits us to read the neumes with exact intervals.

[5] The organa associated with the abbey of St. Martial in Limoges and then particularly with the cathedral of Notre Dame in Paris are based on plainchant material in the tenor and additional new melodies in duplum, triplum, or quadruplum (that is, in one to three new voice parts).

[6] The ambo is the pulpit from where the cantors sing.

[7] Perotinus, organum "Sederunt principes," ed. Rudolf von Ficker (Vienna: Universal, 1930). Also in *Publikationen älterer Musik*, Jg. 11, ed. Heinrich Husmann (Leipzig: Breitkopf and Härtel, 1940).

[8] The *punctus divisionis* is a small comma that indicates feet of two beats (dactyls).

[9] The Montpellier Codex, from the period around 1200 and in the possession of Montpellier University, was a music manuscipt apparently intended for the king.

[10] The *motetus* is a specific, song-like voice line that carries the text.

[11]The contratenor, which crosses the other voices without a special top limit, is a usually unsingable part conceived as a filler. Later it separates into two parts: *contratenor altus* (above the tenor) and *contratenor bassus* (below the tenor), the voice parts subsequently known as alto and bass.

[12]*Hoquetus*: voice parts interrupt their lines with very short pauses — a "hiccoughing" cutting-up of the melos.

[13]The Squarcialupi Codex of the Biblioteca Medicea Laurenziana is a sumptuous manuscript containing over 350 examples of secular trecento music (black mensural notation on six lines).

[14]Francesco Landini (d. 1397) is the principal composer of the Italian ars nova.

[15]Martin Agricola, who died while a cantor at Magdeburg in 1556, composed several works of *musica figuralis*.

[16]Josquin Des Prés, *Werken*, ed. Albert Smijers (Amsterdam and Leipzig: G. Alsbach, 1921-1969).

[17]Jacob Obrecht, *Opera Omnia: editio altera*, ed. Albert Smijers and Marcus van Crevel (Amsterdam: G. Alsbach, 1953-1959).

[18]Thomas Stolzer (d. 1526), "Psalm 37" in *Das Chorwerk*, Bd. 6, ed. Otto Gombosi (Wolfenbüttel: G. Kallmeyer, 1930).

[19]Idem, "Octo tonorum melodiae," in *Reichsdenkmale*, Bd. 22, ed. Hans Albrecht (Leipzig: C. F. Peters, 1942).

[20]G. B. P. da Palestrina, *Werke*, Bd. 4, ed. Franz Espagne (Leipzig: Breitkopf and Härtel, 1875).

[21]Claudio Monteverdi, *Tutte le Opere*, ed. Francesco Malipiero (Vienna: Universal, 1926-1942), vols. 14a and 14b.

[22]*Publikationen*, Jg. 4 and 6, ed. Alfred Einstein (Leipzig: Breitkopf and Härtel, 1929-1931).

[23]Heinrich Schütz, *Sämtliche Werke*, ed. Philipp Spitta (Leipzig: Breitkopf and Härtel, 1885-1927), Bd. 9, or *Neue Ausgabe sämtlicher Werke*, Bd. 22, ed. Hans Joachim Moser (Kassel: Bärenreiter, 1962).

[24]Carlo Gesualdo, *Sämtliche Werke*, ed. Wilhelm Weismann and Glenn E. Watkins (Hamburg: Ugrino, 1957-1967).

[25]Boethius (d. 526), advisor to Theoderich, King of the East Goths. Fifth book *De musica*. His writings preserve for us some of the most reliable knowledge of the music of the Greeks.

[26]See fn. 4.

[27]Dietrich Buxtehude, *Werke*, Bd. 5 (facsimile), ed. Hilmar Trede (Klecken: Ugrino, 1933).

[28]Georg Friedrich Händel, *Werke*, ed. Friedrich Chrysander (Leipzig: Breitkopf and Härtel, 1858-94, 1902), Bd. 32b ("Cantata Spagnuola").

[29]BWV 1007-1012, *Werke*, ed. Bach-Gesellschaft (Leipzig: Breitkopf and Härtel, 1851-1926), Bd. 27/1.

[30]Facsimile in Apel (see fn. 1).

[31]*Musica Divina*, 8 vols., ed. Carl Proske (Regensburg: Friderici Pustet, 1853-1869).

[32]Under the term *contrapunctus floridus* one understands medieval polyphony which *does not* employ the practice of imitation.

[33]See fn. 15.

[34] Schütz, *Werke* (Spitta), Bd. 6, 184.

[35] Jacob Weckmann died in 1689 while organist at St. Thomas. The Konzert on Psalm 126 in *Denkmäler Deutscher Tonkunst*, Bd. 6, ed. Musikgeschichte Kommission (Leipzig: Breitkopf and Härtel, 1892-1931).

[36] Schütz, *Werke* (Spitta), Bd. 1; *NA* (Bärenreiter), Bd. 3 (Facsimile of preface).

[37] Franchino Gafori (1451-1522), chapel master of the Milan Cathedral. His highly valued works deal with the foundations of music theory up to the time of proportions.

[38] Thomas Morley (1558-1603), the important English madrigalist, also wrote the book *A Plaine and Easie Introduction*...(London: P. Short, 1597/R 1971; facs. ed. 1937), on the state of composition and musical practice around the turn of the seventeenth century.

[39] Cf. Jacques de Liége, *Speculum musicae* (c. 1340): "One must know the longa, brevis, and semibrevis can be divided in two and in three, that is, the measure is fast (*cita*), slow (*morosa*), or moderate. Accordingly there are three ways of singing: drawn out (*tractum*), fast (*velociter*), or moderate (*medie*). However one does it, the notation is the same."

[40] Schütz, *Werke* (Spitta), Bd. 4, *Symphoniae Sacrae 1*.

[41] In *Landschaftsdenkmale: Schleswig-Holstein und Hansestädte*, Bd. 1, ed. Fritz Stein (Braunschweig: H. Litolff, 1937-39).

[42] Monteverdi, *Opere* (Malipiero), vol. 11. The *Orfeo* score proves that the tempo can be determined by notational relations. The prelude to the second act and the Orfeo strophe are notated in tempus imperfectum although they are pieces in pronounced triple meter. What matters is the retention of the slower tempo resulting from the duple division of the tactus prescribed for a number of sections in the second act (which must always be integrated strictly into the general movement).

[43] See the facsimile reproduction (Leipzig: Insel, 1924).

[44] *Versuch über die wahre Art, das Clavier zu spielen*, facs. ed. by Lothar Hoffmann-Erbrecht (Leipzig: Breitkopf and Härtel, 1957); Eng. trans., 1949.

[45] The sarabande springs from the harem and was an unequivocally lascivious dance. It stood under papal ban.

[46] J. S. Bach, *Orchestra Suite No. 2*, B minor, BWV 1067.

[47] Schütz, *Werke* (Spitta), Bd. 7.

[48] BWV 1043.

[49] BWV 243.

[50] Neidhart (Nithard) von Reuenthal, minnesinger at the court of the last Babenberger. *DTÖ* (Vienna and Graz: Österreichischer Bundesverlag, 1894-1959, 1960-), Bd. 71, ed. Wolfgang Schmieder, 1930.

[51] Bach, *St. John Passion,* part II, chorale "In meines Herzens Grunde."

[52] In the Schütz *Werke* (Spitta), Bd. 7 (appendix).

[53] Brussels, Bibliothèque Royale Albert 1er.

[54] *DTÖ*, Bd. 70 (dance music of Paul Peuerl and Isaac Posch), ed. Karl Geiringer, 1929.

[55] *Musikalische Werke der Kaiser Ferdinand III, Leopold I und Joseph I,* ed. Guido Adler (Vienna: Artaria, 1892-93).

[56] J. J. Fux, *Concentus, DTÖ*, Bd. 47, ed. Heinrich Rietsch, 1916.

[57] J. S. Bach, Cantata BWV 78, "Jesu, der du meine Seele."

[58] Cf. Schütz, *Werke* (Spitta), Bd. 7, opus X, Konzert "Ich werde nicht sterben."

[59] Heinrich Besseler, ed., *Altniederländische Motetten* (Kassel: Bärenreiter, 1929).

[60]Dufay, "Gloria ad modum tubae," in *DTÖ*, Jg. 7 (Trienter Codices), ed. G. Adler and O. Koller, 1900.

[61]BWV 1079.

[62]Friedrich Smend, "Auflösung zum Canon per augmentationem in contrario motu des Musikalischen Opfers," *Zeitschrift für Musikwissenschaft*, xi/4 (1929), 252.

[63]Bach's *Kunst der Fuge, Ausgabe der Neuen Bachgesellschaft* (Leipzig: Breitkopf and Härtel, 1901-), Jg. 28/1, ed. Wolfgang Graeser, 1927; *Neue Ausgabe sämtlicher Werke*, ed. Johann-Sebastian-Bach-Institut, Göttingen, and Bach-Archiv, Leipzig (Kassel and Basel: Bärenreiter, 1954-), Bd. 8/2, or edition of Hans Th. David (Leipzig: Peters, 1928).

[64]*Beispielsammlung zur älteren Musikgeschichte*, ed. Alfred Einstein (Leipzig: B. G. Teubner, 1917).

[65]In *Chorwerk*, Bd. 19, ed. Heinrich Besseler, 1951 (now Bärenreiter).

[66]John Dunstable, *Complete Works*, ed. Manfred Bukofzer as vol. 8 of *Musica Britannica* (London: Stainer and Bell, 1951, rev. 2/1970).

[67]Guillaume de Machaut, *Musikalische Werke*, ed. Friedrich Ludwig and Heinrich Besseler (Leipzig: Breitkopf and Härtel, 1926-29, 1943), Bd. 4.

[68]Edmond de Coussemaker, *Messe du XIIIe siècle* (Tournai: Malo and Levasseur, 1861).

[69]*Graduale Romanum:* Mass IV "Cunctipotens genitor Deus" (chorale Masses are named after the text of their tropes).

[70]Credo IV of the *Graduale Romanum.*

[71]Machaut, *Werke*, Bd. 1, 102; Siegmund Levarie, *Guillaume de Machaut*, ed. John J. Becker (New York: Sheed and Ward, 1954; reprinted New York: Da Capo Press, 1969).

[72]In Pobé and Roubier, *Das gotische Frankreich* (Schroll).

[73]Machaut, *Werke*, Bd. 1, 35.

[74]Guillaume Dufay, *Opera Omnia*, ed. G. de Van and Heinrich Besseler as vol. 1 of *Corpus Mensurabilis Musicae* (Rome: American Institute of Musicology, 1951-66), or *DTÖ*, Bd. 53.

[75]See fn. 60.

[76]"Ave regina caelorum," Dufay *Opera*, Bd. 5.

[77]*Altniederländische Motetten*, cf. fn. 59.

[78]In *Chorwerk*, Bd. 1. The missing "Agnus secundus" is found in the Alamire Codex at the Nationalbibliothek, Vienna.

[79]Josquin, *Werken* (Smijers), Bd. 1.

[80]*DTÖ*, Jg. 7 (Trienter Codices).

[81]In Archibald T. Davison and Willi Apel, *Historical Anthology of Music* (Cambridge, Mass.: Harvard University Press, 1946), vol. I, 79.

[82]See fn. 13.

[83]See *DTÖ*, Jg. 9/1, 205.

[84]*Locheimer Liederbuch*, ed. Konrad Ameln (Augsburg: Bärenreiter, 1925).

[85]He shows the role of home music-making, for instance in Nuremberg.

[86]Josquin, *Werken* (Smijers), Bd. 3 and 5 (Wereldlijke Werken).

[87]Sylvestro Ganassi, "La Fontegara," Venice, 1535, ed. Hildemarie Peter (Berlin: R. Lienau, 1956).

[88]Gesualdo, *Werke* (Weismann).

[89]Ottaviano dei Petrucci (d. 1539), licensed printer of mensural music with metal type.

[90]Printed by Gardano, Venice, 1611, *Werke* (Spitta), Bd. 9, or *NA*, (Bärenreiter), Bd. 22.

⁹¹See fn. 21.

⁹²ed. Wasiliewski, Bonn, 1874.

⁹³See fn. 87.

⁹⁴Palestrina, *Werke* (Espagne), Bd. 4 (and supplement IV).

⁹⁵See fn. 42.

⁹⁶See fn. 49.

⁹⁷Cantata BWV 6, *BG*, Jg. 1.

⁹⁸BWV 118, *BG*, Jg. 24.

⁹⁹Not yet published.

¹⁰⁰Schütz, *NA* (Bärenreiter), Bd. 3, preface in facsimile.

¹⁰¹Johann David Heinichen, *Der General-Bass in der Composition* (Dresden: by the author, 1728).

¹⁰²Jean-Philippe Rameau, "Plan abrégé d'une méthode nouvelle d'accompagnement pour le clavecin," *Mercure de France* (Paris, 1730).

¹⁰³Johann Mattheson, *Grosse Generalbassschule* (Hamburg: Kissner, 1731/R 1968).

¹⁰⁴Jean-Jacques Rousseau, *Dictionnaire de musique* (Paris: Vve. Duchesne, 1768/R 1969; Eng. trans., 1771).

¹⁰⁵C. J. F. Haltmeier, *Anleitung, wie man einen General-Bass*, ed. Georg Philipp Telemann (Hamburg: J. G. Piscator, 1737).

¹⁰⁶Kunsthistorisches Museum, Vienna; Collection of old musical instruments.

¹⁰⁷Denis Gaultier (called "le jeune") died in Paris in 1672. By means of two collections of lute music disseminated in printed copies, he acquired a decided influence on the culture of lute playing outside the French regions.

¹⁰⁸Lute of Johann Christian Hoffmann, documented in the will proceedings following Bach's death.

¹⁰⁹J. S. Bach, *St. John Passion, BG,* Jg. 12.

¹¹⁰J. S. Bach, *Trauerode*, BWV 198, *BG*, Jg. 13(3).

¹¹¹See fn. 42.

¹¹²Monteverdi, *Opere* (Malipiero), vol. 9.

¹¹³BWV 106, *BG*, Jg. 11.

¹¹⁴Hucbald, Benedictine monk, died 932 at St. Amand in Flanders. Among writings attributed to him, the *Musica enchiriadis* and *De harmonica institutione* are of special note.

¹¹⁵In regard to the Bernelius Codex, see Christhard Mahrenholz, *Die Berechnung der Orgelpfeifenmensuren* (Kassel: Bärenreiter, 1938).

¹¹⁶See fn. 114.

¹¹⁷Dom Bedos, *L'Art du Facteur d'Orgues* (Paris: L. F. Delatour, 1766; facs. ed. 1963-66).

¹¹⁸The organ register *montre*: "standing in the prospectus," hence diapason.

¹¹⁹*Bicinium*: designation for two-voice sections or movements in Josquin-like through-imitation.

¹²⁰Aliquot voices: name for all the partial-tone registers.

¹²¹In Flor Peeters, *Alte Orgelmusik aus England und Frankreich* (Mainz: B. Schott, 1958).

¹²²In Arnolt Schlick, *Tabulaturen etlicher Lobgesang* (Mainz: P. Schöffer, 1512/R 1977; ed. 1924, 2/1957).

¹²³*DTÖ*, Bd. 98 (ed. Milton Steinhardt, 1961-).

¹²⁴*DTÖ*, Jg. 10 (ed. Guido Adler, 1903).

¹²⁵Johann Philipp Kirnberger, *Grundsätze des Generalbasses* (Berlin: J. J. Hummel, c.1781/R 1974).

[126]Andreas Werckmeister, *Die Musikalische Temperatur* (Frankfurt and Leipzig, ?1686-7 [lost], 2/1691; ed. 1983).

[127]See fn. 122. Works by Paumann in *Das Erbe deutscher Musik*, Bd. 37, 38, 39, ed. Bertha A. Wallner (Kassel: Bärenreiter, 1958).

[128]Johannes Ciconia, in *HAM* (see fn. 81), 59.

[129]Norbert Dufourq, *Esquisse d'une historie de l'orgue en France* (Paris: Larousse, 1935).

[130]See fn. 47.

[131]Cantata BWV 169, *BG*, Jg. 33.

[132]Joseph Haydn, *Werke*, ed. Joseph-Haydn-Institut, Cologne (Munich and Duisberg: Henle, 1958-), Reihe xxiii/2. Wolfgang Amadeus Mozart, *Neue Ausgabe sämtlicher Werke*, ed. Internationalen Stiftung Mozarteum, Salzburg (Kassel: Bärenreiter, 1955-), Bd. 2.

[133]In Prado Museum, Madrid. Reproduced by Heinrich Besseler in *Die Musik des Mittelalters*, 184, as Bd. 1 of Ernst Bücken's *Handbuch der Musikwissenschaft* (Potsdam: Athenaion, 1931).

[134]Facsimile in *Documenta Musicologica*, Bd. 4, ed. G. le Cerf and E.-R. Labande (Kassel: Bärenreiter, 1972).

[135]On the echiquier, see Franz Josef Hirt, *Meisterwerke des Klavierbaues* (Olten: Urs Graf, 1955; Eng. trans. 1968).

[136]Robert Haas, *Aufführungspraxis der Musik*, reproduction of title-page woodcut by Hans Nel, or by Pseudo-Eyck, in Bücken, *Handbuch*, Bd. 6, 112.

[137]Sachs took the date of 1409 for a single-keyboard harpsichord from the *Book of Hours of the Duke of Berry* (one copy in the Nationalbibliothek, Vienna).

[138]Curt Sachs, *History of Musical Instruments* (New York: Norton, 1940), 341.

[139]See fn. 134.

[140]On the Ruckers family, see *Hirt* (fn. 135), 451.

[141]Arnolt Schlick, *Spiegel der Orgelmacher und Organisten* (Speyer: Peter Drach, 1511/R 1959; ed. 1931, 2/1951; facs. ed., incl. Eng. trans., 1978).

[142]On piano builders, see *Hirt* (fn. 135), 447, 463.

[143]Albrecht Hass, see *Hirt* (fn. 135), 445.

[144]Cf. Friedrich Ernst, *Der Flügel Joh. Seb. Bachs* (Frankfurt: Peters, 1955).

[145]Michael Praetorius, *Syntagma musicum* (Wolfenbüttel: E. Holwein, 1618, 2/1610; facs. ed. 1959; Eng. trans. 1949), Bd. II, plate III: "Nürnbergisch Geigenwerk."

[146]David Kellner, *Treulicher Unterricht im Generalbass* (Hamburg: C. Herold, 1737).

[147]Daniel Gottlob Türk, *Anweisung zum Generalbassspielen* (Halle: Hemmerde and Schwetschke, 1800/R 1971).

[148]Heinrich Schütz, *Weihnachtshistorie*, *Werke* (Spitta), Bd. 17, *NA* (Bärenreiter), Bd. 1.

[149]BWV 23, *BG*, Jg. 5/1.

[150]Facsimile edition (Leipzig: Deutscher, 1966).

[151]BWV 232, facsimile edition (Kassel: Bärenreiter, 1965).

[152]Cf. Julius Schlosser, *Die Sammlung alter Musikinstrumente; beschreibendes Verzeichnis* (Vienna, 1920), No. 193.

[153]*Trumscheit*, a strangely isolated instrument with one string. The string is not pressed against a fingerboard but merely touched to produce harmonics. One foot of the bridge is turned sideways so as to bear only a fraction of the string pressure. This loose foot then vibrates against the resonance board in the frequency of the tone produced by

the bow, creating a comical, shabby, trumpet-like sound. Hence, and also because the instrument was used in convents as a substitute for the trumpet, the name *nun's trumpet*. As *tromba marina* it also served to give signals, and was perhaps used by early warships in fog and darkness (reportedly at the battle of Trafalgar).

[154]See fn. 42.

[155]See fn. 135.

[156]See fn. 117

[157]Adriaen van Wesel, a music-making angel in an adoration group, in Timmers *Hauten Beelden* (Amsterdam, 1949).

[158]The cister was built by Girolamo de Virchis in 1574 as a fine specimen of princely ambition. See Schlosser *Verzeichnis* (fn. 152), 158.

[159]Ernst Friedrich Chladni (1756-1827) undertook important researches in acoustics. Glass plates sprinkled with fine sand and set in vibration with a bow reveal regular patterns as the sand shifts according to the vibrational system.

[160]Hans Kayser, *Die Form der Geige* (Zürich: Occident, 1947).

[161]The Tourte bow, named after its inventor, the watchmaker Tourte, is constructed to permit a rich array of staccato effects, for it easily bounces off the strings.

[162]See fn. 87.

[163]Musée Mahillon, Brussels: case with krummhorns; Correr, Venice, 1506.

[164]*Chorwerk*, Bd. 6 (ed. Otto Gombosi, 1953).

[165]*Pavanes* by H. Schein, specifying krummhorns, 1612.

[166]Albertina, Vienna, Catalog No. 1884.

[167]*Reichsdenkmale* (Peters), Bd. 22.

[168]*DTÖ*, Bd. 70 (ed. Karl Geiringer, 1929).

[169]Shortly after 1700.

[170]Curt Sachs, *Reallexicon der Musikinstrumente* (Berlin: J. Bard, 1913/R 1962).

[171]See fn. 60.

[172]Gottlieb Reich, in *Die Musik in Geschichte und Gegenwart*, ed. Friedrich Blume (Kassel: Bärenreiter, 1949-), XI, table 13, facing 191.

[173]In Arnold Schering, *Geschichte der Musik in Beispielen* (Leipzig: Breitkopf and Härtel, 1931,2/1954/R 1972; Eng. trans. 1950).

[174]Volgano would probably have designated a large, military trumpet.

[175]See fn. 47.

[176]J. J. Fux, *Concentus musico-instrumentalis*, *DTÖ*, Bd. 47 (ed. Hienrich Rietsch, 1916).

[177]*DTÖ*, Bd. 101 (ed. Camillo Schoenbaum, 1962).

[178]In the Carolino-Augusteo Museum: *trombone doppio* with the escutcheon of Bishop Paris Lodron.

[179]W. A. Mozart, *Sämtliche Werke*, ed. L. von Köchel and others (Leipzig: Breitkopf and Härtel, 1876-1905), Ser. I/ii.

[180]See fn. 99.

[181]Santiago di Compostela, Pórtico de la Gloria.

[182]*Ekmelic* (extra musical) is an ancient term for the overtone positions corresponding to prime numbers (7, 11, 13, etc.). These tones lie outside the tone positions of Western music. They are usually named by approximation to the nearest tone within our system, although this procedure conceals their nature as outsiders.

[183]See fn. 98.

[184]Lorenzo Perosi and his assistant and successor.

[185]See fn. 87.

[186]*Organworks*, BWV 565, "Dorische" Toccata.

[187]For example, op. 23a and b.

[188]See fn. 125.

[189]See fn. 124.

[190]Pythagoras's contemporaries already knew that a series of pure (beatfree) fifths does not return to the starting pitch. To this day, the discrepancy is known as the *Pythagorean comma*.

ABBREVIATIONS

Bd.   = Band
Jg.   = Jahrgang
BG   = Bach Werke (Bach-Gesellschaft, 1851-1926)
DTÖ = Denkmäler der Tonkunst in Österreich
NA   = Schütz, Neue Ausgabe sämtlicher Werke (Bärenreiter)

NOTE

Elizabeth Wright deserves credit and gratitude for coping with the footnotes.

DATE DUE